LOVE
MARRIAGE
AND THE FAMILY

LOVE
MARRIAGE
AND THE FAMILY

YESTERDAY AND TODAY

James A. Mohler, S.J.

Library of Congress Cataloging in Publication Data

Mohler, James A.
  Love, marriage, and the family.

  Bibliography: p.
  Includes index.
  1. Marriage—History. 2. Marriage—Religious aspects
—Christianity—History. 3. Family—History.
4. Family—Religious aspects—Christianity—History.
I. Title.
HQ503.M63   1982   306.8'09   82-8699
ISBN 0-8189-0434-8   AACR2

Nihil Obstat:
James T. O'Connor, S.T.D.
Censor Librorum

Imprimatur:
†Joseph T. O'Keefe
Vicar General, Archdiocese of New York
June 11, 1982

Designed, printed and bound in the United States of
America by the Fathers and Brothers of the
Society of St. Paul, 2187 Victory Boulevard,
Staten Island, New York 10314, as part of their
communications apostolate.

1 2 3 4 5 6 7 8 9 (Current Printing: first digit).

Books by James A. Mohler, S.J.

MAN NEEDS GOD: An Interpretation of Biblical Faith
THE BEGINNING OF ETERNAL LIFE: The Dynamic Faith of
Thomas Aquinas
DIMENSIONS OF FAITH: Yesterday and Today
ORIGIN AND EVOLUTION OF THE PRIESTHOOD: A Return
to the Sources
THE HERESY OF MONASTICISM: The Christian Monks: Types
and Anti-Types
THE SCHOOL OF JESUS: An Overview of Christian Education,
Yesterday and Today
COSMOS, MAN, GOD, MESSIAH: An Introduction to Religion
DIMENSIONS OF LOVE: East and West
SEXUAL SUBLIMATION AND THE SACRED
THE SACRAMENT OF SUFFERING
DIMENSIONS OF PRAYER
LOVE, MARRIAGE AND THE FAMILY: Yesterday and Today

DEDICATION

IN GRATITUDE
TO MY BELOVED PARENTS,
EDWARD FRANCIS MOHLER
AND
GERTRUDE AYLWARD MOHLER.
MAY THEY REST IN PEACE.

Contents

Abbreviations

FOC	Fathers of the Church
ANF	Ante-Nicene Fathers
NPNF	Nicene and Post-Nicene Fathers
SC	Sources Chretiennes
PG	Patrologia Graeca
PL	Patrologia Latina
LCL	Loeb Classical Library
ACW	Ancient Christian Writers

Prologue

When we look at the history of marriage and the family, we find both joys and problems. In many ways marriage and the family are the happiest times in life, for which youth hopes and over which old age reminisces.

Yet there are inevitable tensions between the ideal monogamy and human weakness, tensions which have increased in our high pressure, competitive, urban industrial society.

While the marriage rate has remained rather constant over the years, for example, [9 (1890), 8.5 (1960), 10.6 (1980), divorces have grown from 0.5 (1890) to 2.2 (1960) to 5.4 (1980)].

Several factors have influenced the rise in the divorce rate, including lower death rates and a longer life span of 74 years (70, 1960; 47, 1890). Fewer children 16 (24, 1960) make splitting easier. Moreover, high affluence and dual careers encourage financial and social independence.

But is the modern family worse off than in ancient times? All through history there have been those who predicted the demise of the family.

Marriage counselors say that youth weddings and those of too disparate backgrounds are risky. But if two college graduates make a mature decision and are of similar origins, the prospects are good.

A recent study of Muncie, Indiana, by Caplow, Bahr and Chadwick sounds encouraging for it found increasing family togetherness, a narrowing of the generation gap and more religion.[1] Is Muncie different from the country as a whole? Caplow and his colleagues think not.

Moreover, they are convinced that society and its bureaucracy stimulate anti-familial policies, including higher taxes for married couples, no-fault divorce, ADC for illegitimate children and for those from broken homes, and also the sanctioning of premarital sex, birth control and abortion.

Caplow and colleagues also see the growing importance of the composite or extended family including grandparents, parents, uncles, aunts, etc. This is especially significant because of the growing number of single adults in recent years.

What can we make of the conflicting evidence? Although the divorce rate is high, the majority of marriages still last till death. Moreover, the marriage age is rising (25, 22), which means more mature decisions with a higher assurance of success. Also the church wedding is making a comeback.

The divorce rate seems to be leveling off at 5.3 and most of the divorcees remarry. Furthermore, though unmarried liaisons are a scandal, only 2% of American men and women live together out of wedlock.

To understand the pluses and minuses in today's marriage and the family, it might be helpful to see something of the history of marriage, for today's problems have been faced many times before.

Ancient myths tell us of the primordial hierogamy (divine marriage). Is this an attempt on man's part to make the gods in his own image, or is it rather a certain consciousness of something divine in his nuptials? Is marriage an anthropomorphism in God, or a theomorphism in man by which husband and wife imitate God in their sacred union?

In some early peoples polygamy was necessary to care for widows and other single women for the good of the tribe. But as cultures developed and became more urbanized, monogamy became the rule.

Divorce is found in many early civilizations. But often it is concerned with fertility or harmony necessary for the survival of the family. Since the ancestors oversee with great care the generation of their descendents, this lends a certain spiritual dimension to marriage. So the wedding is not just an agreement between two families or clans, but also that the spirits of the ancestors approve.

In Judaeo-Christian tradition marriage is seen as a consecration or a sanctifying. Even the Roman patricians celebrated their *confarreatio* (solemn marriage) before a priest. By medieval times the church demanded a priestly presence at the sacrament of matrimony.

Though the Reformers do not see marriage as a separate Christian sacrament, nonetheless, they recognize it as a holy union according to divine law from the beginning.

Modern Marxists believe that monogamy is a late capitalistic exploitation of wives and children by their husbands and fathers. However, when Communist Russia eased divorce restrictions, it soon found that the basic family fabric of society was weakened.

So marriage and the family are not just the concern of husband, wife and children, but of the whole society of which they are the foundation stones. Moreover, the family does not derive its meaning from society, as the Marxists claim, but *vice versa*.

Modern marriage faces new vagaries of sexual liberation, easy birth control, abortion, no-fault divorce, inflation, unemployment, high interest rates, longer lives, boredom, etc.

Marriage and the family must rest on a firmer foundation than society or the economy, namely the divine and eternal paradigm. Marriage and the family need safeguards because of man's weakness and the many temptations to slip from the monogamous ideal. Civil and religious laws try to build a fence around it.

Marriage is considered sacred in most cultures, based on the archetypal hierogamy or solidarity with the ancestors. This is especially so in Christianity, where it celebrates the union of Christ with His Church. As the Holy Eucharist is the permanent presence of Christ among His people, the Church, so Christian marriage is the perpetual living of Christ in the family, His domestic church.

PART ONE
YESTERDAY

CHAPTER ONE

The Evolution of Marriage

We find the essentials of marriage in all cultures, namely, a lifelong union of husband and wife, for mutual support and progeny, to continue the ancestral line and promote the welfare of the tribe or clan.

EARLY PEOPLES

In ancient societies though, the good of the individual seems to be subordinate to the prosperity of the tribe, nevertheless, the group protects needy singles, such as widows, orphans, the sick etc. So there are fewer psychological traumas than in modern impersonal urbanized society.

Many primordial myths see man starting out as an androgyne, who, as a punishment for his sins, is split up by God into male and female. So he must seek out his better half in marriage in order to find peace.

Some evolutionists see male and female as environmentally conditioned to tasks of hunting, protecting, gestation, nurturing and planting.

Often, strict sexual mores are found in the close contact of tribe, band, or extended family, where immorality can literally destroy the harmony so necessary for subsistence. Actually, sexuality played a relatively minor role in many early societies, reflecting its subdued place in nature.

R. Mohr remarks[1] that early marriage prevented premarital sex, since marriage soon after puberty rites was common. "The only form of marriage is monogamy in which both partners are pledged to fidelity." Adultery is a capital crime. Moreover, when the rule of monogamy is relaxed for the good of the tribe, the first wife is in charge.

Monogamy can be weakened by either male or female preponderance in a culture. Under male dominance, promiscuity and polygamy flourish and fertility is highly prized. Under female rule, premarital virginity is honored and the wife and children often live apart from the husband.

J. Thiel[2] finds that African tribes have definite forms of sexual morality for the preservation and the increase of society. "There is not and there certainly never has been such a thing as institutional promiscuity."

African marriage is often a tribal contract with the patriarch and his elders supervising and approving the union. "We have taken a wife." So there is little emphasis on romance.

Since the wife's fertility is of prime importance, its guarantee is a part of the marriage contract. Although female sterility annuls the bond, if the husband is guilty, he can bring in a friend to save face. Children not only continue the all-important ancestral line, but also offer filial piety to the ancients, bringing a certain supernatural aura to the marriage.

African nuptials are a drawn out process that begins with the betrothal arrangements between the families. When the bride enters the groom's home or community, the bride price is paid and proper ceremonies are performed. Finally, the contract is fulfilled when children are born. Some tribes insist on virgin brides, for virginity insures fertility and stability in the marriage.

"Virginity is held to be a good thing insofar as it is a promise of a harmonious marriage." If a girl is chaste before her wedding she will probably be faithful after it. Adultery is vicious because it not only steals the wife's fertility, but kills the marriage.

The bride price does not buy a woman, but rather compensates her family for her fertility. In general, a man marries for life. Above all, this applies to the first marriage. Children cement the relationship, for their presence indicates that the contract has been fulfilled.

Among the Gbandes of Liberia the marriage of future offspring is sometimes arranged by good friends even before they themselves marry, or a union can be agreed upon by the parents. Moreover, even romances must have parental approval.[3]

In the nuptial ceremony the two fathers and the groom place their hands on iron money which rests on the bride's head. "May the relationship between these two and between us be as strong and as good as this iron money."

Then the groom and his father request the blessings of their ancestors in the name of Gelewolongala, the Maker of All Things. Those present respond: "May the couple be blessed with good health and with many children."

If the bride proves not to be a virgin, she is rejected, for she has deceived her husband and disgraced her people. Moreover, she must tell who took her virginity, and in former times he was put to death.

Gbandes of high birth want two or more wives, but most have less. The chief reserves his first two wives to himself. His first wife takes precedence over the others and is his most important counselor. His second wife, who is younger, is a secret spouse selected by the ancestors. She is not only the wife of the chief, but of the ancestral spirits as well.

Progeny are the primary purpose of marriage, and polygamy insures many children. "One who has many children, his name will never die." Levirate marriage guarantees the ancestral line, while the sororate union takes care of single women.

Sometimes there is a vast age difference, like a one year old wife for a fifty year old man. She marries a husband, and his family as well. "Sexuality is far less important than having a wife who has the potential of perpetuating and of increasing the family" (92).

In the large extended family the wives live together in the big house, while each husband has his own hut. Since the children are seen as the reincarnation of the great grandparents, they are respected.

Although the wives are not inferior to their husbands, they allow them to assume the leadership of the tribe. Since child bearing and rearing are of the highest priority, the wife abstains from sex for four years while nursing her first boy, and three years, if it is a girl.

While his wife encourages the husband, he in turn consults with her. "He who is wise, is one who listens to his wives" (99).

In general, African marriage is for the good of the clan or the tribe, with a deemphasis on romance. It is a sacred union since it continues the line of the ancestral spirits, who are to be consulted and honored. Of course, any misuse of male-female relationships can be a problem, for it can be harmful to the ancestors.

Among the native American Indians, marriage is usually monogamous and for life. For example, the Aztec boy and girl tie their tilmanti cloaks in a wedding knot, and the clan council approves.[4] Here, too, love and romance are minimized. For example, no love goddess or pornographic symbols are found.

Since the women should set the example in chastity, their infidelity is punished by death. Moreover, a sterile wife may be dismissed. The Nanatl word for wife is "she who owns a husband." Her progeny are called "beloved children."

Among the Indians of North America the nuclear family is universal. Marriage is permanent and public, an arranged contract between two families. Although premarital sex is common, bridal chastity is highly valued and so demands a higher price. As in most tribal peoples, marriage takes place shortly after puberty.[5]

Though monogamy is the norm, polygamy is found among the Plains Indians in the 19th century due to the shortage of men and the need of women to prepare the hides and furs. The extended family shares in hunting, child care, nursing the ill, etc. The mother of a large family is honored.

The spirits do not approve of premarital sex. For example, if a boy indulges himself before his vision quest, the supernaturals will refuse to help him. Although extramarital sex did occur, "faithfulness was the ideal, especially for certain women who were regarded as especially virtuous and good because they had never committed adultery" (538).

Though the Iroquois allowed divorce and remarriage, "chastity in the young and marital fidelity in the mature were regarded as virtues." Some tribes had a public confession of secret infidelities once a year to insure the blessings of the supernaturals on the group. Mohr adds,[6]

> In the oldest groups known to history, we find esteem of premarital chastity and a demand for it, ignorance of sexual perversions, a natural practice of sexual intercourse for the procreation of

children, and monogamy, with the severest punishments for the rare case of adultery.

No early tribes encouraged promiscuity. For strict sexual morals are often necessary for the continued existence of the band.

Affluence, urbanization, class structure, leisure, and male or female dominance tend to shake up the harmony between the sexes.

Marriage has evolved over the centuries from a tribal, social, political, cosmic and spiritual event (involving not only the parents and tribal leaders, but also the whole group including long dead forebearers), to the modern individual romance with little concern for parental or ancestral approval.

MORE COMPLEX CULTURES

The Chinese extended family has always been close-knit and interrelated with the clan.

Jen, love, and *li*, etiquette, begin in the home and only then can they go out to others, as Confucius teaches. These are illustrated vertically in *hsiao*, filial piety between children and parents, grandparents and ancestors, and horizontally in *ti*, brotherly and sisterly respect.

In Chinese society marriage is a family and clan affair, with sexuality and romance having lesser roles.[7] Since a fertile marriage extends the ancestral line and insures their honor, one who refuses to marry is accused of unfilial behavior.

Parents, and fathers in particular, arrange the Chinese nuptials with a serious investigation into family backgrounds. "Marriage, as the beginning of human relationships, deserves the utmost caution" (78).

Marriage for money, fame, child betrothals, engagements to disgraceful persons are frowned upon. Strict exogamy is the rule, so that even those with the same surname may not wed. Unions which are the results of adultery, elopement, or misconduct are forbidden.

The Chinese wife is subordinate to her husband and should cultivate fidelity, prudence, industry and graceful manners. Lao Tzu counsels the wife that by her submission she will conquer her spouse as water wears down the hardest rock.

Although the husband is the head of his family, it is not wise for him to ignore his wife's advice. A wife may be dismissed for: insulting her in-laws, infertility, extreme jealousy, repulsive diseases, garrulousness and theft.

Since being heirless is an insult to the ancestors, a husband may take a concubine if he is over forty and still has no children. The newcomer is inferior for she can neither take the wife's place, nor become the second wife after the first wife's death.

Harmony, *ho*, speaking with one voice, is essential to family life. The father is the head and filial piety smooths the relationship between parents and children. There must also be love and respect between husband and wife, and honor among siblings. Although the individual subordinates his desires for the good of the family, the poor, sick or old are cared for by the group.

Family pride has always been a great crime deterrent in China. If one is disgraced, his name is removed from the clan tablets, for he has insulted his ancestors.

As in other cultures, Chinese marriage is a family and clan concern with stress on harmony, fertility and proper relationships. For if one does not have *jen*, love or humanity, in his family, he will never display it outside.

The supernatural element in marriage often includes the blessing of the ancestors, the continuation of the line, and a guarantee of the perpetual honoring of the family spirits.

Perhaps there is a parallel in the recapitulation of the primordial hierogamy. For example, in Hinduism the human union of husband and wife both celebrates, and, in a sense, continues the divine marriage.

Though all the gods have wives in Hinduism, the prime wedding is that of *Purusha* and *Prakrti*, spirit and nature, *Shiva* and *Shakti*, *linga* and *yoni*, male and female.

The sacredness of sex and its cosmic implications are seen in the holiest sanctuaries where the union of the linga and yoni is venerated, far different from the degrading pornography found in some Western cultures.

In the Upanishads the marital act is called a sacred sacrifice. As the two become one in marriage, so the individual self, *jivatman*, unites with the Universal Self, *Paramatman*, in salvation or *moksha*. For the upper caste Hindu, life is divided into four stages or *ashrams*: student, householder, retired and forest ascetic.

In married life (*grhastha*), husband and wife enjoy *kama* (pleasure) and *artha* (business and property), but both must be moderated by *dharma* (moral discipline). "Thus a man practicing *dharma*, *artha* and *kama*, enjoys happiness in this world and in the world to come" (1.2.ans 4).[8]

> When a girl of the same caste and a virgin is married in accordance with the precepts of Holy Writ, the results of the union are the acquisition of *dharma*, *artha*, offspring, affinity, increase of friends, and untarnished love (3.1).

A man should fix his affections on a girl from a good family with live parents, who is three years or more younger, healthy, beautiful, etc. The husband should have similar qualities, but a girl who is already joined to others should never be loved. Parents and friends help arrange a proper union.

In the Hindu marriage ceremony hymns are to be sung only for virgins. "The hymns (*mantras*) are the established token whereby a (legitimate) wife may be recognized." To complete the rites, the couple take seven steps around the sacred fire (*The Laws of Manu*, 8.226, 227)[9] so they will walk together through life doing *dharma*.

Matrimony is the only real sacrament for women and it includes: the Vedic consecration of women, her obligations to her husband, obedience to her *guru*, household duties, and attention to the sacred fire (2.67). Only once is a girl given in marriage (9.47). "A man is as much as his wife, himself and his children" (9.45) and what a husband is, his wife also is. The sacred fire of the wedding rites originally was carried home and kept burning by the wife till her husband died, when it lit his funeral *ghat*.

The sacred fire witnesses the marriage contract with its prayers, petitions, promises, presents and blessings, and the bride places her foot on a stone, pledging her fidelity. The two may tie a knot or touch a yoke as a sign of their faithful union. Together they will pursue *artha*, *kama* and *dharma* and so attain *moksha*.

The three main aims of Hindu marriage are: to promote religion in
the household by *puja* (worship) and *samskara* (ritual purification);
putra or progeny; and *pitri*, honor to the ancestors. As husband and
wife unite in generation, so they share common religious duties
(*dharma*) as revealed in sacred scriptures (*sruti*) (9.96). They show their
devotion to Brahma, the Creator, by studying and teaching the *Vedas*.
Moreover, they offer food and water to their forebearers, give fire-
offerings to the *devas* (gods), food to animals, and hospitality to men.

Although sex pleasure (*kama*) is good and proper to married life,
nonetheless, the newlyweds abstain for the first three nights to insure
tender beginning, show that sex is of secondary importance, and
heighten their joy of union.

Since the intercourse of husband and wife is a sacred event in
which *Shiva* and *Shakti* are joined, it is preceded by the sacrament of
garbhadhana on the fourth night. Moreover, this is not a sacrament of
the couple, but rather of their child, about to be conceived. As the
husband prepares to deposit his seed (*adhana*) in his wife's womb
(*garbha*), holy *mantras* are recited. Furthermore, Hindu couples believe that by their pious and sacred union they will attract a holy soul
into the womb of the mother.

The wife should honor her husband as a god and obey him and so
be exalted in heaven and not do anything disagreeable to him (5.154).
The husband must reciprocate for "where women are honored, there
the gods rejoice," (3.56) and if they grieve, the family perishes (3.57).

"In what family the husband is pleased by his wife, and so also the
wife by her husband, truly prosperity is ever firm there" (3.60). For if
the wife is not happy, how can she please her husband?

"By a bad marriage, by neglect of the rites and want of study of the
Vedas, families decay," (3.63). On the other hand, "prosperous by the
mantras, families, though of little wealth, attain respectability and
attract great glory" (3.66). A wife, loyal to her husband even after his
death, disciplined and faithful, attains his abode in heaven and is called
virtuous (5.165).

A husband may overmarry his wife if she is ill-tempered, hateful,
infertile, diseased, etc. However, she is never discarded. Rather she
becomes a mother to the new young bride (9.80, 81).

Adultery is severely punished by banishment, castration and even death (8.552). Even meeting the wife of another in a lonely place or touching her improperly is considered adulterous (8.556).

The household stage of life is the most important since it supports both the old and the young. When gray hair, grandchildren and menopause come, earthly occupations are given up for a life of public service. Some Brahmins pursue the life of a forest ascetic, or *sannyasi*.

We have seen in this chapter some love, marriage and family customs in several ancient civilizations in Africa, North America, China and India, and parallel practices may be found elsewhere. In general, promiscuity is frowned upon, marital fidelity is encouraged and adultery severely punished. Monogamy is the rule except where environmental conditions or infertility allow the taking of more consorts. And even here the first wife is the head.

Marriage has a religious and sacramental aspect. It is almost universally sacred, witnessed by the ancestral spirits. Or it is a theomorphy in which the nuptials of the gods are celebrated.

CHAPTER TWO

It Is Not Good That The Man Should Be Alone (Gn 2:18)

ADAM AND EVE

The Yahwist tells the story of Adam and Eve to remind the Israelites of their pristine monogamy which they had too easily forgotten by the time of the monarchy.

Like many primordial archetypes, Adam is split in two by God to be reunited with Eve in marriage. Whereas the dividing in many myths is a punishment, here Yahweh is compassionate (Gn 2:18). "It is not good that the man should be alone. I will make a helper fit for him" (RSV).

So, putting Adam into a deep sleep, He removes a rib and, forming it into a woman, brings her to him. Adam is delighted. "This one, at last, is bone of my bones and flesh of my flesh. She shall be called 'woman' (*ishah*) because she was taken from man (*ish*)."

"Therefore, a man leaves his father and mother and cleaves to his wife, and they become one flesh, and the man and his wife were both naked, and were not ashamed" (Gn 2:23-25).

The Yahwist calls for a return to this primordial monogamy—the one body, which does not mean only the physical part of man, but rather one whole person, body and soul. In this sense, it is a return to his original androgyny.

Adam and Eve's innocent nakedness may reflect the unashamed nudity common among aborigines. But something happened on the road to paradise. The serpent tempts Eve to eat of the forbidden tree in order to be more like God. Then she runs to Adam with this delicious fruit. "The eyes of both were opened and they knew that they were naked" (Gn 3:7). They grabbed a bunch of fig leaves to cover their privates. And when they heard God coming, they ran and hid in shame. God asks them, "Who told you that you were naked?" (Gn 3:11).

What was the sin of Adam and Eve? Pride, selfishness, disobedience, sexuality? The snake is a common symbol of sex and fertility. This together with their bareness and shame might point to a sexual mistake, a deviation from the divine plan.

From this archetypal fault comes the Jewish *Yetzer ha-Ra* and Christian concupiscence, built-in drives which, though good and created by God, are prone to error, especially in sexual matters. This is not due to any error in God's plan, but rather because of man's own fault as described in the Genesis story.

God punishes Eve with painful child-bearing, and Adam with endless toil in the uncooperative soil till death. Cast out of the garden, they must live in a world of pain, sweat and sin.

The Priestly tradition of *Genesis* (5th century BC) stresses more the fertility of marriage *vis-a-vis* the companionship of the Yahwist story. "God created man in his own image, in the image of God he created them, male and female he created them." He blessed their marriage, saying, "Be fruitful and multiply and fill the earth and subdue it" (Gn 1:27-28). And he gave them charge over the creatures of the earth.

In creating mankind God uses Himself as a model, male and female. This is the closest thing we have to a hierogamy in Genesis, namely, the male and female image in God in which humanity is created.

To multiply, fill the earth and subdue it. This is the first *mitzvah* (divine commandment) recorded by the Priest and stressed again later by the rabbis. It is the universal law of tribal society, that is, marriage for the sake of procreation.

Whereas the Yahwist brings out the interpersonal and centripetal, namely, the cure for Adam's loneliness, the Priest speaks of the centrifugal cosmic obligation of continuing God's work of creation.

In *Genesis* we find the basis of the famous threefold good of marriage. First is the mutual love and fidelity described by the Yahwist. Second is its sanctity, modeled on God's holy image and blessed by Him. Third is procreation to fill the earth, the last two stressed in the Priestly tradition.

TORAH

In patriarchal times the family was ruled by the father, with a paternal uncle next in line. The family or house (*beth*) often included three generations plus servants, widows, orphans, etc. Sometimes *beth* was used in a wider sense of tribe, clan or nation. Family solidarity was illustrated by the go'el or protector, such as the paternal uncle. In this sense, Yahweh is the avenger of Israel.

As the culture becomes more complex and urbanized, the family is smaller and less self-sufficient, and the father's authority is limited. And as individualism grows, there is less family solidarity, protection and avenging of the needy.[1]

The common law of the patriarchal East, for example, the *Code of Hammurabi*, is reflected in the Hebrew Torah.

Although the patriarchs had one wife, they could take another if the first wife was infertile. Thus the story of Abraham, Sarah and Hagar (Gn 16:1-2). Abraham also had concubines.

In general, as de Vaux notes (24), there was a relative monogamy. "For there is never more than one lawful wedded wife," but in the time of the judges and kings, restrictions loosened. For example, some kings had harems.

However, in practice the common people had one or at most two wives. Often it is a desire of progeny that leads a husband to seek another wife. Prophets and wise men warned the Israelites to be loyal to the wife of their youth. Far and away monogamy was the most common form of marriage in Israel.

In Hebrew society, the wife, children and servants were under the patriarch's authority, as *baal* or master. The future husband had to pay *mohar* to the girl's father (Gn 34:12), either in money or service. Moreover, he does not buy his bride, but rather compensates her father for her fertility. Probably the father only used the interest on the *mohar*, the principal being saved as insurance against the bride's divorce or widowhood. Patriarchal society was also patrilocal, in which the bride left home to live with her husband's clan.

Hebrew marriage was early, post-puberty, and so arranged by the parents. The boy could make known his preference and could even bypass his parents' wishes.

Virginity had high priority in Israel, as did marital fidelity. Thus, if a bride is found to be a non-virgin, she is stoned to death. "Because she brought folly in Israel by playing the harlot in her father's house" (Dt 22:20-21).

For adultery both are to be put to death, for example, "If a man lies with a betrothed virgin and she does not cry out." Betrothal in Israel is considered as marriage except that the bride lives in her father's house till her husband takes her home for the wedding feast.

But, if someone violates the betrothed, way out in the country where no one can hear her scream, the raper only is to die for it is like "a man attacking and murdering his neighbor" (Dt 22:26).

It was customary for Hebrews to marry their own. Although sometimes they wed foreigners, this is forbidden as a danger to the faith (Ex 34:15-16). Also the marriage of close relatives is not allowed (Lv 18:6).

De Vaux comments (33) that marriage in Israel, as in Mesopotamia, is a civil contract, although it is called a covenant of God (Pr 2:17) and is compared by the prophets to the union of Yahweh and Israel.

The Hebrew marriage formula: "She is my wife and I am her husband, from this day forever." Then the bride enters the groom's house with much rejoicing, feasting and singing.

Divorce was allowed for good reasons in Eastern codes, for example, (Dt 24:1-4) if his wife finds no favor in his eyes, "because he has found some indecency in her, and he writes her a bill of divorce and puts it in her hand and sends her out of his house, and she departs out of his house."

But if she remarries and is divorced again, or her second husband dies, her first spouse may not take her back. There is much speculation over this indecency which makes the wife unacceptable. Some feel that it might be incest, since adultery is punishable by death.

Jesus said that Moses allowed divorce because of hardened hearts (Mt 19:8). The divorce formula: "She is no longer my wife, and I am no longer her husband" (Ho 2:4). Divorce was not to be precipitous, since thought had to be given and a writ of divorce (*get*) carefully prepared and handed over to the wife. In later times rabbinical courts mediated family squabbles.

As we have seen, a man may not divorce his wife whom he violated when she was a virgin (Dt 22:28-9), nor may he divorce her if he falsely accuses her of not being a virgin (Dt 22:13-19).

Although he may not take her back if she remarries and is sent away again, Hosea forgave Gomer who had become a prostitute (2-3). And David welcomes back Mikal since he had never formally divorced her (1 S 18:20-7; 2 S 3:12-16).

How much was divorce used among the Hebrews? Probably not all that much, for it was restricted and the prophets and wise men opposed it. Hammurabi told the husband to pay his divorced wife, if she were guiltless. In Hebrew tradition she probably used her *mohar* for support.

The *Torah* is strict against adultery, for it is a sin against God and man (Ex 20:14; Dt 5:18; Lv 18:20). In the Decalogue the prohibition of adultery is between killing and stealing for it partakes in both (Ex 20:13-15). If marriage is two in one person, then adultery kills the union by going to another. The penalty is death. Although one may go to a prostitute, he may never ravish another's wife, for she is consecrated (*hekdesh*) to her husband.

The levirate marriage is found in Israel as well as among other ancient peoples. Here a man takes in his brother's childless widow to perpetuate his name, house and heritage. When Onan refused this obligation, God killed him (Gn 38:8-10). If there are no brothers-in-law, as in the case of Ruth, another male relative may assume the duty.

Though the Israelite husband is his wife's *baal* or master, she is not his slave. He cannot sell her. And, even if he divorces her, she can remarry and use her *mohar* for support.

Although *ahab*, to love, can have many meanings in the *Torah*, it most frequently expresses the love between husband and wife. Love can mean something more than sexual affection. "Then Isaac brought her into his tent and took Rebekah and she became his wife, and he loved her" (Gn 24:67).

Moreover, there can be degrees of love, especially where more than one wife is concerned (Dt 21:15). This love of preference can destroy family peace and harmony in a polygamous household.

Hebrew marriage from the beginning (Gn 1:28) was child-oriented, and the patriarchs hoped for countless progeny (Gn 24:60, 15:5, 22:17, 26:4). Infertility is to be remedied by the children of another spouse.

Sons are highly prized to carry on the name and house, for the daughters would soon leave to join their husbands' families. Though the firstborn son takes precedence, he can lose his rights by disgrace.

There could be sometimes a tension between the law of primogeniture and the son of one's old age, thus sometimes God chose the younger, for example, Abel, Jacob, David and Solomon.

Under the law of first fruits the firstborn belongs to God. And the Levites are especially consecrated to Yahweh in lieu of the firstborn (Nb 3:40-41).

The parents take God's place in the family. This is illustrated by the Hebrew fifth commandment, the only law with a promised reward, namely, a long life. The parents, as God's surrogates, may bless or curse. While the mother begins the child's moral education, the father teaches him prayers from the *Shema* to the *Tephillah*, and later takes him to the synagogue to learn *Torah*.

Judaism is basically a home and family religion, celebrating the Sabbath and other feasts, and reciting *Shema* and *Tephillah* together. The Sabbath helps to solidify the family in a day of peace, rest, prayer, Torah, feasting and joy, anticipating eternity. The mother is the Sabbath queen, while the father recites the *Kiddush*, or benediction. The *Shema* is the family prayer of Israel (Dt 6:4-5). "The Lord is one Lord, And you shall love him with your whole heart, soul and might, keeping the words in your heart."

> And you shall teach them diligently to your children, and shall talk of them when you sit in your house, and when you walk by the way, and when you lie down and when you rise . . . . And you shall write them on the doorposts of your house and on your gates (Dt 6:7-8).

The family is constantly reminded to love God. If they love him, they will respect his image in the family and neighbor. God is blessed frequently during the day, and especially at meals, which are a holy sharing in his bounty. Later the *Tephillah* or Eighteen Benedictions is recited two or three times a day.

PROPHETS

Since the prophets are God's protectors of the weak and the voices of his anger and compassion, we might expect that their view of marriage would lean more towards reconciliation and forgiveness.

In prophecy, marriage evolves beyond the tribal and patriarchal goals of fertility and lineage. Its sanctity and fidelity reflect the everlasting covenant between Yahweh and Israel. Even though his chosen one continues to wander in sin, Yahweh continues to love her and wants her back.

Though we found no explicit hierogamy in Genesis, in the prophets, the love of Yahweh for Israel is important. For he loved her first and Moses arranged the wedding on Mt. Sinai. The Torah is their contract, and the two lovers honeymoon in the desert.

If Israel is faithful to her marriage testament, Yahweh will bless her. If not, he will punish her and her children. He is a jealous lover, demanding their love in return (Dt 6:5).

Other heirogamies are found in neighboring peoples, such as the Canaanite Baal and Anath, whose marriage is celebrated in human union.

Hosea is the first prophet to use nuptial language to explain Yahweh's covenant with Israel (1:2-3:5). Hosea had trouble with his own roaming wife, Gomer, whom he compares to the unfaithful Israel.

When the mother of his children has become a prostitute, he walls her in and pursues her lovers and she will repent. "I will go and return to my first husband, for it was better with me than now" (Ho 2:7). The Lord tells Hosea:

> Go again, love a woman who is beloved of a paramour and is an adulteress. Even as the Lord loves the people of Israel, though they turn to other gods and love raisin cakes (Ho 3:1).

So Hosea buys back Gomer. "You must dwell as mine for many

days; you shall not play the harlot, or belong to another man; so will it be also to you" (Ho 3:3).

On Yahweh's part, though Israel is faithless, he is ever compassionate and forgiving, calling her back to a second wilderness honeymoon (2:14). There she will respond to him as she did in the land of Egypt. He will betroth her to him forever (Ho 2:21). Yahweh always takes the initiative. Even though his love is unrequited, he still pursues his bride in hope.

There is a parallel between Yahweh and Israel, Hosea and Gomer, hierogamic archetype and human marriage. Though both Israel and Gomer are unfaithful and deserving of punishment, God's forgiveness and reconciliation should be mirrored in Hosea.

In Ezekiel, Yahweh finds a baby girl, Judah, raises her to maidenhood and is betrothed to her, but she, too, is not loyal. So Yahweh delivers her to her lovers, Egypt, Philistia, Assyria and Chaldea, who strip her naked and stone her.

In chapter 23, Ezekiel tells the story of two sisters, Oholah and Oholibah (Samaria and Jerusalem) who also were not true to Yahweh. He will be compassionate if only they show repentance.

Second Isaiah notes that although Yahweh's bride is in exile, she cannot forget him. Judah must overcome her despair, for Yahweh is still her husband. Though she is forsaken, Yahweh still loves her. She hopes that he will take her back as his bride, no longer abandoned, but now called "my delight is in her," and her land "married."

> For the Lord delights in you and your land shall be married. For as a young man marries a virgin, so shall your sons marry you. And as the bridegroom rejoices over the bride, so shall your God rejoice over you (Is 62:4-5).

Like earlier prophets, Malachi also stresses marital fidelity and forgiveness. For example, Judah has profaned the temple and married an idolatrous woman. And so his sacrifice is unacceptable.

> Because the Lord is witness between you and the wife of your youth, with whom you have broken faith, though she is your companion, your betrothed wife. Did he not make one being

with flesh and spirit; and what does that one require but godly offspring? You must then safeguard life that is your own and not break faith with the wife of your youth. For I hate divorce, says the Lord, God of Israel (Ml 2:14-16).

Moreover, to marry someone outside of God's people is to desecrate His temple, since the man generally follows the god of his wife. In the prophets we see that marriage is more than just a civil contract, for it is a holy covenant witnessed by the Lord.

The wife of one's youth is not to be rejected when she is old. The Hebrew girls married after puberty and aged quickly in the hot, dry climate, no doubt a factor in rejecting the old wife for a new and younger one.

The ethical cannot be separated from the ritual. If the offerer is unfaithful and divorcing, the altar is covered with tears and God no longer hears his prayers (Ml 2:13). Furthermore, a divorce is not allowed to a husband who is immoral himself.

SONGS AND PROVERBS

Since the Hebrews preserved their ancient heritage in song for liturgy and home, one would expect to find prayers and petitions dealing with love, marriage and the family. For example, *Psalm 45*. The daughter (queen) is advised to forget her people and her father's house. She is to bow down to her lord and husband.

She wears gold and colored robes, and is let in to the king, accompanied by virgins. And the poet promises them sons, honors and immortality.

A successful marriage can only be founded on God. "Unless the Lord build the house, they labor in vain who build it" (Ps 127). And he will give them progeny. "Like arrows in the hands of a warrior are the sons of one's youth." Happy is the father whose quiver is full of sons.

One who walks in the way of the Lord will be happy and blessed. "Your wife shall be like a fruitful vine within your house; your children shall be like olive shoots around your table" (Ps 128).

Thus is one blessed who fears the Lord. "The Lord bless you from Zion. May you see the prosperity of Jerusalem all the days of your life. May you see your children's children" (Ps 128).

The *Greatest Song,* or the *Song of Solomon,* was probably sung at weddings. In it two young lovers, the shepherd boy and his beautiful Shulamite girl, and Solomon make a *menage a trois.* But Solomon has a change of heart, backing away in favor of the two young lovers.

Tension and repose end in mutual possession. "As a lily among brambles, so is my beloved among maidens. As an apple tree among the trees of the wood, so is my beloved among young men" (Sg 2:2-3). Her lover comes skipping across the mountains and hills like a gazelle or a young stag. "Arise my love, my fair one, and come away" (Sg 2:13), He comes and goes as if testing her love.

"I opened to my beloved, but my beloved had turned and gone.... I sought him, but did not find him. I called him, but he did not answer me" (Sg 5:6). One at last. "I am my beloved's and his desire is for me. Come, my beloved, let us go forth into the fields and lodge in the villages" (Sg 7:10-11).

The prophetic marriage between Yahweh and Israel helped pave the way for the rabbinical interpretation of the Song of Solomon as Yahweh's love song for Israel. Generations of mystics have heard it sing the joys of the love between the individual soul and God.

The story of Tobias and Sarah in the *Book of Tobit* describes a marriage in the intertestamental period (3-2 century B.C.). Raguel, Sarah's father, taking her by the hand, gives her to Tobias, saying: "Take her according to the law of Moses. And take her with you to your father" (Tb 7:12). And he blessed them.

Then Raguel called his wife, Edna. He wrote out the contract, and they set their seals on it. Since Sarah's previous husbands had died on the wedding night at the hands of a demon, they perform the protecting rituals prescribed by the angel Azarias (Raphael).

Then Tobias prays, praising God and recalling the primordial pair, whose union they are about to recapitulate. "And now, O Lord, I am not taking this sister of mine because of lust, but with sincerity. Grant that I may find mercy and may grow old together with her." They both say "Amen" and retire.

Then Raguel gives the newlyweds a fourteen day feast, promising them one half of his property now and the rest when he and Edna die. Sending the lovers on their way, he blesses them. "The God of heaven will prosper you, my children, before I die" (Tb 10:11). Kissing Sarah, he tells her to honor her in-laws as parents. And Edna to Tobias:

> The Lord of heaven bring you back safely, dear brother, and grant me to see your children by my daughter Sarah, that I may rejoice before the Lord. See, I am entrusting my daughter to you. Do nothing to grieve her (Tb 10:13).

The *Proverbs* safeguard marital fidelity. Drink water from your own well. Do not scatter your waters through the streets.

> Let them be for yourself alone, and not for strangers with you. Let your fountain be blessed, and rejoice in the wife of your youth, a lovely hind, a graceful doe. Let her affection fill her at all times with delight. Be infatuated always with her love. Why should you be infatuated, my son, with a loose woman and embrace the bosom of an adventuress? (Pr 5:17-20).

A loving wife will keep her husband faithful. She is more valuable than pearls. "The heart of her husband trusts in her, and he will have no lack of gain. She does him good, not harm, all the days of her life" (Pr 31:11-12).

She makes cloth, buys food, gets up early to fix breakfast, invests in real estate, plants a vineyard. She is strong and stays up late spinning, helps the poor and provides warm clothing for her family in winter time.

Her husband is prominent in politics. She makes garments to sell, and does not fear the future. She speaks wisely and kindly, watching over the conduct of her home. Her children and her husband praise her.

"Many women have done excellently, but you surpass them all" (Pr 31:29). Though her charm and beauty may fade, "the woman who fears the Lord is to be praised" (Pr 31:30).

"Do not deprive yourself of a wise and good wife, for her charm is worth more than gold" (Si 7:19).

Discipline your children and watch over your daughter's chastity. Do not indulge her, and give her in marriage to a man of understanding. "If you have a wife who pleases you, do not cast her out" (Si 7:26). Remember your parents who gave you life. "What can you give back to them that equals their gift to you (Si 7:28).

Fidelity is a constant theme in the wisdom literature. For example, Ben Sira warns about loose women and singers. "Do not look intently at a virgin, lest you stumble and incur penalties for her" (59:5). Never give yourself to prostitutes.

> Keep modesty of the eyes. Turn your eyes away from a shapely woman, and do not look intently at beauty belonging to another. Many have been misled by a woman's beauty, and by it passion is enkindled like a fire (Si 9:8-9).

Avoid dining or drinking with another's wife. Though one may feel that nobody sees him when he secretly defiles his marriage bed, "he does not realize that the eyes of the Lord are 10,000 times brighter than the sun. They look upon all the ways of men and perceive even the hidden places" (Si 23:19).

An unfaithful wife who has an illegitimate son disobeys God's law, wrongs her husband, commits adultery, and disgraces her children (Si 23:22-27). She makes her husband sigh and feel depressed.

> Happy is the husband of a good wife. The number of his days is doubled. A loyal wife rejoices her husband and he will complete his years in peace. A good wife is a great blessing. She will be granted among the blessings of the man who fears the Lord. Whether rich or poor, his heart is glad and at all times his face is cheerful (Si 26:1-4).
>
> While a scolding, lascivious wife is a scourge, a wife's charm delights her husband, and her skill puts fat on his bones. A silent wife is a gift of the Lord, and there is nothing so precious as a disciplined soul. A modest wife adds charm to charm, and no balance can weight the value of a chaste soul (Si 26:13-15).

As the rising sun, the virtuous wife lights up her home. Parents should keep watch over their sons, disciplining and educating them. Although "the father may die, yet he is not dead, for he has left behind him one like himself" (Si 30:4-5), in whom he rejoices in life and in death.

On the other hand, one who spoils his son will find him troublesome and stubborn. Laughter and comaraderie should give way to discipline, "that you may not be offended by his shamelessness" (Si 30:13).

A good father worries over his daughter lest she never get a husband. Or, once married, she prove to be barren, or that she be seduced or be unfaithful. Better harshness now than disgrace later.

THE RABBIS

The *Torah* is the law of love. The rabbis succeeded the priests and the prophets as teachers of the Law. Love of God and love of neighbor are the two pillars of the *Torah*, and both begin in the home. One should love his neighbor as God loves him or her. Love that is only based on bodily beauty will fade away with the inevitable inroads of age.

"*Yetzer* is human desire, imagination, and concupiscence, and can be either good or evil. *Yetzer ha Ra* is desire turned to evil."

Man stumbles into sex sins because of his *Yetzer ha Ra*, the evil influence, which, however, is basically a good drive. Without it one would never marry, build a home, raise children or start a business.

Though the wandering *yetzer* can become unruly, God gave remedies in the *Torah* and marriage.

Marriage is holy and blessed by God. A married woman is prohibited to all others as *hekdesh* or a sacred object, for the *Shekhinah* of God accompanies her.

Marriage for Judaism is a sacred *mitzvah* to be fruitful and multiply (Gn 1:28).[2] The Jewish wedding process included the formal betrothal with its *ketubah* and *mohar*, the taking of the bride to the home of the groom, celebration and consummation.

The wedding is the foundation of the home, signified by the canopy (*huppah*) under which the bride and groom stand and drink wine. Then the groom places a ring on his bride's finger. "You are consecrated unto me with this ring according to the Law of Moses and the people of Israel."

Mutual support is outlined in the marriage contract (*ketubah*) which is read. Then seven blessings are recited to God for marriage and the family, the divine image in man, joy and happiness of the bride and groom. A prayer is said for the restoration of Jerusalem.

Rosenberg concludes. "For all Jews marriage is a sacred act and for that reason it is called *kiddushin*, or sanctification." It is a mutual consecration in the spiritual order of life. "Indeed, if marriage is not sacred, then nothing else in life can ever be" (118, 119).

In Judaism there are no churches, for the home is the church. The *mezzuzah* on the doorpost reminds all that the family is built on the total dedication to the God of the *Shema*. The many family prayers from the *Shema* to the *Tephillah* and the *berakoth* illustrate this domestic consecration in their daily life.

YAHWEH AND HIS SHEKHINAH

Medieval and Renaissance Jewish Kabbalists taught the sanctification of marriage based on the ancient hierogamy of Yahweh and His *Shekhinah*.[3]

God's *Shekhinah*, His Holy Presence, the cloud and pillar of fire, loving companion of Moses in the desert, became the divine spouse among the rabbis. She joins scripture scholars and those in prayer, and she intercedes for Israel with Yahweh.

The *Shekhinah* is at the heart of the Jewish home, where she is personified by the mother. She watches over the sick and lies between the husband and wife in their marriage bed. Her sweet voice is like the tinkling of a bell or the chirping of a bird.

When the husband goes on a journey, the *Shekhinah* accompanies him so that he will be male and female, as God intended. Upon his return, he gives his wife pleasure, for she has obtained the *Shekhinah* for him. This is a religious joy, giving happiness also to the *Shekhinah* and spreading peace in the world (Bahir 1:50a).

If his wife becomes pregnant in this sacred union, "the celestial partner imparts to the child a holy soul, for this covenant is called the covenant of the Holy One, blessed be He." Moreover, peace comes to the house in which the religious duty of conjugal intercourse is enjoyed in gladness in the presence of the *Shekhinah*.

Husband and wife celebrate the hierogamy of Yahweh and His *Shekhinah*. So the husband has two women, mother and wife. The one blesses him, while the other supports and joins him. While he is alone, his heavenly mother accompanies him. But when he is with his wife, the upper and lower *Shekhinoth* are joined.

As the divine union is recapitulated in marital love, so it is destroyed in adultery with the tempting *Lilith*. *Matronit-Shekhinah* and *Lilith* personify sexual dualism and the ambivalence of the *Yetzer*.

Sex can be divine when it joins the *Shekhinah* with her King, or illicit when her spouse unites with *Lilith*.

Whereas Pentecost each year celebrates the marriage of Yahweh and Israel, the Sabbath is a weekly observance, so that at midnight the *Shekhinah* mates with her divine partner in the temple.

On the Sabbath eve the husband must choose between the *Shekhinah* and *Lilith*. The Sabbath rite in 16th century Safed resembled a wedding—walking around the table, singing, reciting proverbs.[4] During the meal they sang of the union of the King with His Sabbath bride. Then at midnight husband and wife retire as the King and His *Shekhinah*, from whose union the soul of their child comes.

Thus in Jewish tradition marriage is ordained by God and blessed by Him to fill the earth and subdue it, and to join husband and wife in mutual love and support. Moreover, it is sacred, *theomorphy*, recapitulating the eternal hierogamy.

CHAPTER THREE

"From the Beginning It Was Not So" (Mt 19:8)

HOLY FAMILY

The family of Jesus has long been the paradigm of Christian marriage. Moreover, their prominent role in the early Church may be seen in the apocrypha, filling in the details of the early life of Jesus, Mary and Joseph for the edification of Christian families.

We know that Mary was betrothed to Joseph. And Galilean betrothal, which included *ketubah* and *mohar*, precluded sexual contact until the bride was brought to the groom's home—often a year later—with great celebration and festivity. So Joseph, understandably upset at Mary's pregnancy, decided to put her away quietly, until the angel told him that the child was of the Holy Spirit (Mt 1:18-25).

Christians believe in a preexisting archetypal divine family of Father, Son and Holy Spirit, which is mirrored in the Holy Family of Nazareth and indeed, in all Christian families. Mary is the spouse of the Father through the Holy Spirit, and, as a Jewish mother, is the special representative of the Spirit in the home. Mary begets God's Son as the child Jesus.

Moreover, Joseph's adoption of Jesus imitates God's fatherhood of man. Joseph acts as the family protector through the trips to Bethlehem, Egypt and Jerusalem. And, although he is not Jesus' natural father, he is, nonetheless, His real father, since he guards, teaches and guides Jesus in His early years. For Jesus learned *Torah, Shema* and *Tephillah* from Joseph, and was known as Jesus, son of Joseph, or the carpenter's Son.

Mary also teaches Jesus by word and example. She is queen of the Sabbath, as Joseph recites the *Kiddush*. Together they celebrate with joy the many feasts from *Rosh Hashanah* to *Shavuot*. Often they went to Jerusalem for the Passover. And once when they found Jesus missing on the return trip, they went back and found Him studying with the doctors of the law. Then He returned obediently with them to Nazareth.

When Joseph died, Jesus worked as a carpenter to support Mary. And Mary, as a good Jewish mother, worried over her son, following Him to Cana and Capernaum. There are times when He seems impatient with her solicitude. "Who are my mother and my brothers? Those who do the will of my Father" (Mt 12:46-50).

But Mary still follows Him to Jerusalem and the cross. In His last agony Jesus gives His young disciple John to His mother as a son. As Mary, through the Holy Spirit, is the mother of Jesus Christ, the head of the Mystical Body, so the Christian mother, by the same Spirit, is the parent of new members of the Mystical Body, adopted sons and daughters of God and Mary and foster brothers and sisters of Jesus.

Mary's pain and bravery at Calvary inspire all mothers of sorrow. One might wonder if the Holy Spirit would have come to the little *haburah* in Jerusalem on the first *Shavuot*, if Mary were absent. For, according to Jewish tradition, the mother of the family brings Yahweh's *Shekhinah* home.

The apocrypha describe Mary's leadership in the early Church, advising the apostles and departing from their midst to join her son and husband in heaven.

THE BRIDEGROOM COMES

Jewish apocalyptic literature sees Israel as the betrothed of Yahweh, but not yet his wife in full union. So she waits expectantly for his coming.

Jesus describes the kingdom or days of the Messiah as a joyful wedding feast. For example, the virgin companions of the betrothed anxiously await the arrival the groom to take his bride home for the feast. When he comes at Sabbath midnight, the five wise maids rush out to greet him with their lamps brightly burning. While their unprepared sisters go off to buy oil, the prepared virgins accompany bride and groom to the wedding feast (Mt 25:1-13).

Jesus also spoke of the coming of the bridegroom Messiah. When His disciples were criticized for not fasting, Jesus asked: why should they mourn when they are with the bridegroom? (Mt 9:14-15).

Another time He compares the kingdom to a wedding feast that a king plans for his son (Mt 22:1-14). Those who are invited are ungrateful, even killing the messengers of the king. So he invites others to this eschatological feast, but they should come attired in a proper wedding garment.

The kingdom will be a time of joy, an eternal Sabbath. As the King meets his Sabbath-Bride-*Shekhinah* at midnight in the temple, so it will be in the eschaton. The guests will have eternal happiness.

In these parables we can get a glimpse of some of the wedding customs of the times: betrothal, procession to the groom's home, feast, guests, joy, etc. Clearly it is the happiest event in Jewish life.

John the Baptizer describes himself as the best man of the bridegroom, Jesus Christ, at whose side he stands full of joy (Jn 3:28-30). The bridegroom must increase, while the best man fades into the background for his job is finished when the bride and groom unite.

JESUS TEACHES ON LOVE, MARRIAGE AND THE FAMILY

Jesus, as a wandering teacher, a *maggid*, spent much of His time preaching to the *am-ha-aretz*, who were mediocre observers of the law compared to the strict Pharisees.

In anticipation of the Messianic age, continent and celibate groups sprung up during the intertestamental period. For example, the Essenes of Qumran, the Therapeuts of Egypt, the Baptists of the Jordan Valley. Some rabbis left home and family to marry Torah and *Shekhinah*.

So prevalent was this that a *mitzvah* had to be passed, requiring marriage and children. "No man may abstain from keeping the law 'Be fruitful and multiply' (Gn 1:28), unless he already has children" (M Yev 6:67).

Though tradition has Jesus and most of His *haburah* as single, he taught the holiness of marriage. For example, in (Jn 2:1-12) we see that

Jesus and Mary, along with friends, relatives and disciples attend the marriage feast at Cana. This is, as we have seen, the celebration of a holy event, *kiddushin*, the joining of man and woman according to the Law of Moses in the groom's home. The wine is the harbinger of happiness as it is in the *Sabbath kiddush*. Moreover, the changing of water into wine mirrors the miracle of the vineyard.

At Cana we have the prototype of the Christian marriage, in which husband and wife unite as Christ joins His Church in the feast. The theme of Jesus' marriage ethics is love, *agape*. Correlating with the total love of God of the *Shema* is the love of neighbor, the two great commandments. Our closest neighbors are our spouse and family. And the love of God flows to them through us (Mt 22:37-40).

Jesus says to love even those who hate us, for it is easy to love those who are nice to us, and of course, when we love our enemies, they become our friends. Love of those who have done us wrong ties in with forgiveness and reconciliation of spouses, as taught by the prophets.

If God forgives our many faults, why should we not forgive others, as the Lord's Prayer teaches? Refusal to forgive implies that we are sinless. *Agape* is the message of Jesus' parables from the prodigal son to the good shepherd. We should freely pass on the *agape* of God which we have so abundantly received.

Just as the adoration of false gods destroys our love of Yahweh, so going to another in adultery tears down marital love. Echoing the wisdom writers, Jesus teaches that lustful desires are also wrong, for "he has already committed adultery with her in his thoughts" (Mt 5:28).

In the prophetic line of forgiveness and compassion, Jesus saves the adulteress (Jn 8:7). Let the sinless ones throw stones at her. Concerning divorce Jesus follows more the strict school of Shammai than the liberal views of Hillel. "Everyone who divorces his wife and marries another, commits adultery. And he who marries a woman divorced from her husband likewise commits adultery" (Lk 16:18; Mt 5:31-32).

In Mark the Pharisees remind Jesus that Moses allowed divorce (Mk 10:2-12). Jesus replies that this was just a concession to the hardhearted. Also there was the influence of Middle Eastern codes, as we have seen.

From the beginning 'God made them male and female'; 'for this reason a man shall leave his father and mother and be joined to his wife and the two shall become one. So they are no longer two but one.' What God has joined, let no man put asunder (Mk 10:6-9).

This harkening back to Adam and Eve is common in the age of Messianic expectation, for the *eschaton* (the last age) will recapitulate the *archon* (the first age). Indeed, the Messiah is to be the last Adam, preaching a return to the pristine days before the fall. The ideal monogamy of Adam and Eve is to replace the polygamy, infidelity and divorce of more recent times.

Mark links Jesus' teaching against divorce with the story about the people bringing their children to Him. Divorce harms these little ones the most for they are the one flesh of the parents, split in two. The kingdom of heaven is for children and woe to anyone who scandalizes them. Then Jesus blesses them.

In Matthew Jesus also speaks of the marriage of Adam and Eve, but He allows divorce for *porneia* or lewdness. Jesus' strict interpretation of marital fidelity makes His disciples think that perhaps it would be better not to marry at all.

This leads Jesus to speak to them of the eunuchs for the sake of the kingdom. As we have seen, at the time of Jesus some Jewish monks and rabbis were following the celibate way in expectation of the Messianic age. Jesus recommends this (Mt 19:10-12).

In the *eschaton* there will be no need of marriage and procreation. For example when Jesus was asked which husband an oft-married woman will have in heaven, He replies: "When they rise from the dead, they neither marry nor are given in marriage, but are like angels in heaven" (Mk 12:25).

In the same theme Jesus says (Mt 10:34-39; Lk 12:51-53). "I have come to set a man against his father." And "He who loves father and mother more than me is not worthy of me."

These enigmatic sayings may reflect early conversions to Christianity, causing ill feelings in the families. The new Christian is reborn in the family of Christ. Also if necessary, he leaves his old family behind.

Marriage and the family, though good and blessed by God, are only temporary, so that in the light of the kingdom and eternity one may leave them behind. The first Christian Jews naturally followed the Jewish home-centered liturgies of prayer, Sabbath, feasts, etc., but according to the teachings of Jesus.

YOUNG CHURCHES

As an apostle-rabbi and circuit judge, Paul sends his advice and decisions by mail to his *diaspora* communities. As a good Pharisee in the tradition of Gamaliel, Paul draws the Christians' attention to the Holy Spirit who brings God's love into their homes. This is the special loving Presence of Yahweh which guarantees peace in the family. And the mother personifies this healing Spirit. Paul tells the Galatians that *agape* (love) is the essence of the ethical code (Gal 5:13-24). Though Christ calls us to freedom, "do not use your freedom as an opportunity for the flesh. But, through love, be servants of one another." The whole law may be summed up by "Love your neighbor as yourself."

"But if you bite and devour one another, take heed that you are not consumed by one another. . . .The fruit of the Spirit is love, joy, peace, patience, kindness, goodness, faithfulness, gentleness, self-control. Against such there is no law."

What better advice to Christian families than to curb the flesh, serve one another, refrain from devouring each other, in order to enjoy the peace and gentleness of the Holy Spirit?

Paul writes to the Corinthians with some sound advice in a difficult situation. Corinth, a busy port city, had plenty of prostitutes, lewd shows, baths, etc. to lure young local maidens and visiting sailors and travelers.

The sexual promiscuity of Corinth prompts Paul's comments on the sacredness of the human body, in which the *Shekhinah*, God's Holy Presence, dwells.

They forget that as Christians their bodies are members of Christ, Do we take the modest limbs of Christ and touch them to the bold bare body of a prostitute? If we have intercourse with her, we are one body with her and sin against our own body.

You must know that your body is a temple of the Holy Spirit, who is within, the Spirit you have received from God. You are not your own, you have been purchased, and at a price. So glorify God in your body (1 Cor 6:19-20).

The Shekhinah dwells in one who is united with God, but flees when he joins Satan. Sexual abuse of our or others' bodies desecrates the body of Christ. As Christ is the head of the Mystical Body, His Spirit is its soul. But when we are impure, His Spirit leaves.

In response to the Corinthians' concern about the loose morals of the city, Paul replies: "A man is better off having no relations with a woman. But to avoid immorality, every man should have his own wife. And every woman should have her own husband" (1 Cor 7:1-2).

Here we have the healing remedy of marriage which controls the wandering *yetzer*, as taught by the rabbis. Paul may also be idealizing the single life as some of the other rabbis and monks of the time. Paul himself was probably a widower who could devote his full time to the apostolate.

Since marriage is total self-giving, husband and wife no longer have rights over their own bodies. In their mutual exchange, they become one person (1 Cor 7:3-4).

Paul also notes that it is well for husband and wife not to be united too much. In fact, it makes good sense to abstain from sex from time to time, to bring freshness and enthusiasm to the marriage. Paul says that they may practice continence for a while for the sake of prayer. But then they should come back together again, for too long a separation encourages temptation (1 Cor 7:6).

Prayer, as Paul reminds the Corinthians, is important to marriage and the family. These short respites can have a spiritual dimension as well. He would like others to imitate his celibate apostolate. But if one is not called to this way of life, it is better to marry than to burn with passion (1 Cor 7:8-9).

As Jesus, Paul teaches strict monogamy and marital fidelity.

> To the married, I give charge, not I, but the Lord, that the wife should not separate from her husband. (But if she does, let her remain single or else be reconciled to her husband), and that the husband should not divorce his wife (1 Cor 7:10-11).

This is the forgiveness, healing and reconciliation taught by the prophets and the Lord. Paul next addresses himself to the problem of mixed marriages. In general, Judaism forbade union with Gentiles because of the danger to the faith. Yet in the *diaspora* (the Jewish dispersion) it was inevitable. In Jewish tradition, when a Gentile became a proselyte, his Gentile marriage could be annulled.

Paul respects the pagan marriage, telling them to live together as long as the unbelieving spouse is willing. "For the unbelieving husband is consecrated through his wife." And the unbelieving wife is also consecrated through her believing husband. The children are made holy, too, by their parents' union (1 Cor 7:14).

What if the unbelieving partner rejects his or her spouse? "The believing husband or wife is not bound in such cases. God has called you to live in peace." If there is no *shalom* in the home, the union is not fulfilling its purpose.

Paul adds: "Wife, how do you know that you will not save your husband; or you, husband, that you will not save your wife?" (1 Cor 7:16). Do not give up so easily. God's grace is invincible. God is ever compassionate and forgiving, and we should imitate his mercy.

In the light of the impending crisis (persecution?), Paul advises the Corinthians to stay the way they are, either married or unmarried, though it would not be wrong to marry. Historically, in times of crisis, wise people tend to put off their marriages till the climate is more conducive to raising a family.

Since the form of this world is passing away, we should act for eternity. "Let those who have wives act as though they had none" (1 Cor 7:29). Is Paul expecting the immediate coming of the kingdom, in which there will be neither marriage nor the giving in marriage? Jewish expectations were high in the first century and had led some to eschew marriage, as we have seen.

Some mistakenly try to pin down the *eschaton* in chronological time, when obviously it applies to *kairos*, sacred time. It is in this light of kairos that Paul speaks of continence and celibacy. The many practical cares of job and family leave the married man or woman little time for the kingdom. So Paul feels that an unmarried person is freer for the Lord's things (1 Cor 7:32-34).

Far from downgrading marriage, Paul is just facing the fact that marriage and the family are full time vocations, as also is the Lord's service. Some of Paul's fellow rabbis saw the incompatibility of marriage with *Torah* study and the apostolate.

But, once one's family is raised, he or she will have more time to serve the Lord (1 Cor 7:35). In fact, the practice of the early Church was to call to ministry men or women of mature age who had already raised their families well.

The lonely widows were encouraged by Paul to serve the community. Since marriage is for life, a woman is free to marry when her husband dies. "She will be happier, though, in my opinion, if she stays unmarried. I am persuaded that in this I have the spirit of God" (1 Cor 7:39-40).

Here again Paul is realistic, for few widows remarry. Also, the man of one wife and the woman of one husband were highly respected even among the pagans.

Paul compares the union of husband and wife to the archetypal hierogamy of Christ and the Church paralleling the Jewish betrothal of Yahweh and Israel.

As Christ is the head of His Church, so the husband is over his wife. And as man reflects the image and glory of God, the woman is the glory of her husband, for she was created from and for man. Husband and wife should be mutually supportive. The debate over who is head is hardly relevant, where the two are one.

> In the Lord, woman is not independent of man or man of woman. For, as woman was made from man, so man is now born of woman. And all things are from God (1 Cor 11:11-12).

Judaism, like most Eastern societies, is patriarchal. Authority lies in the husband. And the veil is a sign of his wife's consecration to him as a holy object, *hekdesh*.

Agape is the enduring, self-giving love that permeates the Christian family. Indeed, family and community meals are often called *agape*, for they illustrate family solidarity and care in the practical order.

It is *agape* that builds up the Christian family. *Oikodomei (oikon demo)* means literally to build a home. This is precisely what *agape* does, namely, fortify home and family, whereas hate tears down and knowledge puffs up (1 Cor 8:1-2).

Thus husband and wife must constantly love and support each other. Parents and children likewise reciprocate in affection. This makes family (*oikodome*), towards which the *oikonomia*, the management of the home, is geared.

Though it is true that many gifts support the Christian family and community, including prophecy and authority, *agape* is the main builder. "Therefore, encourage one another and build one another up, just as you are doing" (1 Th 5:11). Paul specifies *agape* in chapter 13 of First Corinthians. Prophecy, faith and renunciation are fruitless without love.

> Love is patient and kind, love is not jealous or boastful; love does not insist on its own way. It is not irritable or resentful; it does not rejoice at wrong, but rejoices in the right. Love bears all things, hopes all things, endures all things.

All other gifts pass, but faith, hope and love perdure, and the greatest is love, *agape*. *Agape* is self-giving, disinterested, theomorphic, eternal.

Paul calls his Corinthian church the bride of the Messiah, including both Jews and Gentiles. He jealously guards their betrothal as the best man who arranged the union. "I feel a divine jealousy for you, for I betrothed you to Christ, to present you as a pure bride to her one husband." But Satan deceives her.

To be a pure virgin, *parthenos*, is a high priority for a Jewish bride. Corinth is divided, and more like the woman with seven husbands: Apollo, Cephas, Paul, etc. But she is only betrothed to one, Christ. Betrothed to the Messiah, the Church anticipates with great joy the happy marriage feast of the kingdom.[1]

Paul shares nuptial imagery with apocalyptic Judaism which hopes for a Messianic age in which Israel will return as a bride from her exile to the peace and security of divine union. Whoever labors to prepare for the wedding will partake in the nuptial banquet.

While in their betrothal, the King promises gifts; as a husband, he will present them to his bride. As Moses arranged the betrothal of

Yahweh and Israel, so Paul joins Christ with His Church. Cleansed in the waters of Baptism, the Church is presented to the King as a pure and holy bride.

Paul is a very human person, sympathetic with the problems of others, for he himself has been tempted. Probably a widower, Paul feels the urge of the flesh, the evil inclination (Rm 7:14-25), with the law of the flesh fighting against the law of the Spirit.

Jewish tradition sees the Spirit fleeing illicit sex and being a part of holy marital relations. Only the law of the Spirit of Jesus Christ can set Paul free from the slavery of the law of sin and death (Rm 8:2). With the love of God in the Spirit, we can do anything so that nothing can separate us from the love of God in Jesus Christ (Rm 8:37-39).

It is not enough to be united to his *agape* unless we show it to others, since this is the real test of whether we have it, and of course, this begins in the family. "Love one another with brotherly affection; outdo one another in showing honor" (Rm 12:9-10). This is the key to success in the Pauline theology of marriage, namely, husband and wife outdoing each other in love and honor. A holy rivalry.

Since the *Torah* is the law of love, the only way it can be fulfilled is in love. "Owe no one anything except to love one another," for we fulfill the law by loving our neighbor.

All the commandments against adultery, stealing, coveting, etc. are summed up in: love your neighbor as yourself. "Love does no wrong to a neighbor. Therefore, love is the fulfilling of the law" (Rm 13:10). God's love for us must be shared with our neighbor, beginning in the family (Rm 15:7).

In his letter to the Colossians Paul gives some suggestions for moral conduct, especially in the home.

For example, put away harmful passions, immorality, impurity, covetousness, walk in Christ, leaving behind anger, wrath, malice, slander and foul talk, lying and divorce, for all are one in Christ.

As God's chosen ones, be holy, compassionate, putting up with each other's faults, forgiving as the Lord forgives us. "And, above all, put on love, which binds everything together in perfect harmony. Let the peace of Christ rule in your hearts, to which you were called in one body, and be thankful" (Col 3:1-15). Family love, *agape*, brings harmony and peace in Christ.

Families should teach and admonish each other in wisdom, singing psalms and hymns in thanksgiving. The wife should be subject to her husband in the Lord.

> Husbands, love your wives, and do not be harsh with them. Children, obey your parents in everything, for this pleases the Lord. Fathers, do not provoke your children, lest they become discouraged (Col 3:19-21).

Whatever they do should be as if they are serving Christ, seeing Christ in all. He will reward them (Col 3:16-25).

The firm foundation of faith, love and peace in the family is common prayer, as in the *Shema, Tephillah, Torah* and *Berakoth.* "Continue steadfastly in prayer, being watchful in it with thanksgiving." Paul asks for prayers for himself, that he may proclaim the mystery of Christ as clearly as he should.

The Pauline letter to the Ephesians also urges *agape* which fills with the fullness of God's love, especially in the Christian family. Human marriage is built on the divine archetype.

I bow my knees before the Father from whom every family in heaven and on earth is named (Ep 3:14-15). The Father will inspire the family through his Spirit who dwells in our soul, and Christ who lives in our hearts, "rooted and grounded in love" (Ep 3:14-19).

Here we see the trinitarian archetype of the Christian family; adopted sons and daughters of the Father, brothers and sisters of His Son, Jesus Christ, inspired by the Holy Spirit.

Agape builds up the family, the moral person of Christ. When each part of the family is working properly, "it makes bodily growth and builds itself in love" (Ep 4:15-16).

As members of Christ, we are also members of each other. So "do not let the sun go down on your anger" (Ep 4:26). Speak only good, build up graciously, not grieving the Holy Spirit. Get rid of bitterness, anger, clamor, and slander. "And be kind to one another, tenderhearted, forgive one another, as God in Christ forgives you" (Ep 4:27-32).

The Christian family, as children of God, must be imitators of him, walking in love, as Christ did, without immorality or impurity, filthiness, silliness or levity. Walk (*halachah*) as children of the Lord, walking carefully without foolishness and drunkenness, but filled with the true Spirit, singing hymns and psalms and giving thanks to God in the name of our Lord, Jesus Christ (Ep 5:1-20).

Though the patriarchal family prevails among the Ephesians, they should "be subject to one another out of reverence for Christ" (Ep 5:21). This remark prefaces the rules for family behavior. Husband and wife should sacrifice for each other, as Christ did. As members of the body serve each other, so husband and wife should anticipate each other's wishes.

As in Colossians (1:18) and Second Corinthians (11:2), the Messiah-King is espoused to His Church—the hierogamy upon which Christian marriage is modeled. Wives should be subject to their husbands as to the Lord, for the husband is head of his wife, as Christ leads His Church.

But "husbands love your wives, as Christ loved the Church and gave himself up for her," to sanctify her, cleansing her first by the washing of water with the word to make her a spotless and holy bride, paralleling Jewish bridal customs.

"Husbands should love their wives as their own bodies. He who loves his wife, loves himself" (Ep 5:28). Two in one flesh, or one person. He cherishes this one body, as Christ has great affection for His mystical body, the Church. A man leaves his home to join his wife.

> This is a great foreshadowing. I mean that it refers to Christ and the Church. In any case, each one should love his wife, as he loves himself; the wife, for her part, showing respect for her husband (Ep 5:32-33).

The sanctity of Christian marriage recapitulates the union of the Messiah-King with His people. And so the fidelity and the indissolubility of Christian marriage are based on this eternal hierogamy.

Whereas children should obey their parents, their fathers should not harass them, but rather correct them in the Lord (Ep 6:1-3).

Paul condemns those, probably the Gnostics, who tear down marriage, or forbid certain foods. Since God created these good things, they should be received with thanks.

Everything God created is good, nothing is to be rejected when it is to be received with thanksgiving, for it was made holy by God's word and by prayer (1 Tm 4:4-5).

Paul and his followers so highly regarded monogamy as the Christian ideal that they refused to consider anyone for the clergy who was not *mias gynaikos*, a man of one wife, following the Roman requirements for high officials and priests.

The elder-guardian of the Church must be a model father, keeping his children submissive and respectful. Moreover, he should be: temperate, sensible, dignified, hospitable, a good teacher, sober, gentle, peaceable, not money-grubbing, well thought of, and not a recent convert.

If he cannot run his own home and family properly, how can he oversee the whole Church? The Romans used the same arguments (1 Tm 3:1-7).[2]

The elder-bishop should be mature, educated, successful, probably possessing a substantial home in which the congregation can meet for the Eucharist. In a sense, his little domestic church expands until it includes the whole Christian community.

The church leader has raised his family well; and now he is at the age when he can devote his full time to the Church. It would be unfair to expect a younger man with a growing family to shoulder such heavy responsibilities.

If the bishop has been a good parent to his children, then he may well become an outstanding father to his church in lieu of God the Father, while his deacons and deaconesses represent Christ and the Holy Spirit, an ecclesial family mirroring the heavenly one.

The bishop's spiritual paternity is through the rebirth of his church in Baptism. As a good father, he also reconciles, presides at the Eucharist, blesses marriages and teaches by word and example.

It seems that from the beginning the Church, like the Romans, considered successive bigamy as an impediment to religious leadership. Thus the custom that clerics may not marry. The presbyter-bishop must be a man of one wife, a living illustration of the faithful union of the Messiah-King with his people.

Peter also advises his young churches on marriage and the family (1 P 3:1-7). The Christian wife should obey and give good example to her nonbelieving husband. "They have only to observe the reverent purity of your way of life." No fancy hairdos, cosmetics or expensive clothes are necessary, "Your adornment is rather the hidden character of the heart, expressed in the unfading beauty of a calm and gentle disposition. This is precious in God's eyes." Imitate the holy women of old. For you are Sarah's daughter.

Husbands should treat with respect the women with whom they share their lives. If they do so, their prayers will be answered.

John writes later, stressing the love theme so strong in Jesus and Paul. "A new commandment I give you, that you love one another, even as I have loved you" (Jn 13:34-35). Thus all will know that you are my disciples, says the Lord.

As Jesus laid down His life for His disciples, husband and wife should be willing to do the same for each other. This love is shown by keeping the commandments, the law of love.

Jesus prays for unity among His followers. This begins in the domestic church, the family where the two become one. "That they may be one, even as we are one, I in them and you in me, and that they may be perfectly one" (Jn 17:22-26). As the divine family is one, so should the human household live in harmony.

Jesus tells them His Father's name. "And I will make it known that the love with which you have loved me may be in them and I in them" (Jn 17:26).

The love with which the Father loves His Son is the *Shekhinah* or Holy Spirit. This loving presence of God will be in a Christian home, personified by the mother who walks in his love (Jn 2:4-6). Hate has no place in marriage and the family, for he who hates is still living in darkness (Jn 2:9-10).

John equates lust with love of the world, whether it is lust of the flesh or lust of the eyes. But the world quickly passes away, whereas God's love lasts forever (1 Jn 2:15-17).

Hate is the equivalent of murder. Rather we should be willing to die for those we love, as Jesus did. Love builds up even at the expense of our own lives, whereas hate tears down and kills.

If we love each other, God's presence will abide in us and his love will be perfected (1 Jn 4:7-12). Since God is love, if we abide in love, we abide in God and he is us.

Love of God and love of husband or wife are the same. "If anyone says 'I love God' and hates his brother, (or sister) he is a liar. For if he does not love one whom he sees and lives with every day, how can he love the invisible God? He who loves God, should love his brother (or sister) also" (1 Jn 4:16-21).

One who loves a parent, loves his child. We love God's children, husband, wife and offspring, when we love God and keep his commandments (1 Jn 5:1-3). As adopted sons and daughters of the Father, and stepbrothers and sisters of Christ, we are integrated into the divine family, whose loving Presence pervades our Christian home. Where two or three are gathered together in his name, Jesus' Spirit is there.

Jesus, Paul, and their followers teach marital fidelity, based on the archetypal unions of Adam and Eve, and Yahweh and Israel. Yahweh sends His Son as Messiah-King and Bridegroom of the New Israel, a hierogamic model for Christian spouses.

Jesus and Paul, like the prophets, want to protect wives from the easy divorce of patriarchal Judaism. Husbands should love their wives perpetually, as Christ loves His Church. And wives should honor and respect their husbands, as the Church obeys Christ.

Parents should teach their children by word and example. In their turn, children should submit to their mothers and fathers. *Agape* should permeate the Christian family, as the Spirit of love is present in the faithful and affectionate home.

The Christian family is the basic organ of the Mystical Body of Christ, necessary for the generation of new members. Christian marriage both recapitulates the betrothal of Christ and His Church, and anticipates the joy of the wedding banquet of the Lamb with His bride in the new temple of the New Jerusalem (Rv 19:7-9).

CHAPTER FOUR

"A Community Of Human And Divine Law" (Modestinus, D 23:2-1)

Besides Jewish marriage traditions, Roman nuptials also influenced the evolution of Christian matrimony.

EARLY ROMAN MARRIAGE

Etruscan marriage and families seem to have been matriarchal, with the children belonging to the mother's family. As later patriarchal society developed, absolute authority rested in the father of the family.[1]

The three main types of Roman marriage are: *confarreatio*, the solemn marriage of patricians with witnesses, high priest and sacrifice; *coemptio*, a mock purchase of the bride, common among the ordinary people; and *usus*, cohabitation for one year with the intention to live as husband and wife, and used to regularize a marriage between a Roman and a foreigner. The most common form of matrimony in later times was the *coemptio*.

In the Roman betrothal the groom gives a ring to the bride, and the marriage contract is drawn up. The marriage formula: *"Quando tu, Caius, ego Caia.* Then the *pronuba* (patroness) joins the hands of the bride and groom, and a sacrifice is made. Next the groom escorts his bride to his home (*deductio*) with songs and felicitations. Upon arrival, he carries her over the threshold, and together they light the new fire.

There seem to have been few divorces from the patrician *confarreatio*. However, a husband could send his wife away for adultery, though his wife did not have equal rights when he erred. The punishment for adultery varied in early Rome from death to exile. In the later

Republic, divorce became easier as the status of women improved.

As early as the fourth century, B.C., there was seen a certain reluctance to assume the burdens of marriage. So bachelors and childless couples were taxed to encourage marriage and the family.

Kiefer (40) sees the end of the Second Punic War (201 B.C.) as a turning point in Roman morality and social life. With extensive military expansion, the old Roman families declined. Conquest brought in large numbers of slaves with consequent luxurious idleness. Chastity disappeared, and women became liberated economically and politically. Prostitution and unnatural vice grew.

Were the good old days better? Seneca (L 97) and Cicero (*Speech For Caelius*) are doubtful. Perhaps in immoral times people tend to idealize the past. Orgies and the deification of sex were popular. For example, rites honoring: Cupid, Mutunus, Tutunus, Pertunda, Venus, Priapus, Juno, Genius, Dionysius, Bacchus, Cybele, and Isis.

Some of the philosophers reacted to the sexual promiscuity. The Stoics, Orphics, Pythagoreans, Gnostics and Neo-Platonists taught the beauty and strength of continence over indulgence.

Some have described mankind as trying to balance on the wobbly fence of morality and falling either on the one side into promiscuity, or on the other into rigid moralism.

OVID: LOVE IS WAR

Ovid, born in the midst of decadent Rome, soon became its prophet. Although he was exiled by the Emperor Augustus, he was to become the patron of the medieval troubadours.

Ovid praises Cupid, the god of Romance, in contrast to the Judaeo-Christian hierogamy. He describes romance as a sickness, torture, a craze in which conscience and modesty are chained. Ovid lauds furtive adultery over marital love (*Amores*, 1.4.22, LCL). In fact, the more barriers between the lover and his beloved, the better.

Love is war with long vigils and pursuits (1.9.1). It is never bought or sold. The ever watchful, jealous husband only escalates his wife's desires. Ovid is ambivalent, desiring the immoral beauty or the chaste harlot. He wrote his *Art of Love* for beginners, telling them how to find, win and hold their beloveds; the proper time, place, words, etc.

To hold onto your beloved, be lovable and cultivate the mind, for bodily beauty quickly wanes. Be gentle, indulgent with soft words. Yield, agree with her, laugh, cry, etc. Do little things such as putting on her slippers, warming her hands, and giving her small gifts.

Praise her beauty, clothes, hair, skills, etc., but make it an unobtrusive flattery (314). Be concerned over her health. Let her see much of you, then not, for a rested field repays its trust. But do not be too submissive nor too complimentary. Hearts grow flaccid when all is smooth. So fight, but then make up (464), and overlook flaws.

Ovid warns young maidens to take advantage of their youth. However, bodily beauty is ephemeral, but good character is lasting. "Goodness endures and lasts for many a day. And throughout its years, love securely rests thereon" (50).

Enhance your good points and cover your faults. Be seen. Beauty is best seen in peace, humility, cheerfulness. Keep your lover in suspense and jealous, but romantic love can be delibitating. So Ovid tells how to heal it. Resist beginnings, for once love is advanced, it is difficult to halt, and deaf to counsel.

Since leisure fosters love, keep busy (140). Cupid hates the busy. Take a trip. Stress your beloved's faults. Flee loneliness. Avoid young lovers and lewd shows, and depart from her in peace. Thus Ovid tries to cure ailing love. Ovid's influence was strong in the medieval and Renaissance periods, not only in love poems and romances, but also in ethics, theology and medicine.

MATRIMONY AND THE FAMILY IN ROMAN LAW

The Roman family included all who were under the patriarch's power. For example, wife, children and slaves. The *pater familias* must be a Roman citizen and not under the power of another.[2]

The *pater familias* is the undisputed head of the family, master of his house. His power lasts for life, limited only by custom and tradition. He alone can dispose of family property. Not only does he have authority over his wife and children who are *in manum*, (under his authority) but also over the wives of his sons who are still under his power.

Though originally the *pater familias* jurisdiction was absolute, even including life and death, gradually it was moderated for the protection and sustenance of his subjects.

The *mater familias* is not under the power of another. She can be married, a widow, free born or a freed woman. As a revered *matrona*, she has the right to wear a stole with a purple border.

The *filius familias* is a son under his *pater familias*. His sons and grandsons have the same status. Although the *filius familias* may not own property, he has the use of it. Furthermore, he is not allowed to marry without his father's permission, though Justinian limited this power. He can be *sui juris* (his own master) only if his father dies or he himself is emancipated.

A *filia familias* is also under her father's authority. She can only become *sui juris* through emancipation or matrimony,—*in manum conventio*,—by which she enters the family of her husband as a *filia familias*. Although in ancient times the *pater familias* promised his *filia familias* in the matrimony through the *sponsio* (betrothal), later the mutual consent of the bride and groom sufficed.

The betrothal, *sponsalia*, obliged under Roman civil law. And it is assumed through oral response, *spondeo*, to the question, *spondesne?* (do you espouse?) So the *sponsalia* consists of a promise and counterpromise of a future marriage (D 23.1.1).

Although the *sponsalia* were not binding as a marriage, nonetheless, it had certain legal effects. For example, taking another betrothed at the same time was considered as infamy. Moreover, the promised one could be accused of adultery. However, the *sponsalia* could be dissolved by mutual consent.

Matrimony means motherhood, whereas nuptials signify the veiling of the bride. Modestinus describes matrimony as "a union between a man and a woman, an association for the whole of life, a community of human and divine law" (D 23.2.1), a moral ethical and social bond.

Roman matrimony is based on *affectio maritalis*, the cohabitation as husband and wife in a legitimate marriage for life, and the propagation of legitimate children. If there is no marital affection the union is considered as concubinage. Under Justinian, concubinage with a free woman was seen as a valid marriage unless otherwise declared (C 5.26).

Dos, or dowry, is given to the husband by his bride or her father to be used for household expenses. And it must be returned to her or her heirs when her husband dies.

The husband acquires authority *manus* over his wife by the marriage contract, *conventio in manum*.

The main purpose of marriage according to Roman law is—*liberorum quaerundorum causa*-the procreation of legitimate children. At census time the head of the family was asked if he was living with his wife *liberorum quaerundorum causa*. As we have seen, many Romans were reluctant to take on the responsibilities of raising a family. Augustus had to take measures to try to restore the child orientation of matrimony.

Roman marriage was monogamous and began with the *deductio in domum mariti*, a solemn introduction of the bride into her husband's home with religious ceremonies.

The legal prerequisites for Roman marriage are: the *ius conubii*, or the right to marry; and *consensus* or consent.

Although the *ius conubii* was originally limited to patricians, it later allowed nuptials between patricians and plebians and even foreigners.

Consensus facit nuptias (D 50.17.30). If one is still under the *manus* of a parent, the parent's approval is required. Consent must be complete, on one and the same matter, and free. It can be either spoken or written, or by any other sign.

Those under the age of puberty, blood relatives, lunatics, or soldiers do not have the *ius connubii*. Affinity is an obstacle, plus some other restrictions. For example, senators were not allowed to marry freewomen.

Roman divorce, *divortium*, was informal—"a definitive cessation of the common life of the consorts, initiated by common agreement or by one" proving that there is no longer marital affection between them. When the wife suddenly runs off in a fit of anger, *per calorem*, this is not considered as a divorce.

If a marriage is accompanied by *conventio in manum*, dissolution is by a contrary act. Usually Roman divorce was a unilateral declaration by the divorcing spouse, *repudium*, following the separation. It could be either written or oral.

Christian emperors made restrictions and imposed fines on those who divorced without a just cause. For example, Justinian required a written notification, *libellus divortii*, but he upheld the dissolubility of marriage (D 24.2, C 5.24).

In *divortium bona gratia*, no fault divorce, neither party is to blame. E.g., if a mother is childless after three years due to physical deficiency, or if the husband is absent as a prisoner of war for five years. Also, mental illness, disease or a denial of the *liberorum quaerundorum causa* can be causes.

Also, divorce can be *ex iusta causa* because of the immoral behavior of one of the spouses, such as the adultery of the wife or the husband living with a concubine. Here Justinian ordered the guilty party to be fined. In *divortium sine causa*, there is no reasonable cause. While the divorce is valid, the divorcing spouse must pay a fine. Also, if one of the spouses loses the *ius connubii*, a divorce must be obtained. The Christian doctrine on the indissolubility of marriage helped mitigate Roman divorces (Inst 1.10, D 23.2, C 5.4, 6. 7).

Remarriage after the death or divorce of a spouse was permitted, though both the Romans and the Christians idealized the man of one wife (C 5.9, Nov 22). However, in their campaigns for more progeny, some emperors encouraged remarriage. Moreover, they exempted fathers of families from onerous public duties. Women with three children were freed from guardianship. On the other hand, unmarried men and women were barred from succession under a will.

Roman officials foresaw that the decadence of broken family life eventually would spell the end of the republic, as it had for so many empires and civilizations before. Solid moral marriage and family life mean survival as much in the nation as in the tribe.

Although the Roman matrimony was basically monogamous, with the wife under the *manus* of her husband and the couple living together in marital affection for the purpose of procreation, by the beginning of Christianity the ideal is rare, for the Augustan reform had by and large failed.[3]

> Yet the thought embodied in the Modestinus precept could still serve early Christianity as a point of departure for the development of its new ideal of marriage from the spirit of revelation and the wisdom of philosophy.

Syncretism between Roman law and Christian dogma on marriage was inevitable. "Historians of Roman law tell us that Roman marriage was not in the first place a legal relationship, but a social condition or state." Since it is primarily based on marital affection, it is a social arrangement, rather than juridical, and so it can be terminated by either party.

Though the Christian influence before 600 A.D. tied Roman divorce to very specific reasons, a divorce could be granted even without a valid cause.[4] But penalties such as fines or monastery stays were levied against the guilty ones. The *Ecloga* (8th century), though quoting the Sermon on the Mount, allows divorce for the attempted murder of a spouse, impotence, leprosy, etc. Divorce was not the main concern, but rather remarriage after divorce, and *porneia* (indecency or lewdness. See Mt 5:32, 19:9) was widely interpreted. In Byzantine society, the state was the ultimate judge in marital matters, as it was in Rome.

Orthodoxy tended to interpret the Bible leniently, because of human weakness and the difficulty in measuring up to the ideal of the Sermon on the Mount. Widows and widowers were allowed to remarry, but third and fourth marriages were frowned upon. Moreover, if a spouse enters a monastery or becomes a bishop, his wife may remarry.

Leo the Wise (9th-10th centuries) declared that marriages should take place in the Church and with the Church's blessing (Nov 89). Though the codes of Theodosius and Justinian had been followed in the East, the West was only awakened to the Roman codes by Gratian and the decretalists in the early Middle Ages. We will see more of this in chapter VI.

ROMAN MARRIAGE CEREMONIES

As we have seen, the Romans distinguished betrothal from nuptials. The two parties were engaged by a set formula and a ring was given by the groom to his bride (*subarrhatio*), or a contract is drawn up. Then he gives her other presents in a happy social occasion with friends and relatives in attendance.[5] The evening before the wedding, the bride puts on (*nubere*) her bridal dress with a red veil (*flammeum*). And she is crowned with flowers. The groom wears a similar crown.

On the morning of the wedding the gods are consulted. Guests arrive and the diviners forecast a happy marriage. Then the couple give their consent and sign their marriage contract. The *pronuba* (patroness) joins their hands, and then they offer fruit and bread, *confarreatio*.

Next the bride and groom sit on two chairs bound together and covered by the skin of a sheep, slaughtered for the divination. Then, while a priest recites the prayer, the couple circumambulate the altar, and an ox or a pig is sacrificed on the temple altar. The guests cheer *"Feliciter!"* (Good Luck!), and the father of the bride gives a huge banquet. Then, at nightfall, the groom takes his bride to his home and *manus*.

The Christians adopted the Roman marriage rites, substituting the unbloody sacrifice of the Mass for the animal offerings. Though they kept the veil and crowns, a Christian priest and prayers replaced the Roman, but the presence of a priest was not required till early medieval times. As du Quesne notes (434), "Essentially conservative, the Church in these matters merely modified that which was incompatible with her faith."

CHAPTER FIVE

Dearest Companion In The Service Of The Lord (Tertullian to His Wife)

The early Fathers of the Church followed Paul's leadership in applying the teaching of Christ on marriage to the Roman traditions. For example, Ignatius of Antioch writes to Polycarp (5.1-2) that husbands should love their wives as Christ cherishes His Church. Moreover, those contemplating marriage should seek the blessings of the bishop, the *pater familias* of the Christian community. In general, the Apostolic Fathers say that although a husband may put away his wife for adultery, he may not remarry (e.g. Hermas, *Mandate* 4.1-8).

Athenagoras of Athens in his *Apology* (33), echoing Jewish and Roman law, writes that marriage is for the sake of children. As the farmer plants his seed, and then patiently awaits the harvest, so "the generation of children is the measure of our appetite." Athenagoras, like others of his time, honors the man of one wife, for he believes that marriage lasts even after death. One who does not respect his spouse's memory is a hidden adulterer.

CLEMENT OF ALEXANDRIA: TIMELY SOWERS

Clement (2nd-3rd centuries), head of the Christian catechetical school in Alexandria, naturally is concerned with the theology of marriage. Where two or three are gathered together, there is the Lord's Presence (*Strom* 3.10-68) (ANF). Marriage is not just the joining of two bodies, but the sacred union of man and woman (3.12-84). Though Clement praises virginity, he notes that married couples have more trials and so can surpass the single one in virtue (7.12-20).

Condemning those who would degrade marriage, he steers a middle course between them and the lusters (3.17, 18). Since marriage is good as scripture tells us, any defamation also censures its Creator. Following tradition, Clement names the purpose of marriage as procreation. "And its end is that the children be good." Just as the goal of agriculture is a fruitful harvest. Marriage is holy since in it man imitates God's creation by his procreation.

Clement decries the sexual aberrations of Alexandria, including: homosexuality, adultery, fornication, and lasciviousness, all condemned by the scriptures (*Instructor* 2.10). He recommends modesty and temperance in marriage. However, time does not always withhold from nature. Above all, avoid a dishonest union. "He violates marriage, who uses it in a meretricious way."

One who sins sexually really harms himself. For, "he who has been overcome by base pleasures, has now licentiousness wholly attached to him." The fornicator is dead to God, since the holy abhors the polluted.

> Do not, I pray, put off your modesty at the same time that you put off your clothes, because it is never right for the just man to divest himself of continence.

One is not just, who is conquered by venery, who gapes stupidly at pornography, or who is torn from reason by his desire for pollution. "For him alone who is married and who is a farmer, is it allowed to sow, when the time allows the sower."

TERTULLIAN: TO HIS WIFE

Tertullian, North African contemporary of Clement, gives us some good insights into the development of Christian marriage in the second and third centuries. He shows the Church's growing influence in matrimony and defends its indissolubility, even after death. In his treatise on the soul (203) (ch 27) (ANF), Tertullian comments on the sanctity of marriage. "The normal condition of marriage (not the excess) has received a blessing from God, and is blessed by him." In this holy union, body and soul work together.

Tertullian sees three degrees of chastity (204): lifelong virginity; virginity after baptism; and monogamy. God ordained monogamy from the beginning, when he made a companion for Adam, two in one flesh. When we remarry, we are no longer two in one, as Christ and His Church. Though there was polygamy among the patriarchs, the priest could not marry a widow. Moreover, monogamists are chosen for the Christian clergy.

Although remarriage after the death of a spouse is licit, it is not desirable. For even the pagan *flamen* and *pontifex maximus* (Roman religious officials) are men of one wife, and the vestal virgins are faithful. *A fortiori*, Christians of the royal priesthood of Christ should be steadfast.

Tertullian addresses his beloved wife as (207) (ACW), "My dearest companion in the service of the Lord." Just as Paul and Ignatius spoke of walking in Christ and marrying in the Lord, so a good Christian marriage is one in which Christ's holy Presence lives, and the service of Christ is the primary goal.

Monogamy was blessed by God for procreation. "Be fruitful and multiply." Tertullian asks his dear wife not to remarry when he dies. "This is what many a pagan woman does in order to honor the memory of her beloved spouse." Moreover, there are chaste pagan virgins and widows. Some even practice continence in matrimony. If they can do it, *a fortiori*, Christians should.

It is true that Paul allows young widows to marry, but in the Lord. For, if she marries a pagan, she will act like a pagan. How can she observe the stations, fast, attend evening devotions, paschal solemnities, the Lord's Supper, visit martyrs' shrines, and receive the kiss of peace, when she lives in a divided home? Early Christian opposition to mixed marriages parallels the Jewish attitude, namely, a fear of danger to the faith.

A Christian wife in a pagan home is always on edge, concealing her sign of the cross, night prayers, holy communion, etc. On the other hand, there can be great happiness and peace in a marriage in the Lord, which the Church arranges, the sacrifice strengthens, "upon which the blessing sets seal, at which the angels are present as witnesses, and to which the Father gives his consent." For even natural children do not marry without their father's approval.

"How beautiful, then, the marriage of two Christians, two who are one in hope, one in desire, one in the way of life they follow, one in the religion they practice," as brother and sister, serving the same Master (35).

Nothing divides them, for they are two in one flesh, and one in spirit. They pray, worship and fast together, encourage and strengthen each other. Side by side, they walk to church, receive holy communion, face difficulties and share consolations. There are no secrets between them, neither do they avoid each other or cause each other sorrow.

Together they visit the sick, give alms and attend church and say their daily prayers. Together they make the sign of the cross, greet fellow Christians, ask God's blessing and sing psalms and hymns. Christ rejoices in them, giving them peace. "Where there are two together, there he is present. And where he is, evil is not."

Tertullian opposes Marcion, who looks down on marriage (207) (ANF). Those who glorify virginity sometimes forget that virgins receive their pure bodies from the nuptial bed. Furthermore, anyone who attacks marriage insults its Creator.

> For he bestowed his blessings on matrimony, also, as an honorable estate, for the increase of the human race, as he did indeed on the whole of His creation for wholesome and good uses, despite the many misuses of sex (1.29).

Marcion destroys the material of sanctity, for "if there is no marriage, there is no sanctity." Strength is made perfect in weakness. How can Marcion want salvation, if he takes away the institute of its birth? How can you love someone whose origin you hate (4.34)?

Paul, though professing continence, "permits the contracting of marriage and the enjoyment of it, and advises the continuance therein, rather than the dissolution thereof."

Paul tells wives not to leave their husbands, but if they do, they should either remain single or be reconciled. Christ confirms the sanctity of marriage by first forbidding its dissolution. And if there is a separation, the bond is to be renewed once again.

Paul advises marriage in the Lord. Even in a mixed marriage, the Christian spouse should sanctify the pagan one. Christ says that if one puts away his wife and marries another, and if one marries a divorced woman, both are guilty of adultery. However, divorce would seem to be permitted in cases of adultery.

As Tertullian is attracted more to Montanism, he takes a harder line against remarriage and further glorifies chastity. Thus he writes on monogamy (after 213) (ANF) that God alone can separate husband and wife. "Marriage is had when God joins two together in one flesh, or, finding them already united, blesses their union." But in adultery the two are separated and mingled with another. Tertullian feels that the marriage bond is stronger than death. If a divorced wife is bound to her husband, *a fortiori*, a widow should be "bound to him even after his departure, to whom, even in death she owes a debt of undivided affection."

Since she is not divorced from her husband, she is still with him in spirit. If she is not at peace with him, she should settle their differences. Moreover, if she is already at peace, she would never separate herself from him. The widow should pray for her husband's soul, eternal rest and resurrection, and offer Mass on his anniversary. If she doesn't do this, it is the equivalent of divorce, and she must give an account at judgment.

Although there is no marriage in heaven, there is an even tighter bond, a special spiritual fellowship. "God will no more separate those whom he has joined together than he would have them separated in this lesser life below" (93).

How, then, can a widow remarry, for she would have one husband in the flesh and another in the spirit, a type of adultery, for her first husband still possesses her soul. Though Paul permits young widows to remarry, he by no means commands it.

No doubt Tertullian reflects here the Roman ideal of monogamy, the one spouse required for priests and officials. Since all Christians are of the royal priesthood of Christ, they should not only be monogamous, but also sober, blameless, hospitable, etc.

JOHN CHRYSOSTOM: LOVING WELD

Chrysostom, bishop of Antioch and later of Constantinople, was concerned about the family life of his flock. For example, in his *Homily 20 on Ephesians* (5.22-24) (NPNF), he says, "There is nothing that so welds our life together as the love of husband and wife. For this many will lay aside their arms, for this they will give up life itself."

A husband should seek in his wife affection, modesty, and gentleness, and should not be infatuated with the fleeting prettiness of her face and figure. "Let him make her fair in God's light, not in our own." When a man leaves his father and mother, he is knit to his wife as one flesh. And "by the mingling of their seeds is the child produced, so that the three are one flesh." A man should love his wife as he loves himself for the two are one flesh,—he the head and she the body. He honors her and prays that they so live that they will be united in heaven.

Honor your wife, pray with her, address her with respect and love. "Teach her the fear of God and all things will flow from this, as from a fountain, and the home will be full of blessings."

Chrysostom was a forthright defender of the sanctity of marriage, and a condemner of adultery and fornication. Indeed, it was his criticism of the Worldly standards of the Imperial Court that earned him an exile.

AMBROSE: HEAVENLY SACRAMENT

Ambrose, bishop of Milan and friend of Augustine, stresses the consent and progeny orientation of Roman marriage. Also, he sees matrimony as a healing remedy for man's wounded soul, according to the Judeao-Christian tradition.[1] Marriage is a divine gift to man, sanctified in a special way by Christ. We should be especially careful not to destroy this sacred presence through divorce, for one who sins against marriage loses the grace of this heavenly sacrament (*On Abraham* 1.7.59).

Ambrose, as most of his predecessors, follows Paul's theology of marriage, basing its sanctity on the union of Christ with His Church. The wife, as mother Church, brings forth new members, to be received and baptized.

We know God, as the watcher and guard of marriage, does not suffer the marriage bed of someone else to be defiled. And if anyone does this, we know that he sins against God, whose law he violates, whose grace he loses.

God's presence remains with the couple as long as they are at peace. But mixed marriages cause disharmony. How can the nuptials be sanctified if one spouse does not believe (L 19.7)?

Husband and wife have equal rights and duties, for neither is allowed intercourse with strangers. But preserving mutual love for the whole of married life is not easy.

Affection, service, harmony and cheerfulness help preserve love. The husband should never lord it over his wife, for she is not his servant, but his spouse (L 63.107). What if the husband has to go away alone on a business trip?

> The same bond of nature links together the rights of conjugal love between those who are far apart, as well as between those who are together. And they are both united by the yoke of the same blessing (*Hexameron* 5.7.18) (D 40).

In Hebrew tradition, the heavenly Mother, the *Shekhinah* of Yahweh, who binds husband and wife, accompanies the husband when he travels alone.

Ambrose stresses marital chastity, the man of one wife and the woman of one husband; and also temperance, especially in old age, which is more suitable for governing than procreation (*Exp on Lk* 1.43). He suggests moderation in sex, for excesses can draw one away from his faith.

Since the purpose of marriage is the generation and education of children, abortion and child abuse are counter-productive, for even animals guard their own progeny. The parents' obligations are only beginning at the birth of their children, for they must feed, care for, give good example to, and train their youngsters. They, in their turn, should support their mothers and fathers in their old age.

Ambrose opposes easy Roman divorce. Though husband and wife may separate for adultery, they may not divorce, for this makes the children rootless, and the unborn suffer even more.

The divorced spouses are subject to grave temptations. How cruel it is for a husband to abandon the wife of his youth, when she gets old and wrinkled, for a young and pretty face and body.

Though Ambrose honors virginity, he notes that if there were no marriage, there would be no virgins since virgins are the fruit of marriage. Chastity is required of all Christians according to their different gifts: virgins, widows or spouses.

AUGUSTINE: CHILD, FIDELITY, SACRAMENT

Augustine, educator, rhetor, philosopher and spiritual son of Ambrose, lived in an unequal marriage for twelve years and had a brilliant son, Adeodatus. Monica, Augustine's *mater familias*, felt it would be in his best interest if he would leave his companion in order to wed the daughter of a wealthy patrician in an equal union.

When he was bishop of Hippo, he looked back on his youthful wanderings and wrote them out in his *Confessions* to help others who were going through the same problems.[2] His insatiable sexual desires dragged him down. "They clouded over and darkened my soul so that I could not distinguish the calm light of chaste love from the fog of lust" (2.2.2).

There is a natural attraction in human bodies, "For the sense of touch, what is suitable to it affords great pleasure." Each of the other senses delights in bodily indulgence as well.

"I was tossed about and split out in my fornications; I flowed out and boiled over in them, but you kept silent." But the Lord allowed him to wallow in his impurities. "For you fashion sorrow into a lesson for us" (2:2-4).

> In those years I had a companion, not one joined to me in what is named lawful wedlock, but one whom my wandering passion, empty of prudence, had picked up. But I had this one only and I was faithful to her bed. With her I learned first hand how great a distance lies between the restraint of a conjugal covenant, mutually made for the sake of begetting offspring and the bargain of a lustful love, where a child is born against his will, although, once born, he forces himself upon our love (4.1, 2).

However, his union with his peregrine consort was not unusual for the time, and later could be considered a marriage, unless stated to the contrary. "Even the Catholic Church was prepared to recognize it, provided that the couple remained faithful to one another" (*Ser* 312.2).

Alypius, Augustine's friend and fellow philosopher, tried to convince him not to marry so that he could devote his full time to speculation. Augustine, too, feared the obligations of a permanent marriage. "For whatever conjugal dignity there is in raising children, it attracted neither of us, unless very lightly" (6.12).

Monica wanted Augustine baptized, and settled into a good matrimony. But the girl she had picked was two years below the age of consent (10). It was only with reluctance that Augustine asked his dear companion to leave. "This was a blow which crushed my heart to bleeding. I loved her dearly" (6.15). She returned to Africa, loyal to her cherished Augustine, "vowing never to know man again" (6.15).

Two years is a long wait for his new bride, so Augustine found a new friend. "By her my soul's disease would be fostered and brought safe, as it were, either unchanged, or in a more intense form, under the convoy of continual use into the kingdom of marriage" (6.15).

But fear of death and judgment call him back. He could not see inner beauty because his eye was too busy searching for bodily charms. However, he hears a voice calling him: "Run forward, I will bear you up" (6.16).

In his *Soliloquies* at Cassiciacum (386-7) (FOC), Augustine debates whether to marry or continue his philosophical leisure. Would not a well-placed, fair, modest, obedient, intelligent wife be nice?

> If it is a part of a wise man's duty to devote himself to children, the man who takes a wife for this sole reason can seem to me to be worthy of admiration, not imitation (1.10.17).

In the past he had often longed for a wife who would "in good repute bring me sensual satisfaction." Though Augustine spurns feminine embraces during his daytime reveries, at night, lying awake,

you realized how differently from your claims those imagined caresses and their bitter sweetness excited you, far, far less than you were wont to do, but also far different from what you had expected.

The hidden Physician pointed out to Augustine not only what he had escaped under his guidance, but also what remained to be healed. Augustine makes no claim to soundness "until I shall have looked upon that Beauty."

Adeodatus joins Augustine and Alypius in baptism by Ambrose at Milan in 387. "In that boy I owned nothing but the sin. That he was brought up by us in your discipline, to that, you and none other inspired us. Your gifts I confess to you" (*Confessions* 9.6). God took Adeodatus home to heaven shortly after. Augustine would always remember him as a virtuous youth, the same age as his father in grace.

As bishop, Augustine defends the sanctity and indissolubility of marriage. For example, he challenges the Manichees who downgraded the body, sex and marriage. God created all things good. The battle is not between the evil body and the good soul, but the weak flesh (man) confronts the Spirit of God within. Continence, far from despising sex, rather sublimates something good for something better (*On Continence*).

Augustine calls man's tendency to sin concupiscence, originating in the fall of Adam and Eve, similar to the Jewish *Yetzer*, which, though good, is prone to error, especially in sexual matters.

In this Commentary on the Sermon on the Mount (393-6) (FOC) (Mt 5:27-28), Augustine notes that Jesus not only condemned adultery in deed, but also adultery of the heart, "which is the giving of such full consent that the aroused desire for it is not suppressed, but would be satisfied if the opportunity presented itself."

The three steps to sin: suggestion, pleasure and consent, parallel the garden story: the temptation of the serpent, the sin of Adam and Eve, and the expulsion from the Garden. The three degrees of sin: heart, deed and habit reflect: death, carrying out the body, and burial.

Jesus was against divorce because it causes adultery (Mt 5:31-32). Moses ordered a written bill of divorce to moderate the husband's anger and to delay the separation. Only for a grave reason such as fornication can a wife be put away, "and he commands that all other annoyances be steadfastly borne for the sake of conjugal fidelity and chastity." Paul also preaches reconciliation.

What about the puzzling paradox of preferring Christ to our own family (Mt 10:34-37)? Since there will be no marriage in the kingdom, temporal relationship should be seen as really transitory. Can he love his wife as a human being, but abhor the shortness of their union?

> The disciple of Christ must hate the things that are transitory in those persons whom he wishes to come with him to the things that endure; the more he loves those persons, so much the more must he hate those things.

A Christian can live in harmony with his wife in procreating union or in companionship as a brother. "At all events, he can live with her in such harmony that in her he loves the hope of eternal blessedness, even though he dislikes that in her which goes by the relationship of time."

Perhaps Augustine is facing here the myth of growing old together. There is an underlying fear of the finiteness of marriage, of widowhood and loneliness. Time is the enemy of love. In fact, most extramarital liaisons are futile attempts to turn back the clock. However, if matrimony is seen in the light of eternity, anxiety will disappear.

In his work *On Christian Teaching* (397) (1.4, 12, 22), Augustine speaks of two types of love: *uti* and *frui*, use and enjoyment. *Uti* is preferable because by it one uses his spouse to help him attain heaven, and does not make of her an object of selfish pleasure (*frui*). Thus husband and wife are instruments of each other's salvation. For in marriage two are saved as one.

Marriage is good, writes Augustine against the Manichees (*On the Good of Marriage*) (401) (FOC). God made the first natural tie of human society, man and wife. "They are joined to each other, side by side, who walk together and observe together where they are walking."

In our earthly life, "the marriage of male and female is something good." The Lord confirmed this by forbidding divorce and by participating in the marriage feast of Cana. Moreover, "this does not seem to me to be a good solely because of the procreation of children, but also because of the natural companionship between the sexes."

Thus the marriage of old people is also good. For, when the ardor of youth wanes, "the order of charity still flourishes between husband and wife" (ch. 3).

Perhaps it might be a good idea occasionally to refrain from intercourse early in married life so that, as the couple ages, "the chastity of souls rightly joined together continues the purer,"—the more proved and secure, if valued. Procreation tames lust. "For a kind of dignity prevails when, as husband and wife, they unite in the marital act, they think of themselves as mother and father."

Husband and wife owe each other fidelity to the marriage debt, "even if they demand its payment somewhat intemperately and inconstantly" (ch. 4). Violations are adulterous, for marital fidelity should be valued even over bodily health. However, some men are so incontinent and inconsiderate, that they do not even spare their pregnant wives.

> Married people owe each other not only the fidelity of sexual intercourse for the purpose of procreating children, but also the mutual service in a certain measure of sustaining each other's weakness, for the avoidance of illicit sex (ch. 6).

Augustine sees marital intercourse solely for the satisfaction of personal lust as selfish and faulty. This would seem to imply the positive and deliberate exclusion of procreation from the act. Augustine lauds marital chastity. The marriage pact is a kind of sacrament, not nullified by separation. "The bond of fellowship between married couples is so strong that, though it is tied for the purpose of procreation, it is not loosed for the purpose of procreation." This tight union is a symbol of something greater, so that they are wedded even when apart (ch. 7).

Marriage and intercourse promote friendship, "for from this comes the propagation of the human race in which friendly association is a great good" (ch. 9). "For this reason it is good to marry since it is good to beget children, to be the mother of a family."

Augustine, like the other Fathers, and the Romans, too, see virginity as an ideal. But it is far better to marry than to be tortured by passion. Intercourse for generation belongs properly to matrimony, while outside it, is for passion rather than for reason (10).

Even the immoderate use of sex in marriage is tolerable lest lust break out into something worse. But what if a husband wants to use his wife in a manner against nature? She is more shameful if she permits this than if she allows him to go to another woman.

Augustine sees the crown of marriage as "the chastity of procreation and faithfulness in rendering the carnal debt" (11). The bodies of husband and wife are temples of the Holy Spirit, and holy if they remain faithful to themselves and to the Lord. Paul adds that the believing wife sanctifies the body of her unbelieving husband.

Paul reminds us that the virgin has more time to think of the Lord. It is not that the faithful and chaste wife is not trying to please the Lord, but rather that she is too busy with family problems. Augustine, like many of the Fathers, recognized the crushing burden of family responsibilities, especially in the time of the collapsing Roman Empire.

However, some married women are very concerned with pleasing the Lord in reverence and chastity with the "inner life of your heart, in the imperishableness of a quiet and gentle spirit, which is of great price in the sight of the Lord." Thus Sarah dwelt in peace and chastity (12).

When marriage is entered in the city of God, "from the first union of the two human beings matrimony bears a kind of sacred bond. So it can be dissolved in no way except by the death of one of the parties." This bond remains intact even if one of the two is sterile (15).

Just as food is for our health, so sex promotes the welfare of the race, and both are made attractive by pleasure, but, just as the misuse of food may be harmful, so also the abuse of sex. However, what if a couple cannot have children? It is better to die childless than to seek progeny from unlawful union.

Furthermore, just as good children of an adulterous marriage do not excuse it, so bad offspring from a good union do not condemn it. Marriage among all peoples is for procreation, "so that children might be born properly and decently."

In the Roman and patristic tradition, Augustine praises the man of one wife. Why? If one has two wives, he loses "a certain standard, as it were, to the sacrament, necessary not for the reward of a good life, but for the seal of ecclesiastical ordination." While the single marriage of clerics signifies the union of Christ with his Church, the one wedlock of the laity reflects the unity of all under God in the heavenly city.

Just as apostasy from the one, true God is adultery, so "in the marriage of our women, the sanctity of the sacrament is more important than the fecundity of the womb" (18). A marriage is good insofar as the couple "fear God more chastely and more faithfully, especially if they also nourish spiritually the child whom they desire carnally" (19).

Though Augustine lauds virginity, he also teaches that the obedient wife is superior to the disobedient virgin, and that the chaste mother surpasses the drunken celibate (23).

The good of marriage among all peoples "is in the cause of generation and in the fidelity of chastity." For the people of God the good of matrimony also includes the sanctity of the sacrament. So Christian marriage contains a threefold good: *proles*, (child) *fides* (fidelity) and *sacramentum* (sacrament) with all three elements inseparable. Thus it is wrong to leave a spouse in order to beget children (24).

In his *Literal Commentary on Genesis* (9:7-12) (PL), Augustine changes the order of the threefold good to: fidelity, child and sacrament.

> In fidelity one is careful not to lie with another outside the marriage bond. In the child, that it be lovingly received, kindly nourished and religiously educated. In the sacrament, however, that the union never be split, and the disowned one not be vowed to another for the purpose of childbearing. This is the rule of nature by which either the fecundity of nature is honored, or the depravity of incontinence is controlled.

Just as a priest's ordination for the people is still valid without a congregation, or if he is removed from the ministry, so the marital bond still holds, though the union is childless.

Augustine argues against many traditions, including some in his native Africa, that hold that childbearing is necessary for the validity of marriage, or that at least allow the taking of concubines to insure offspring. Augustine reflects the Church's position in defending the rights of sterile women from dismissal in a patriarchal society. This is unjust because male sterility is overlooked.

When Pollentius asks Augustine to clarify the problem of divorce and remarriage, he responds (*On Adulterous Marriages*) (419) (FOC), that the indissolubility of marriage is based on its sacramentality.

Just as matrimony heals man's errant sexuality, so divorce spurs his libido to adultery. Moreover, even if a wife leaves him to pursue the continent way, she may be the cause of her husband's sexual wanderings. Separation should never be attempted without mutual consent of husband and wife (4).

But what if one spouse is immoral? The innocent mate may separate, but not remarry, and of course, it is wrong to separate, if there is no immorality.

Augustine sees that adultery is less serious if one's unfaithful wife has been put away, but she is still his wife. Husband and wife are bound to each other for life, and adultery is not death. "The woman begins to be the wife of no later husband, unless she has ceased to be the wife of the former one" (2.4). Augustine rejects the double standard common in patriarchal society, namely, punishing the erring wife, while looking the other way at the husband's antics.

Since husbands should be examples of virtue for their wives, they should be punished more severely for adultery (2.8). Thus Emperor Antoninus "did not allow a husband whose conduct did not furnish an example of chastity to accuse his wife of the crime of adultery." How much more true should this be in the holy city of God (2.8)? Since the marriage bond is valid till death, it renders any other marriage adulterous. But it is a worse sin to divorce and remarry for a lesser cause than fornication (2.9).

Christ's law displeases the incontinent who want to divorce a quarrelsome, domineering spouse. "It is this weakness, namely, incontinence, that the apostle wished to remedy by the sanctity of marriage" (2.12).

Since Augustine sees procreation as the primary purpose of matrimony, it is shameful and unlawful "whenever the conception of offspring is avoided" (2.12).

A husband should remain continent even if his wife is an adulteress or is ill. Moreover, a husband should not be vengeful against his erring spouse. Rather he should keep himself chaste and not rail against the mistakes of his wife. "In the knowledge that they are not without sin, they forgive, in order that they may be granted forgiveness. Likewise, kindness and love will not be withheld from them" (2.14).

Husbands should take the lead in chastity. For they go on long journeys and expect their young wives to remain chaste. Some men tend to confuse the male image with the license to sin. Christian clerics and virgins should give good example by their chaste lives. In this same vein, Augustine writes on *Marriage and Concupiscence* (419-420) (PL). True chastity is a gift of God, inspired by faith (ch 3).

The generative act of matrimony can be misused if it is performed only for selfish pleasure (4). Husband and wife should take special care not to defraud each other. Christian marriage is not only aimed at generation, but at a regeneration, in which the children are reborn as sons of God, transforming human members into the members of Christ.

The natural shame connected with carnal pleasure does not condemn marriage. Adam and Eve, whose marriage God blessed, were nude, yet not flustered. Nor did they feel any disturbance in their young bare bodies, "because since nothing preceded which was illicit, nothing followed which was shameful" (5). But when they disobeyed God, shame came. However, the evil inclination towards pleasure does not take away from the good of marriage.

Marriage is indissoluble, and in this, secular law differs from the *Gospels*. Not only fertility, whose fruit is the child, or chastity, whose link is fidelity, but also a certain sacrament of marriage is recommended to the faithful (Ep 5:25).

The *res* of matrimony (legal relationship and rights) is the inseparable union till death, except for cases of fornication (Mt 5:32). This bond is guarded by Christ and his Church. The sacrament of marriage is observed in the city of God, the Church of Christ, whose faithful married couples are the active limbs of his body.

There remains between the couple a living link which neither separation nor union can take away. Even when fidelity is lost, the sacrament of fidelity is not (10). The Holy Family of Nazareth is a model of the threefold good.

Augustine believed like the Jewish *Yetzer ha-Ra*, that original sin is passed down through intercourse, though the act itself is good.

Intemperance among married people may be tolerated, but Augustine feels that the use of marriage solely for selfish delight does not avoid some guilt. But because of the good of marriage, this is small (14) (16).

Again he praises marriage's threefold good: the child born for rebirth; fidelity to a spouse who is a member of Christ's body; and a sacrament which even adultery cannot destroy. This sacrament of matrimony, which is great between Christ and His Church, is mirrored in human union.

Augustine is a notable theologian of concupiscence, love and marriage. Since he had lived with a common-law wife for many years, he speaks from experience. In his work as bishop of Hippo his pastoral care comes to the fore. Condemning the Manichees who looked down upon marriage, Augustine stresses, rather, its threefold good.

Upon the permanent sacramentality of matrimony Augustine bases its indissolubility, opposing the pagan policy of easy divorce. And he puts more responsibility on the husband to give good example to his wife and family.

Augustine accepts the child-orientation of Rome, Israel and other cultures, as well. It is wrong to frustrate this end, although fidelity to one's wife takes precedence over progeny. Like Paul, Augustine reflects the Jewish *Yetzer ha-Ra* in his doctrine of concupiscence, the daughter and mother of sin. However, since marriage is good, libido may be used well there.

In a sense, the threefold good of matrimony mirrors the divine image. For example, procreation imitates the creativity of the Father. Fidelity reflects Christ's loyalty to His Church. And the sacrament points to the Holy Spirit who sanctifies the union.

Augustine considers intercourse for pure pleasure, excluding altogether the generative aspect, as a slight deviation in marriage. This is probably because of the selfishness of the act, without any reference to God, regeneration of the Mystical Body of Christ, or salvation. Certainly this is a lesser fault than enjoying sexually one who is not his wife.

Married love can also reflect the divine triad of lover, Love and beloved, where God is the Love between the spouses. "If he loved him (her) whom he sees by human sight, with a spiritual love, he would see God, who is love itself with that inner sight by which he can be seen" (*Trinity*, 8.8.12) (FOC).

Since God is love, there cannot be true affection in marriage without Him. Like God, the Christian marriage is creative, faithful and holy. So it cannot tolerate the harmful threesome of contraception, adultery and desecration. Christian marriage is indissoluble because God, who is love, is at its core.

Although Augustine praises virginity, he also tells the virgin not to lord it over the God-fearing housewife. Virginity and marriage support each other. Christian marriage generates virgins, who, in their turn, encourage chaste spouses.

Augustine sets the pace for the Western medieval theology of love and marriage, which in turn lay the groundwork for Renaissance and modern thought.

CHAPTER SIX

The Greatest Friendship (Thomas Aquinas, Summa Contra Gentiles, 3.123.6)

Several cultural elements contribute to the evolution of love, marriage and the family in the Middle Ages. These include the penitentials, strict monastic confessional guides of sexual mores; the courtly love of the troubadours; the romantic stream of the North, idealizing married love; the mystical marriage found in monasteries and convents; the rediscovery of Roman law and its effect on medieval canons; and finally, the dogmatic treatises on marriage taught in the universities.

Penitentials, drawn up in the Dark Ages to aid monastic confessors and missionaries, are particularly hard on sexual errors. For example, Theodore, a Greek monk who became archbishop of Canterbury, (7th century) says that fornication with a virgin deserves one year of penance, while with a married woman it gets four years, and with a man or animal ten years (1.12.3, 5).

Theodore allows divorce and remarriage for: adultery, slavery, impotence, desertion, etc. Continence is recommended for three days before receiving the Eucharist, and also during Lent, the last three months of pregnancy, and in the time of purification (2.12.3).

Theodore also penalizes masturbation and abortion, but the long penances were often commuted to shorter periods of fasting, alms or psalms. Although the penitentials were important in Ireland, Britain, France and Saxony, they usually were limited to local situations.

THE TROUBADOURS

Courtly love was a popular theme in the Middle Ages, when lonely knights pined for their unapproachable ladies, whose husbands may well have been away on the Crusades. Many medieval noble marriages were arranged for convenience or for political expediency, which encouraged unhappiness and adultery.

Some see the Cathars of southern France as the first troubadours, with Ovid as their patron saint and his *Art of Love* as their gospel. Courtly love in 12th century France fostered humility, courtesy, love and adultery. It prospered in the courts of Eleanor of Aquitaine and her daughter, Marie of Champagne.

Provencal love poems rejoice in the rising up of Europe from the Dark Ages. They are lively and pleasing, with Ambrosian and Ovidian tones, and happy clowns and jugglers accompany. The early Middle Ages were millennial times, with Crusades and a plethora of monasteries, convents and cathedrals, plus the troubadours, singing of moderation, service, bravery, expectancy, pity and love.

For example, Marcabrun contrasts low, lusty love, leading to hell, with good love, charity, which draws us to heaven—probably the refined love, *fine amor* of knight and lady. Andrew, the chaplain at the court of Marie of Champagne, wrote a love manual based on Ovid's *Art of Love*.[1]

Love, *amor*, he notes, is like a hook, *amus*, capturing one in desire. Now he sees only beauty, where before he perceived ugliness. Love can make a man chaste, for he is now thoroughly committed to his beloved—the opposite of unbridled passion.

Excellence of character is more important than beauty. Andrew's rules for love stress: lack of avarice and shame, chastity, service, modesty, kindness, courtesy and consideration. Courts of love punish violators of the code. Andrew sees love and marriage as incompatible, because love implies something furtive, even forbidden. There are no barriers or jealousies involved in marital affection.

In the forced convenient marriages of medieval times, the option of hidden liaisons is enticing. Whereas pure love is controlled, mixed love gives in totally to lust. This only uses and injures the beloved and leads to remorse.

Andrew cautions in Ovidian manner how to keep a love, once won. Secrecy, restraint, kindness, generosity, courage, selflessness, separation and jealousy can escalate love, whereas too much togetherness, foolishness, cowardice, and uncharitableness can destroy it. Infidelity, a new liaison, or marriage can terminate love. Like Ovid, Andrew, prescribes a remedy for love sickness, since love is short-lived, suffering and jealous. Moreover, God punishes love outside of wedlock, because fornication stains both body and soul.

Chastity is a high virtue, while illicit love breaks up marriage and can lead to murder, adultery, theft and damnation. However, chastity brings rich rewards. Eleanor of Aquitaine brought courtly love North in her first marriage to Louis VII of France, and to England in her second nuptials with Henry II.

Northern romances include: beginnings, development, betrothal, ordeal and separation, and union, with the goal married love in contrast to the unmarried affection of courtly love.

Romantic love is tested by separation, restrictions and even rumored death. Moreover, the wider the discrepancy of ranks and the more parental opposition, the better. Sometimes it is even immoral.

While some romances stress love, others tell of chivalry, with the brave knight winning his fair lady. Both hero and heroine are idealized in a worldly sense. Northern love stories of Erec and Enide, Lancelot and Guinevere, Tristan and Iseult and the *Romance of the Rose* set the pace for later novels.

Jean de Meun, in the latter part of the *Romance of the Rose*, sees love's purpose in procreation, perhaps reflecting the theology of marriage of the University of Paris. Moreover, he calls love irrational mirroring some of his Parisian colleagues. And he rates inclusive love over exclusive love. At the end of the *Romance* the dreamer rejects reason for love, but when he wakes, what does he have?

The *Romance of the Rose*, with its love reveries, allegory and satire, influenced later medieval writers such as Chaucer, who saw courtly love as an escape from reason and morality. Though Chaucer describes the romantic love of Troilus and Criseyde, he knows that human love is at best risky, whereas divine love never fails.

Spencer in his *Faerie Queene* writes of the triumph of married love over courtly affection, mirroring changing mores. But marriage evolved from courtly love. Though love was divorced from marriage by chivalry, it was restored by chastity. Love may have been forced out of marriage by the artificially arranged court marriages of medieval times, to return with more freedom of choice between the lovers. Spencer's romances would inspire later authors from Shakespeare to Meredith.

Dante, beginning with courtly love, ends with a higher love of his resurrected Beatrice, and so to divine love, which wins out over its weak human image. Even married love has a certain sadness, for it is destined for death and separation.

MYSTICAL MARRIAGE

The matrimonial theme is strong in medieval mysticism, following a stream flowing from the *Song of Solomon*.

In the Hebrew tradition there was a marriage contract between Israel and Yahweh. And Paul described the hierogamy between Christ and the Church. Under the influence of Greek individualism as seen in mystics such as Plotinus, pseudo-Dionysius and Gregory of Nyssa, the human soul is the bride of God.

Far from being a condemnation of human marriage the union of the soul with God is an interior wedding, upon which the external matrimony is modeled in theomorphy. Most mystics from pseudo-Dionysius to John Climacus, Maximus the Confessor and John Scotus Erigena teach the marriage of God and the soul.

Bernard of Clairvaux is a medieval knight of his virgin queen and her divine son, and his chivalry to Mary parallels that of the courts. For example, the *Slave Regina* was sung in both castles and monasteries. Bernard is a troubadour of our Lady, as Francis was after him.

He writes of the mystical marriage in his sermons on the *Song of Solomon*. "If, then, love is especially fitting to a bride and groom, it is not unfitting that the name of bride be given to the soul which loves" (*Ser* 7). The divine kiss which Christ bestows on his Church is the Holy Spirit (8).

God loved us first, and his soul-bride loves him in return. My beloved is mine and I am his. Pure love cannot be commercial. The very being of the bride, and her only hope, is love. He seeks nothing more, and she can give nothing more (83).

How can the bride not return the love of God? Yet she loves less than he does because she is less. Though she loves him with her whole soul, he both anticipates and surpasses her love.

Bernard's friend, William of St. Thierry, remarks on the Song of Songs that carnal love must migrate into the love of the spirit in order to grasp spiritual things. Divine love is the love from which all love is named. The kiss of the beloved is like a divine fragrance, not just the joining of bodies, but a spiritual union as well. The Church reached for the divine kiss, when God became man. Bride and groom rest in the mind: memory, intellect and love.

The Holy Spirit is the divine embrace of the Father and the Son, and a hug of grace between God and the soul. While here below the kiss is partial, there it will be full. "The kiss will be full, and the hug, too, whose strength is the wisdom of God and the sweetness of the Holy Spirit, the perfect and full enjoyment of divinity and God, all things in all." Love alone remains (PL 180.520).

The vagaries of human romance mirror divine love. For example, when God goes away, seemingly never to return, sometimes He calls from afar, and then goes away again while His bride begs Him to come back.

Ramon Lull, influenced by Francis, the Sufis (Islamic mystics) and other medieval love themes, writes of mystical love in his *Lover and Beloved*. Here the lover suffers, as in the medieval romances. Although he falls in pain, he delights as if he were in a bed of love.

When deity and humanity open the doors, the Lover goes in to his Beloved, and he will endure anything: thirst, hunger, heat, cold, sickness, and trials, for his Beloved. This is a suffering love, proved by pain, trial, and even death. We see in medieval mystical marriage parallels to human love. Or, perhaps, it is better stated the other way around, namely, that human sacrifice and affection are weak theomorphies of the divine hierogamy.

THE CHURCH AND MATRIMONY

In the Roman empire, matrimony was a social contract regulated by law. When Rome fell, the Church had to step in more and more to protect marriage and the family. Local churches tended to follow the customs of the place, with some guidance from Rome by medieval times. Popes, decretalists, and canonists tried to get some uniformity in the Church's marriage customs.

Pope Alexander III (12th century) was a leader. As the schism healed and papal authority became more respectable, he was able to synthesize the thought of Gratian and Peter Lombard on matrimony.[2] Cathedral schools applied dialectic to the canons. The rediscovery of the *Roman Digest*, plus the Gregorian reform, spurred the study of marriage law. Roman law was to be a major influence in the evolution of classical canon law.

Before the systematization of medieval marriage law, there were two trends. First, the popular view, based on scriptures, said that marriage is a sacrament formed after the union of husband and wife. But the Parisian masters claimed that matrimony is formed after the *desponsatio*, when bride and groom manifest their will to marry. This latter bears similarities to Jewish betrothal.

Some, such as Anselm of Laon, see marriage as only perfect and indissoluble after consummation, but most, such as William of Champeaux and Hugh of St. Victor, claim that consent about the present forms matrimony, as in Roman law. Christian marriage is irrevocable and constitutes a sacrament, mirroring the union of God with the soul, while consummation reflects the nuptials of Christ with His Church.

In Gratian and Peter Lombard, we have two great syntheses of the medieval theology of marriage. Gratian, at Bologna, sums up ancient laws, trying to resolve differences in canons and relationship of consent to consummation. Moreover, he feels that espousal is not indissoluble, since it points to the future.

Peter Lombard (12th century) calls free consent the efficient cause of matrimony (4 S,D. 27), for it directs the whole of marriage. Although present consent is both sacramental and indissoluble, it does not fully reflect the union of Christ with His Church, as in intercourse.

Alexander III (Bandinelli) follows Gratian in saying that although marriage is initiated in the *desponsatio*, and the conjugal pact is born, it is not yet matrimony. For it is only the later consent in the present, *"Ego te recipio in meam-in meum,"* ("I receive you in mine") that forbids future marriages.

Alexander III also wants a solemn marriage consent witnessed by a priest or notary *"in facie ecclesiae,"* enforcing its indissolubility. The oriental church had a similar regulation.

The growing problem of clandestine marriages in the West prompted Alexander III to require matrimony *"in facie ecclesiae"* (before the Church). However, this was not yet acceptable to the people. So he does not require it for validity, although the nuptials still should be witnessed. After 1163, Alexander III sees two ways of forming the bond: consent about the present, and consent concerning the future with intercourse.

Engaged couples may freely break up. But what if only one reneges? *"Monenda potius quam cogenda,"* for matrimony ought to be entered freely. If an engaged party marries another the betrothal is nullified, but a penance is to be given for infidelity.

Alexander III's successors applied Gratian's doctrine on the marriage bond, that is, a penance for a broken *desponsatio* and that the bond is cemented by intercourse and the presumption of present consent. But they did not buy his twofold method of forming the marriage bond.

After Hostiensis (13th century), consent about the present, ratified in faith, forms matrimony, and it is consummated by intercourse. Hostiensis says that since marriage is a sacrament, *res simplissima* (a most indivisible thing) it cannot be divided into parts. Though consent concerning the present is essentially perfect and a sacrament, it is completed by intercourse, which reflects the union of Christ with His Church, and so is indissoluble (D 79).

Intercourse has a confirmative and supportive role in marriage. For example, it presumes present consent, annulling conditions that might suspend the matrimony, and confirming a doubtful consent due to error or fear.

Consummated marriage alone is indissoluble and affects affinity and bigamy. This is what scripture means by the one flesh which God joins and man cannot separate.

Marital consent both creates a contract and is an instrument of grace. Most medieval canonists saw matrimony as a consensual, personal contract, based on Roman law. This free consent concerns the exchange of conjugal rights and is exlusive and perpetual. Of course, fear, force or error can nullify the contract.

To forestall clandestine marriages, many local synods and the Fourth Lateran Council demanded matrimony before a priest, and ruled that the ceremony should be preceded by bans. The exchange of vows should be public, before the doors of the church. Then bride and groom enter the church to receive the nuptial blessing from the pastor.

Both Gratian and Peter Lombard defend the indissolubility of marriage. But the *desponsatio* can be broken for a good reason. For example, a new *desponsatio* which is consummated, fornication, illness, etc.

Till the end of the 13th century, divorce was practiced in certain countries and churches. Though the popes fought for the indissolubility of a ratified and consummated marriage, they allowed separation for a serious reason.

The Byzantines, however, allowed divorce for adultery and for other reasons based on Novel 117 of the *Code of Justinian*. For example, a husband may divorce his wife if she plots against the emperor, commits adultery, plots against her husband, if she eats or bathes with strangers without the permission of her spouse, etc. And a wife may divorce her husband if he plots against the emperor, makes her commit adultery, falsely accuses her of adultery, etc.

Also, the Roman *"bona gratia"* (no fault) divorce was recognized for three years of impotence, entrance into religion, etc. However, the Trullan Council (7th century) rejected this. *De facto*, the reasons for divorce tended to increase over the years, including spiritual affinity, insanity, a scolding wife, lack of virginity, infidelity, heresy, etc.

What about successive marriages? Though most of the Fathers discouraged successive marriages, the Byzantines allowed second and third marriages with some limitations. The Roman Church felt that, though Paul did not forbid a second marriage after death of a spouse, it does not perfectly reflect the union of Christ with His Church, his one spouse. A second marriage after a divorce simply is not recognized as sacramental.

The spirit of Gratian inspired the popes and classical canon law. Huguccio synthesized the modern view, namely, that the marriage bond is formed by present consent and that a ratified and consummated matrimony is absolutely indissoluble.

The medieval period is important because canon law became fixed and was explicated by the decretalists and theologians. They rejected local customs that were against natural or divine law such as polygamy, divorce, and the forbidding of successive marriages.

The popes tried to unify the impediments to marriage, e.g. ordination, mixed religion, etc. Medieval canon law paved the way for modern legislation. Actually few contemporary problems were not anticipated by the popes, decretalists, canonists and theologians.

THEOLOGY OF LOVE AND MARRIAGE

Bonaventure recognizes the strong bond of marriage based on the creation of one sex from the other. This is relaxing because Eve was created while Adam was asleep, and since she was made from his bone, he gives her strength. They share mutual society, as they partake of the same rib.

In his commentary of Peter Lombard's *Sentences* (4S, d. 26, a.1, q 1),[3] Bonaventure describes the twofold purpose of marriage, namely, duty before the fall and remedy after. Although intercourse fulfills the marriage and signifies the interior consent of the two souls, reflecting the union of Christ and the Church, God and the soul, it is not essential to the sacrament.

Bonaventure sees marriage as a sign, duty and remedy, signifying the nuptials of Christ with His Church in charity, and conformed with nature. It is a duty of mutual education, mitigation and the generation of children. Also, it is a remedy for lust and concupiscence.

He compares marriage to baptism. "So there is something permanent in marriage, and this is the bond, through which male and female are bound." Also, there is something transient, such as the union first made by the external word or act (d. 27, a. 1, q. 1).

The root meaning of matrimony is mother's duty, *matris monium*, for the begetting and feeding of the children mostly pertains to the mother (27.1.2). As patrimony indicates the possessions acquired by paternal solicitude, so by matrimony a child is acquired.

Bonaventure also teaches Augustine's threefold good of marriage:

fidelity, a child and sacrament, but often it is mixed with sorrow and anxiety (31.1.1). In his *Breviloquium*, Bonaventure discusses the integrity of marriage, based on Justinian's "marriage is a legitimate union of a man and woman, establishing an indissoluble community of life."[4]

While originally matrimony was functional, imitating the union of God and the soul, now it is remedial, reflecting Christ and the Church, or two natures in one Incarnate God. Marriage is a free, public consent, consummated by intercourse. "God decreed from the beginning that propagation would be brought about by means of a singular and individual union of male and female."

In the two in one flesh of matrimony "is the body of the one fully surrendered to that of the other in virtue of each one's respective power toward the procreation of offspring" (13.3). Thomas Aquinas, fellow student and colleague of Bonaventure, quotes Aristotle on the naturalness of marriage. "A son cannot be educated or instructed, unless he has determined and certain parents, and this cannot be, unless there is an obligation of a man to a certain woman as in marriage."

The second end of matrimony is the mutual service of the spouses. As men live together because of their insufficiencies, so man and woman are not sufficient for themselves. Thus each completes the other in marital union (4S, d. 26, q. 1, a. 1).

Aquinas includes matrimony among the sacraments which God has given man for his health (26.2.1), granting husband and wife the graces necessary for their state of life.

Thomas, like Bonaventure, teaches Augustine's threefold good of marriage: child, fidelity and sacrament (31.1.2). Whereas child and fidelity pertain to the duty of human nature, marriage is a sacrament insofar as it is instituted by God (31.1.3). These goods make matrimony and its acts honest and holy (31.2.2).

Aristotle taught that you cannot separate pleasure from operation (10 *Eth* 5.8). So, if pleasure in marriage is pursued for its own sake, there is a light sin (31.2.3). Marital rights pertain to the mutual exchange of bodies. Is a husband obliged to please his wife if she does not request intercourse? Yes, says Thomas, for he should anticipate her needs (32.1.2). Although the husband may be the head of the house, husband and wife are equals in seeking and giving the debt (32.1.3).

How about polygamy? Although many children are produced, there is little fidelity or peace, since it is hard for one man to please many wives. Moreover, polygamy can scarcely reflect the unique marriage of Christ and His Church (33.1.1).

Aquinas sees the inseparability of husband and wife as a natural good because of the lifelong association of parents and children (33.2.1).

In his catechetical work, *On the Truth of the Catholic Faith*, written for missionaries in Spain, Aquinas calls any deliberate misuse of human seed a sin. Also, it is proper for a man and woman to remain together after intercourse in order to raise their child (3.122.6).[5]

Concerning divorce, Thomas writes that a wife may not put away her husband, because she is subject to him. Nor may a husband discard his wife, for then marriage would not be an association of equals (3.123.4).

> The greater the friendship is, the more solid and long-lasting will it be. Now there seems to be the greatest friendship between husband and wife. . . . Therefore, it is fitting for matrimony to be completely indissoluble (3.123.6).

In his *Summa Theologiae*, an aid for students, Thomas discusses appetite and love (ST 1-2, qq. 26-30).[6] First the object impresses itself on the appetite. Then the appetite loves the object and moves to enjoy it (26.2).

Love is affection produced in the appetite by its object, and so is called a passion and spurs toward union with its object. Love also includes delight, which indicates a special choice. And charity means one highly prizes the object of his love.

Aristotle defines love as wishing good for someone (2 *Rhetoric*, c. 4, n. 4). There are really two loves. The first is the love of friendship by which I love the person to whom I wish well. The second is the love of concupiscence by which I love the good which I wish for them or for myself (1-2.26.4).

Friendship is useful and delightful when I wish something good for my friend, insofar as the good furthers the delight and usefulness of friendship. Since Aquinas calls marriage the most perfect friendship, we may have here a clue to his theology of marriage.

For example, if one loves his wife with the love of friendship, he wishes for her all the goods of matrimony, namely: fidelity, child and sacrament, and other goods as well, including sexual pleasure. If he uses his wife only for his own selfish enjoyment, this is the love of concupiscence, and is wrong.

The good, knowledge and similarity are causes of love (27). But we can only love a good which we know and in which we see a similarity. Thomas sees two types of similarity: a similarity of qualities, and another similarity in which one has the potency to receive the other's act. The first causes the love of friendship, or the love of good will.

> For the fact that two people are alike in having some form means, in a sense, that they are one form. . . . The result is that the affections of the one are bent upon the other as being one with himself, and he wishes well to the other as to himself (27.3).

The greater the dissimilarity in marriage, the greater the risk. Moreover, the similarity which seeks to fulfill our own selfish needs is also chancy. Love brings union, mutual indwelling, ecstasy and jealousy. It is the union of the lover with his beloved, a friendship in which he wants good things for her as for himself, since she is his other self (28.1).

Mutual indwelling can be by knowledge or desire. For example, when the beloved is absent, as in courtly or romantic love, her lover follows in reverie and song. "Perfect love allows but one life to subsist in two. Each speaks of his self and his other self" (28.2).

Another effect of love is ecstasy, by which the lover is carried out of himself. His mind withdraws from others and goes out to his beloved. But appetitive ecstasy can be selfish; for example, a desire by which we go out in order to bring a good back to ourselves.

> In the love of friendship, the ultimate term of the person's feeling is located outside him completely, for he wants some good thing for his friend, and works for it, exercising thought and care about his friend's interests for his friend's sake (28.3).

The more intense the love, the deeper the jealousy and resistance to obstacles. Jealousy can be selfish when we envy another's good fortune, or it can be selfless in friendship. Here we are apprehensive lest someone hurt our friend. Love is excellent when it brings us to a union with an appropriate good, but can be harmful if it aims at lower pleasures. Moreover, physically and psychologically, immutable love can be detrimental.

Some proximate effects of love are: melting, pleasure, languor and fever. Frigidity is a common obstacle to love (28.5), "whereas melting or warmth suggest a certain softness which means the heart will be quick to let the loved object enter into it." If we possess our beloved,— joy and pleasure. If not,—languor and fever.

Love inspires action since we act for the loved good, either of friendship or desire. Hate, although the opposite of love, is caused by it, since we hate what opposes our love (29.1, 2). But love is stronger than hate.

Though sense pleasures are attractive, they are also ephemeral (31.5), whereas beauty of the mind endures.

Is sex a rational act? Tradition has Adam and Eve as perfectly rational at all times until their fall, when their minds became clouded. However, no one can live without some sensible or corporeal pleasures, of which some are good and others bad. In pleasure the appetitive virtue rests in the loved good, following the action of love.

There are two reasons for pleasure. First from the part of the good in which we rest insofar as it is in accord with reason, and second, from the operation which is closer to the pleasure than the preceding desire. Though pleasures which are against reason are wrong, in some pleasures, such as sex, the use of reason is truncated. Here, although there is something reasonable in the act, nonetheless, it hinders reason because of its corporeal connection.

But this does not mean that there is a moral fault. For example, sleep is good and necessary for health, if done in a rational manner, even though our reason takes a rest during our slumber. Our reason does not have to be constantly operative. In fact, it would be counterproductive if it did. Furthermore, although in a moment of sexual passion, our reason may be on vacation, it is not an unreasonable act, since we reasonably enter marriage for the purpose of intercourse, for mutual healing and progeny. The intense delight experienced in marital intercourse does not exceed the limits of reason prior to the act (*ST*, Sup 49.4.3).

Of course, the love of a Christian man and wife should transcend bodily union into charity, love of God. For although bodily attraction and its child-orientation wane in God's good providence, charity remains, directing all their acts Godward. Love of God and neighbor are one, so Christian spouses love each other in God. "We ought to love our neighbor (spouse) because he (or she) is in God. Thus it is clear that by the same species of act we love God and neighbor. And because of this habit of charity the act not only includes love of God, but also love of neighbor" (25.1).

Naturally, our love for our family is greater than our affection for those outside. Our wife and children are "to be loved more out of charity, because they are loved more intensely, and because they are loved for many reasons. The intensity of the love is from the closeness of the loved and the lover." But what about in-laws, and the inevitable clash of loyalties. Do parents or spouse come first? Thomas cleverly responds.

> One's parents should be loved more than his wife as the princi- ples of his origin. But his wife should be loved more than his parents by reason of closeness—two in one flesh.

The contractual concept of marriage came from the commentators on Roman law and the glossists, and was used by the canonists and the classical theologians. Thus the marriage consent both makes a con- tract, is an instrumental cause of grace, and is a type of obligation.

Duns Scotus (14th century) calls marriage a state, contract and sacrament. It is an indissoluble bond between male and female, a mutual gift of their bodies for the procreation and education of children.

The marriage contract is the efficient cause of the bond, just as baptism or ordination cause a character to be imprinted on the soul. Among Christians the sacrament is united to the contract and state of matrimony.

Nicole Oresme (14th century)[7] notes in the romantic theme that the lord of the house should have first concern over his wife, for this is natural, loving, profitable, divine and harmonious. When two young people love each other freely and joyfully with a reasonable love, sometimes this is chaste, leading to marriage. But at other times it is humanly errant. However, to seek pure pleasure without love is bestial.

Marital friendship includes the good of usefulness, pleasure, virtue, enjoyment, and a permanent and stable friendship, as Aristotle and scriptures teach. Moreover, sex pleasure was given to man "not only for reproduction of its kind, but also to enhance and maintain friendship between man and woman"—two in one.

Far from downplaying marital intercourse, popes and theologians made it the *sine qua non* of nuptial indissolubility, even specifying or making explicit an internal or doubtful consent. Moreover, it celebrates the hierogamy of Christ and His Church.

A husband's love for his wife should seek to satisfy her desires, so that she will not wander. Yet, on the other hand, he should not smother her with affection, lest she pine away in his absence, a common problem in medieval times and a contributing factor to courtly love.

A husband should be courteous, modest, restrained, sensitive, honorable—the refined love, *fine amor* of the courts. Moreover, this courtliness should perdure throughout the marriage, constant, faithful and considerate.

Though he is master of the home, a husband should love and revere his wife, giving good example by his chaste life. A husband's faithful companionship builds a peaceful marriage. Both spouses should try to outdo each other in love and friendship, each considering the other the better one.

Matrimony is based on this mutual love of husband and wife. Their coition is blessed if it is decent and loving, bringing generation and encouraging love and fidelity. We have seen some dimensions of medieval love and marriage. The troubadours, inspired by Ovid and the Sufis, sing of unrequited love, and the romances tell of a tested and chivalrous affection. The mystics see human love reflecting the soul's union with God, as sung in the Song of Solomon.

Marriage law evolved in the Middle Ages, based on the rediscovered Roman codes. Led by Peter Lombard, Gratian and Alexander III, universal canons were adopted, protecting the consent, validity, sacramentality and indissolubility of matrimony. The theologians also call marriage a sacrament, seeing it as both a means of generation and a healing remedy. Aquinas describes marriage as the love of friendship, in which each spouse wants something good for the other.

The Middle Ages are important because the love and marriage concepts of the courts, romances, canonists, mystics and theologians are the foundations of modern western literary and theological traditions on matrimony.

CHAPTER SEVEN

A Truly Noble, Important And Blessed Condition
(Martin Luther: On the Estate of Marriage, 13)

Though the Reformers generally follow the scriptural teaching on marriage, they tend to diminish its sacramentality, and so its absolute indissolubility, torn between the gospel ideal and human weakness.

LUTHER: VOCATION OF MARRIAGE

Luther's theology of marriage can best be understood in his teachings on vocation, *beruf*, or call (klesis, *ekklesia*).[1] Although all people have a stand, station or estate in life, the Christian has a special vocation to spiritual and worldly work.

Luther sees vocation as a stand for the service of others. This fits his doctrine on love by which the Christian is called to be a channel of God's love for others. Vocation for Luther is not just one's occupation or job, but also his or her place in the family: husband or wife, mother or father, son or daughter. Most people wear many hats, e.g. son, husband, father, worker; serving others inside and outside the home.

There is an inevitable tension between selfishness and selflessness.

> When husband and wife, in marriage, serve one another and their children, this is not due to the heart's spontaneous and undisturbed expression of love, every day and hour. Rather in marriage, as an institution, something compels the husband's

selfish desires to yield, and likewise inhibits the egocentricity of the wife's heart. At work in marriage is a power which compels self-giving to spouse and children. So it is the station itself which is the ethical agent, for it is God who is active through the law on earth (6).

This is very close to sacramentality, with marriage as an instrument of God's grace. The gospel of Christ amends the wayward human heart, so that the order of marriage serves God's mission on earth. Man's vocation channels God's gifts to others and thus he helps extend God's creation for man's use. For example,

> God creates the babes in the mother's body—man being an instrument in God's hand—and then he sustains them with his gifts, brought to children through the labors of father and mother in their parental office.

Although God is the author of life, man is his helper in procreation (9) (*On the Estate of Marriage*, 1522). Luther sees man's vocation as descending to man and the world, rather than ascending to God, and so it carries on God's creation. Marriage must be pointed to the welfare of the neighbor here on earth, since there is no marriage in heaven. The marriage vocation is to love and work for others, even to be willing to die for our families.

In his *Large Catechism*, Luther describes parents as God's hands, through which he gives us all. God hides behind the masks of human beings and their marriage vocation. It is God who really brings children into the world, but it takes faith in order to see God behind the human. Marriage is a true vocation. If someone interferes, such as Satan, a neighbor, our family, or our own weakness, call upon the Lord and he will help.

While the Reformers called for ecclesiastical *laissez faire* in marriage, leaving decisions up to the state, the people still went to the Church to heal their nuptial pains. German customs considered consent to a future marriage plus intercourse, as the equivalent of marriage, following medieval tradition. Although divorce was not encouraged, annulments were common for various reasons.

Though Luther is reluctant to include marriage among the sacraments of the Church, because it obviously preceded Christianity, nonetheless, he is not hesitant to call it God's gracious gift, in which husband and wife seek God's help. Like his predecessors, he calls matrimony a healing remedy whose chief end is generation.

Genesis tells us how God gave Eve to Adam as a helper (*On the Estate of Marriage*, 1519, LW). We should emulate Adam in asking God to help us find a suitable spouse. Although a lusty, light-hearted youth has little interest in the spiritual side of marriage, "marriage is, nevertheless, a weighty matter in the sight of God" (8).

Luther sees three kinds of love: the first is false and selfish, the second is the natural love between father and son and the third is married love, which is the greatest. While all other love seeks something besides the beloved, "this kind wants only to have the loved one's own self completely."

Whereas before the fall married love was the "loveliest thing," now it is not pure since it is tinged with selfishness, and it is more like a "hospital for incurables."

Luther teaches Augustine's threefold good of marriage: sacrament, fidelity and child. Matrimony is a sacrament, a sacred sign of the holy and eternal, namely, the unity of the divine and human natures of Christ, God and man, Christ and Church. God gives himself to man, as husband to wife, and marriage blesses and sanctifies man's fleshly desires.

Matrimony is also a covenant of fidelity, a self-gift and a promise to remain faithful. Following the German custom of seeing betrothal and intercourse as marriage, Luther wants the engagement, matrimony and consummation on the same day. "I am yours and you are mine." Moreover, the parents' advice should be sought before entering marriage. The begetting and raising of children to serve, honor and praise God is the chief reason for marriage. Unfortunately, some people rush into marriage and have children, without even knowing what the commandments are.

"O what a truly noble, important and blessed condition the estate of marriage is, if it is properly regarded" (13). But how pitiable and dangerous it is, if it is not used properly. Well-raised children are a better testimony than endowed churches, altars, Masses for the dead, etc. In his *Babylonian Captivity of the Church* (1520), Luther questions the sacramentality of marriage, and sees matrimony rather as an allegory of the mystery of Christ and the Church (LW).

Furthermore, he recognizes no impediments to marriage that are not mentioned in the Bible. Moreover, he feels that the Church overstresses the importance of consummation in relation to the promise. If Paul allows the unbelieving spouse to be put away, why not the deserting believer?

In his *On the Estate of Marriage* (1522) (LW), Luther dreads the prospect of preaching on matrimony, for he thinks that the Church has been too involved in marriage in the past. But he is ambivalent. On the one hand, he would like the civil government to handle marriage problems, but, on the other hand, people come to him for help. Timidity is no solution. "I must try to instruct poor bewildered consciences and take up the matter boldly" (17).

As in his earlier works, Luther feels that the Church has too many ways of preventing or dissolving marriage. He himself would allow divorce and remarriage for three reasons: impotence, adultery, and refusal of the conjugal duty of cohabitation. However, if the couple do not get along, he would allow divorce but no remarriage.

What if one's wife is incurably ill? "Blessed and twice blessed are you when you recognize such a gift of grace, and therefore, serve your invalid wife for God's sake" (35). God will provide His grace. Not all who are married recognize the estate of marriage, and for them life is bitter, boring, an anguish, a complaining, and a blasphemy. "But he who recognizes the estate of marriage will find therein delight, love and joy without end. As Solomon says, 'He who finds a wife, finds a good thing' " (Pr 18:22).

In order to see the estate of matrimony, one has to believe that God formed it, and brought husband and wife together for the sake of children (Gn 1:28). They can be sure that marriage and everything in it: works, suffering, etc., is pleasing to God. What could give us greater joy?

If a husband believes this, he would not see his wife as hateful, ill-tempered, sick, etc., and would not fail to find his heart's delight. We make a mistake if we judge God according to our own feelings, for although our marriage may be painful to us, it is pleasing to Him.

But is it not better to be free than to be burdened with diapers, rashes, discipline, work, cooking, sewing, etc? Sometimes we feel unworthy to serve God through marriage and the family. Yet God and His angels smile as the father washes his baby's dirty diapers in faith.

In the estate of marriage we find God's word and good pleasure "by which all the works, conduct and sufferings of that estate become holy, godly and precious" (Pr 5:18; 9:9) (41). Some married folk become bitter and anguished because they have no knowledge of God's word and will about marriage.

> No one can have real happiness in marriage who does not recognize in firm faith that this estate together with all its works, however insignificant, is pleasing to God and precious in His sight (42).

In a good marriage, husband and wife cherish one another, become one, serve one another, and check unchastity. Moreover, the estate of matrimony not only benefits the body, property, honor and soul of an individual, but aids whole cities and countries by the controlling of passions.

The greatest good of marriage is offspring, brought up to worship and serve God. If we only bring a single soul to God, "you can see how rich the estate of marriage is in good works." When they teach the gospels to their children, mother and father are like bishops and priests.

When one is about to marry, does he worry how he can support his family? Depend on Providence. Moreover, one should not be ashamed to do menial work (Mt 6:25; Ps 37:25). "Let God worry about how they and their little ones are to be fed. God makes children, he will surely also feed them" (48).

Luther sees marriage as a mixture of sin and grace, because it is an earthly work. Though we are still sinners, with God's grace we can win. As a scripture scholar, Luther applies the teachings of the Bible (for example, Paul in his first letter to the Corinthians) to marriage (LW). "The state of marriage is constituted in the law of love, so that no one rules over his own body, but must serve his partner as is the way of love." Fornication, on the other hand, seeks its own pleasure, while adultery gives away another's body and takes one which is not ours.

A Christian wife should not separate from her husband, and if she does, she should either remain single or be reconciled. And a Christian husband should not divorce his wife. However, false Christians divorce and remarry (13). St. Paul allows divorce for anger and hatred between husband and wife where they can neither pray nor work together, but does not allow remarriage.

What if the other party refuses to reconcile? Luther would allow the willing spouse to remarry, since God does not demand the impossible (32). If an unbeliever hinders the faith of his believing spouse, divorce and remarriage is allowed. "For one must honor Christ, the spouse of the soul, more than the spouse of one's body" (34). The unbeliever can be consecrated through his spouse, as long as he doesn't interfere with her faith, but if he leaves, she may divorce and remarry. The Christian spouse should do everything to influence the non-Christian one by word and example.

In 1525 Luther marries an ex-nun, Katherine von Bora, and from then on he speaks on marriage from experience. In his *Large Catechism* (1529)[2] he comments on the fourth and sixth commandments, so central to marriage and the family.

In the fourth commandment God raises mother and father up next to Himself. The children owe love, deference, humility and modesty "toward a majesty hidden within them."

Even if they are feeble and poor, father and mother are still given by God, and "they are not to be deprived of their honor because of their ways or their failings" (108). Be respectful and courteous, serving, helping, caring for them cheerfully and humbly when they are old, feeble and poor.

If all would obey the fourth commandment, "parents would have more happiness, love, kindness and harmony in their houses. And their children would win their parents' hearts completely" (124). Unfortunately, this is not the way it is with today's wayward youth, and their parents are not much better.

God has appointed parents to be His representatives on earth, but we are no more grateful to them than to God Himself, even though God has promised the reward of a long life. From parental authority all other jurisdiction on earth flows.

On their part, parents have the duty of raising their children and servants to praise and honor God. "Therefore, do not imagine that the parental office is a matter of your pleasure and whim" (169). If parents raise their young ones to serve God and man, they, in their turn, will become responsible leaders and good citizens and exemplary husbands and wives, fathers and mothers.

Though the fifth commandment forbids harming the neighbor, in the sixth, "they proceed to the person nearest and dearest to him, namely, his wife, who is one flesh and blood with him," and this is not only in action, but in heart and mind as well (200). Whereas God honored marriage in the fourth commandment, in the sixth He protects it. God raised the estate of marriage above all others.

> It is of the highest importance to him (God) that persons be brought up to serve the world, promote knowledge of God, godly living, and all virtues, and fight against wickedness and the devil (208).

Husband and wife should live together in harmony and fidelity. In his *Commentary of the Sermon on the Mount* (1530-32) (LW), Luther remarks that lusting leads to loving, for the heart follows the eye (87). When a man tires of his wife, he sees only her faults, and other women seem more attractive to him.

A safeguard is "to look at his spouse correctly according to God's Word, which is the dearest treasure and the liveliest ornament you can find in a man or woman. If he mirrored himself in this, then he would hold his wife in love and honor as a divine gift and treasure."

Then, if he spies a ravishing woman, he will say: "In my wife at home I have a lovelier adornment, one that God has given me and has adorned with His Word beyond the others," even though she may not be perfect. And although others may seem more attractive,

> This is the one whom God has granted to me and put into my arms. I know that He and all the angels are heartily pleased if I cling to her lovingly and faithfully (87).

Luther rejects the total avoidance of women of his monastic days, and the evil intimacy of adultery for a third way of friendship without lust. He admits that this is not easy, because of the wiles of Satan. So he must fight the battle through the Word of God. It is easy to get bored with one's wife and be attracted to another. Rather, he should see the special beauty and adornment which God has given her for him.

Marital love is necessary for the health of the union. Otherwise dullness sets in. The devil cannot stand the sight of affection between the spouses, preferring fights, hatred etc. It is a special Christian art—"loving one's husband or wife properly, or bearing the other's faults and all accidents and troubles" (89). In the first fervor of romance, everything seems rosy, but sooner or later comes boredom and the seeking of new thrills, so evil desires have to be fought. Jesus allowed no divorce, except for fornication. Luther feels that if Moses allowed divorce for the hard-hearted, so should the civil government. "Frequently something must be tolerated even though it is not a good thing to do, to prevent something worse from happening" (94).

If one wants to be a true Christian, no divorce is allowed, or if there is a divorce, no remarriage. "He has given every man his spouse, to keep her and for his sake to put up with difficulties involved in married life." Since they think it is only a secular contract, they terminate it when they get fed up. Afterwards they go from bad to worse.

If one wants his marriage to be blessed, he should pray to God. "It is no small gift from God to find a wife who is pious and easy to get along with. Then why not ask Him to make it a happy marriage?" Our own initiative, curiosity and romance will not last long "unless He adds his blessing and success and helps you bear the occasional troubles." This is clearly the grace of marriage, which for Roman Catholics is the grace of the sacrament.

Although Luther leaves divorce up to the secular courts, he advises Christian couples to reconcile and forgive. However, sometimes reconciliation is refused by the unrepentant adulterer.

> Whoever wants to have a wife and children, must stay with them. He must bear the good and the ill with them as long as he lives. And if he refuses to do so, he should be told that he must. Otherwise he will be separated from wife, family and home permanently (98).

Minor faults and foibles should be overlooked. Luther advises patience, for we will never have anything just right, since even in our own bodies we have both good and bad. Christian marital love is between two members of the same body (Rm 12:4-5), accepting, sympathizing, bearing, helping, forgiving as God forgives (98).

As Bainton notes[3] Luther believed that marriage "was indeed instituted by God and approved by Christ, and should be blessed by the Church." Moreover, he knew that matrimony is not purely a civil contract. However, he did not see it as strictly sacramental either, and so not totally under the Church's jurisdiction.

As we have seen, Luther would rather not deal with marriage at all, but his pastoral concern could not avoid it, since so much of Christian life revolves around this holy estate.

Luther's theology of marriage accepts the biblical and medieval view of betrothal as binding. Though he stressed freedom of consent, he also wanted parental approval of the union. He also sees marriage as a healing remedy, and though he is against divorce, his yen for freedom from Church control led to a certain ambivalence about it. However, though the Roman Catholic canons were too restrictive, there had to be some regulations for pastors and faithful alike (*kirchenordnunger*).

TRENT: THE SACRAMENT OF MARRIAGE

Martin Luther had called for a council to try to settle some of the theological differences of the time. Eventually the Council of Trent was called, lasting from 1545 to 1563 with some interruptions. Both scripture and tradition were used as sources.

Adam, the Council notes,[4] instinctively pronounced marriage a perpetual and indissoluble bond, two in one flesh (Gn 2:23-4), and Christ affirmed this (Mt 19:6)—what God has joined, let no man separate.

Christ, the founder and perfecter of the venerable sacraments, by His holy passion merited for us the grace which perfects natural love, and confirms its indissoluble unity and sanctifies the spouses (Ep 5:25, 32).

Since Christian matrimony, by the grace of Christ, surpasses ancient nuptials, it should be numbered among the sacraments of the New Law. This is what the Fathers, councils and the traditions of the Church have always taught, but some of the Reformers opposed this view.

The Council reaffirms: that marriage is a sacrament, instituted by Christ; that polygamy is forbidden by divine law; that there are more grades of consanguinity and affinity than mentioned in *Leviticus* 18:6-18; and that the Church has power to add to and dispense from the impediments to marriage.

Moreover, marriage is not dissolved by heresy, concubinage or absence. A ratified but not consummated marriage can be dissolved by solemn profession in a religious order. Although a marriage cannot be dissolved for adultery, the Church can allow spouses to separate for a good reason.

Furthermore, clerics in sacred orders and solemnly professed cannot marry, and to assert this is not to condemn matrimony. They may not marry even if they feel that they have lost the gift of chastity, for God does not deny purity to those who seek it, and he does not allow us to be tempted beyond our strength.

The Council rates virginity and celibacy over marriage, and defends the Church's right to prohibit marriage at certain times, such as during Lent. Moreover, it encourages special blessings and rites for matrimony. Church courts have the power to interpret marriage cases (1-12).

Since marriage needs renovation, the solemn ceremony recommended by the Lateran council is to be renewed. Although the bishop may dispense from the public banns (for example, for older people), matrimony must be contracted before the parish priest and other witnesses.

The Church recognizes the validity of clandestine marriages, and also those contracted without the permission of the parents. However, the Church frowns on clandestine marriages because sometimes a public union was celebrated with another after the hidden nuptials were consummated. The Lateran council required banns in order to find out about any impediments. If there are no obstacles to the wedding, the couple may proceed to marriage *"in facie ecclesiae."* Then the pastor, after accepting their mutual consent says, "I join you in matrimony in the name of the Father, Son and Holy Spirit."

Though the banns may be adjusted according to need, the priest and witnesses are necessary for validity. The pastor should enter the wedding record in a special book. Both bride and groom are encouraged to confess and receive Holy Communion before their marriage.

Then the Council of Trent lists the impediments to marriage, including: spiritual relationship, especially through baptism; public honesty to the first degree; affinity through fornication to the second degree; prohibited degrees of consanguinity and affinity; and abduction while in the power of the abductor (1-6).

There is a special caution about transients who have a woman in every port.

"Multi sunt, qui vangantur et incertas habent sedes, et ut improbi sunt ingenii, prima uxore relicta, aliam et plerumque plures, illa vivente, diversis in locis ducunt." (There are many who wander and have no permanent abode, and, being of unprincipled character, after having abandoned their first wife, marry another, very often several in different localities during the lifetime of the first.)

Be cautious and inquire (7). Concubinage is a grave sin for singles, but most serious for married people. After three warnings, they are to be excommunicated, and if they persist for one year, criminal proceedings should begin (8). Temporal lords and magistrates have no business interfering in marriage (9).

Whereas solemn marriage may be forbidden in certain sacred times, the rest of the year it may be celebrated with solemnity, decency and honesty. *"Sancta enim res est matrimonium et sancte tractandum"* (10). (Matrimony is holy and is to be treated in a holy manner.)

The Church in the Council of Trent defends its position as the guardian of marriage. Like Luther, perhaps it might wish it otherwise, but troubled consciences and pastoral concern take precedence for the protection of the innocent spouse, as in the case of the wandering bigamist.

Trent set the pattern for Church marriage law for the protection of the sanctity and indissolubility of matrimony, for the next 400 years.

CHAPTER EIGHT

A School of Christian Charity
(John Paul II, October 12, 1980, 6)

POPES

The modern Church continues to teach the sacramentality and indissolubility of marriage.

Benedict XIV (1740-58) quotes *Genesis* and the *Gospels* against the easy divorce of the time.

> Since the matrimonial contract was instituted by God, inasmuch as it is a natural institution, whose aim is the education of offspring and the conservation of the other benefits of marriage, it is suitable that it be perpetual and indissoluble.[1]

Some governments require marriage before civil magistrates or clergymen of other faiths, undermining the sacrament of marriage, but this is just a civil act in the eyes of the Church, and not a true matrimony. "They should know that until their marriage is celebrated before a Catholic priest and two witnesses, they will never be true and legitimate spouses before God and the Church" (37).

Benedict also teaches the Pauline privilege, allowing the Christian spouse to divorce and remarry if the non-Christian spouse hinders the practice of the faith. Although he discourages mixed marriages, when they are allowed, the faith of the Christian spouse and the children should be safeguarded.

Pius VI (1775-1799) answers those who say that since marriage is only a civil contract, it can be easily broken. Rather, marriage is a natural contract, created and ratified by God and previous to any civil society. The family came first and then government, not *vice versa* (67).

Pius VIII (1829-1830) writes that "this intimate society, which is formed by means of a marriage between a man and his bride, is a sacrament, a sacred image of the immortal love of Jesus Christ for His Church, his spouse" (84).

Leo XIII (1878-1903) worries because the contemporary family is in trouble. However, the sacrament of matrimony gives strength and grace to the family to be faithful to their duties.

If marriage is nothing more than a civil contract, there is little care for fidelity or children. If matrimony is established in Christian life, religion, piety, virtue, respect and unselfishness will flourish (124).

In the 19th century, Socialism and Communism began to undermine marriage and the family, by placing the state over these two pillars of society, weakening them, rather than serving and fortifying, as it should.

Christ gave husband and wife the power to obtain holiness in the married state (Feb. 10, 1880), completing natural love and making the union of husband and wife "more perfect through the bond of heavenly love."

Moreover, Christ gave marriage a new purpose, namely, "the bringing forth of children for the Church," to worship the one, true God and our Lord, Jesus Christ (140).

Christ gave the Church the right to protect the sacrament of marriage. "The marriages of Christians have become far the noblest of all matrimonial unions" (146). This is seen "by their lightening each other's burdens through mutual help; by constant and faithful love; by having all their possessions in common; and by the heavenly grace that flows from the sacrament" (152).

Furthermore, the sacrament of matrimony builds up the family, strengthens the union of mother and father, supports a holy education of the children, tempers the authority of the father, and spurs the obedience of the youngsters, making them good, God-loving citizens. But all of this flows only from a marriage that is holy, one and indissoluble under the guidance of the Church.

However, when the Christian religion is rejected, or slips into decadence, new evils come to the family and the state, leading to a loosening of morals and free divorce.

In revolutionary France, God was abandoned and divorce was rampant, and this is still true in Leo's time. Easy divorce weakens the marriage contract, mutual affection and fidelity, harms the children, breaks up home and family, degrades women, weakens the state and undermines morality. Both Church and state should cooperate for the good of marriage.

Pius XI in his encyclical *Casti Connubii* (1930)[2] stresses Augustine's threefold good of marriage: child, fidelity and sacrament. God uses men and women as his helpers to propagate the human race and educate members of Christ's Church.

Marital fidelity, guided by Christ and called the faithfulness of chastity by Augustine, blooms in "the love of husband and wife, which persuades all the duties of married life and holds pride of place in Christian matrimony," joined in pure love as Christ loves His Church, seeking only the good of his spouse. Love is proved in action.

The prime end of marital love is the daily reflection of the interior life in virtue, and love of God and neighbor. This is the "mutual inward molding of husband and wife." This is the chief purpose of marriage in a wider sense beyond mere generation and education of children. It is "the blending of life as a whole and the mutual interchange and sharing thereof" in justice and charity (23).

Although the husband, is the head of the family, he should respect his wife, not as a servant, but as his companion in the Lord. Conjugal fidelity includes: unity, chastity, charity, and obedience, and brings peace, dignity and happiness to the home (29).

The sacrament of matrimony makes the bond holy and indissoluble by Jesus Christ, guaranteeing: stability, intimate fellowship, loyal chastity, security, dignity, mutual help, a sharing of the burden of parenthood, and a building up of the nation.

The sacrament of matrimony sanctifies husband and wife with sanctifying grace, and gives actual grace as well. The spouses have to cooperate with God, in order to be strengthened and made holy by the sacrament. Just as baptism and orders are permanent aids, so also is marriage (40).

The modern media are destroying the sanctity of matrimony by encouraging adultery, divorce, premarital sex, etc. Many claim that marriage was founded by man and not by God. Since it is just a natural form of propagation, it is subject to the will of man.

Pius is against companionate marriage, sterilization, abortion and adultery. Moreover, he warns that a false emancipation of women can abrogate motherhood and wifehood, so that woman can easily become a mere instrument of man (73). Though husband and wife are equal in their marriage rights, there has to be a certain amount of accommodation for the good of family and home (74).

Some would "substitute for that true and solid love, which is the basis of conjugal happiness, a certain vague compatibility of temperament" (76). When this wanes, the marriage dissolves, for since it is just a civil contract, they feel free to terminate it any time they please.

The innate sacredness of matrimony is of divine origin, with the parents as God's ministers and the Christian sacrament adds dignity. But faith can be endangered in a mixed marriage (82).

Modern divorce destroys the indissolubility of marriage, and whatever might make the union hard or unpleasant is considered grounds for splitting. Or else, they say that a fractious marriage is bad for both family and society. However, the indissolubility of marriage is taught by the Bible and the Church.

We cannot hold our passions in check unless we first submit to God and make use of his supernatural help, for example, prayer, sacraments and devotion. Nature alone cannot handle our drives. Moreover, we are not good judges in our own case.

Parents should keep the commandments, observe chastity, respect the marriage bond, and use their marital rights properly and prudently. They should meditate on the sacrament of matrimony, "the efficacious power of which, although it does not impress a character, is undying," In this it is similar to the Eucharistic Presence (108).

Moreover, the couple should prepare diligently for marriage, the state providing material assistance and the Church moral support.

Marriage is for the generation and education of children, Pius reminds us in his *Christian Education of Youth* (1929). "God directly communicates to the family, in the natural order, fecundity, which is the principle of life and hence also the principle of the education of life, together with authority, the principle of order" (45).

Since father and mother have a mission from God to educate their children, they have priority over the state in this matter. The family is the first educator of the child, so his training will be better received "in a well-ordered and well-disciplined Christian family," starting with the good example of the parents.

In modern times parental education has slipped, since mother and father have little preparation for this, and the children are sent at an early age to the public schools.

Church and family, working together in Christian education, "may be said to constitute together one and the same temple of Christian education" (59). From this milieu comes the true Christian, who thinks and acts according to reason, illuminated by the teachings of Christ, not neglecting natural learning, but rather supernaturalizing it.

Pius XII (1939-58) reminds newlyweds (10/23/40), (1/24/41), (7/30/41)[3] that human love is "the delicate witness and interpreter of the union between body and soul."

Beauty is added "when its song is harmonized with the hymn of two souls vibrating with supernatural life," with a mutual exchange of gifts, tenderness, affection and spiritual union. The total self-gift of marriage reflects that of Christ and the Church, partaking in the divine nature and given supernatural help to shoulder superhuman obligations. But mutual affection is not enough. Only supernatural charity, a bond of friendship between God and man, can tie knots strong enough to resist all the shocks, all the vicissitudes, all the inevitable trials of a long life spent together.

Charity alone will help the couple to rise above the daily miseries, differences and foibles. This divine charity, the fruit of the sacrament of matrimony, perfects nature.

Love and fidelity create intimacy and confidence. Charity surpasses nature, for it is selfless, solicitous, affectionate, tender, and gracious. While the husband should give an example of moral dignity and courage in performing his parental duties, his wife should be wise, prudent and reserved, with a spotless reputation.

Mutual trust brings peace and love to the family. On the other hand, jealousy can be the fruit of selfishness. Christ alone is the source of true, pure and strong love, which is spiritual, warm, tender, affectionate and selfless.

Pius XII speaks to newlyweds of popular personal love (10/29/51). As we have seen, love and marriage, which in the beginning were social and family oriented, became more personal in the Middle Ages and Renaissance, with courtly and romantic love. Although marriage is a personal affective union of husband and wife, Pius XII calls its primary end the generation and education of children. God wills that the spouses cleave to each other, but their one flesh includes the child.

The conjugal act expresses their mutual self-gift. The Creator who intended procreation in matrimony, "also disposed that in this function the couple should experience pleasure and happiness in body and soul" (29). Thus only within marriage are these pleasures licit, where the joy is subordinate to the generation.

Happiness in marriage is not dependent on sexual prowess, but rather on the reciprocal respect of husband and wife. Talking to married couples (1941-42), Pius XII calls the sacrament of matrimony a yoke of grace, "which before the priest and the altar of Christ, unites two lives into one, with an indissoluble bond."

God joined Adam and Eve for the sake of children and common family life. It has an unbreakable link which Christ elevated by His Incarnation and His holy presence at Cana, so that it reflects His marriage to His Church.

> Having been elevated to the pure and sacred dignity of a sacrament, imprinted and bound up in such a close connection with the love of the Redeemer and the work of redemption, the marital union can only be indissoluble and perpetual (33).

However, man tends to cast off this yoke as an unbearable burden. Nevertheless, God promises the grace of the sacrament to help sustain them in their trials and sacrifices.

While the marriage contract may seem cold and abstract, fidelity is "the heart and soul of the contract, its open proof and its clear witness," giving one's pledged body to the other spouse. True Christian fidelity rules lovingly over all love.

This mutual gift is honored for life, through the burdens of parenthood to old age, when they care for each other's infirmities.

When youthful beauty and figure fade away to the reality of faults and irritations, true love still sees hidden virtues and qualities. "Love is ready to see what brings together and not what divides" (36), righting wrongs toward an enduring spiritual union. When one enjoys the marital rights without the duties, he displays the sterile selfishness of a closed heart. On the other hand, mutual trust, reciprocity and sharing nourish happiness.

Speaking on the family (11/27/51), Pius XII notes that unemployment, poor housing, etc. undermine family morality, which is essential to the welfare of both the home and society. He recognizes the need to regulate progeny through legitimate means, but faith, prayer and sacraments help parents to make good decisions.

By raising himself in society and in his profession, the father brings credit to his family and treats them with dignity.

Speaking to newlyweds (1941, 42, 44), Pius XII calls the mother the center of the home. But what if she is away on an outside job? This can lead to the neglect of home and family, where she is needed "to spread gentleness and sweetness" (52).

The cradle consecrates the mother of the family and honors her before her husband, children and society. "The heroism of motherhood is the exaltation and glory of the Christian bride" (57). The mutual sacrifices of mother and father build up the house and home, and the mother who out of necessity works outside the home sacrifices doubly.

VATICAN II

In their *Constitutions on the Church*, the Second Vatican Council fathers say that by the sacrament of matrimony the spouses help each other "to attain holiness in their married life and by the rearing and education of their children" (11).[4]

Through baptism the family perpetuates the people of God. Indeed, the Christian family is a domestic church, the primordial cell of the local and universal Church. Father and mother minister to each other and to their children, teaching by word and example.

The health of society depends on the strength of marriage and the family, which can be weakened by self-love, pleasure-seeking, frustration in generation, and by economic, social and psychological pressures.

Children can contribute to the holiness of their parents by their gratitude, love and trust, and by standing by them in their old age or sickness. Thus the Christian family can more clearly mirror the loving union of Christ and His Church.

Married love is eminently human, affectionate and personal, concerned with the good of the whole person and with a special friendship. "This love the Lord has judged worthy of special gifts, healing, perfecting and exalting gifts of grace and of charity" (49). Marital love merges the human and the divine. It is a mutual self-gift, perfected in the marital act. So "the actions within marriage by which the couple are united intimately and chastely are noble and worthy ones" (49).

Steadfast and true in the sacrament, married love will never be profaned by the couple. They should strive and pray for constant love, tenderness and sacrifice. Children are the supreme gift of marriage, the aim of conjugal love and family life, cooperating "with the love of the Creator and the Savior, who, through them, will enlarge and enrich his own family day by day" (50).

Parents participate in God's loving creation and interpret that love. Trusting in divine Providence, they should, with due consideration and advice, plan their family.

When intimacy is broken in marriage, infidelity is encouraged. There cannot be a contradiction between God's laws on transmitting life, and the fostering of conjugal love (51). From the moment of conception life should be guarded, and sex treated with great reverence.

Mutual self-giving and procreation must be pursued in true love. "Such a goal cannot be achieved unless the virtue of conjugal chastity is sincerely practiced." The family should be planned licitly, since the transmission of human life has eternal implications.

The family is "a school of deeper humanity" in which all cooperate so that children may grow up to be responsible adults and parents. Thus it is that the family is the foundation of society. Various social groups such as the Church, state, science, family associations, etc. should aid the family to achieve its ends.

Spouses should strive for mutual affection, harmony and satisfaction, and by their joys, prayers, sacrifices and faithful love, witness to the mystery of love of Christ and the Church.

HUMAN LIFE

In his encyclical on *Human Life* (7, 25, 68)[5] (*Humanae Vitae*), Paul VI recalls some new dimensions of the problems of the transmission of life, such as overpopulation, poverty, low education levels, women's emerging role in society, the value of sexuality and intercourse, and the scientific control of ovulation.

Does not the principle of totality require wise birth control? Does not procreation pertain to the whole of conjugal life, and not just to single acts? Reason should control biology. Jesus gave His apostles and Church the power to interpret marriage law, so John XXIII commissioned a study on the matter.

Conjugal love is from God, who instituted marriage as its vehicle. Through their mutual self-gift, husband and wife collaborate with God in the generation and education of new lives. For the baptized, matrimony is a sacrament reflecting the union of Christ and the Church (8).

Married love is human, of sense and spirit, free, lasting, growing, total, "a very personal form of friendship," unselfish, sharing, faithful, exclusive till death, not exhausted, but continuing in new lives. Children are the supreme gift of marriage.

Responsible parenthood means regulating the family according to conscience, morality, and duties to society, family and God. The Church teaches that all marital acts should be open to the transmission of life. Thus union and procreation are inseparable.

> By safeguarding both these essential aspects, the unitive and the procreative, the conjugal act preserves in its fullness the sense of true, mutual love and its ordination towards man's high calling to parenthood (12).

Forced and selfish intercourse is not true love. Frustrating nature in the marital act destroys intimacy and contradicts the plan of God. Man does not have absolute control over his body or his genitals, only God does. Artificial birth control, sterilization and deliberately frustrated intercourse are objectively immoral. The Church however, allows the rhythm method for good reasons (16).

Moreover, artificial birth control encourages marital infidelity, irresponsible pleasure and a loss of respect for women, treating them rather as sex objects. Also, governments can use artificial birth control for genocide. The Church, on the other hand, defends the divine law and the dignity of husband and wife.

Furthermore, the misuse of women warned about by Paul VI has been proved by the many ailments such as thrombosis, infections and even cancer, stemming from artificial methods of birth regulation. Women have also suffered psychological problems, arising from the loss of self-esteem when treated as an object of pleasure. Since it is difficult to control instinct by reason alone, prayer and asceticism help and give dignity to husband and wife, bringing peace and selflessness, and giving good example to their children.

The Christian vocation is specified and fortified by the sacrament of marriage. The Lord entrusts to Christian spouses "the task of making visible to men the holiness and sweetness of the law which unites the mutual love of husband and wife with their cooperation with the love of God, the author of human life" (25).

The Holy Spirit offers grace to married couples through prayer, the Eucharist and penance, so that they can support each other by good example. Moreover, society, the Church and science should cooperate.

Initially *Human Life* was received with reluctance by a drug-oriented society. But once the dangers of artificial birth control became clear, many saw the wisdom of the letter.

THE ROLE OF THE CHRISTIAN FAMILY IN THE MODERN WORLD

On the feast of Christ the King, 1981, John Paul II gave an apostolic exhortation on *The Role of the Christian Family in the Modern World* (ORIGINS, 12, 24, 81, 437-468), synthesizing the teachings of his predecessors and the findings of the 1980 synod on the family.

"The Christian family is the first community called to announce the gospel to the human person during growth," and to lead through education and catechesis to full human and Christian maturity (2). The family is the chief educator in interpersonal relationships of justice and love.

The Church feels that only in the *Gospels* can be found hope for marriage and the family, which are ordered to fulfillment in Christ and His grace (3). Through evangelical discernment the Church joins families, seeking truth towards the full dignity of marriage and the family through faith and the word of God (5). Pastors and laity must work together for this end, each sector contributing expertise in the process of evangelical discernment.

There is a modern awareness of personal freedom, interpersonal relationships, the dignity of women, responsible procreation and education of children, an awareness of the need of interfamily relationships, reciprocal spiritual and material assistance, a renewal of the Church's mission to the family, and a building up of justice. There are also many problems facing the modern family, such as too much independence of the spouses, a lack of proper relationship between parents and children, poor value transmission, divorce, abortion, sterilization, contraception, and selfish freedom outside of the divine plan.

In the third world are found poverty, malnutrition and lack of work, housing, medicine and freedom. Prosperous nations fear war and economic recession. All these anxieties "deprive married couples of the generosity and courage needed for raising up new human life." Thus fresh life is often seen not as a blessing, but as a threat.

Growing dangers to marriage and the family include: divorce and remarriage, civil marriage, the sacrament of matrimony received without faith, and immorality within marriage (7).

However, the new humanism, with its emphasis on rights and justice, can lead to God when properly evangelized. There is a great need today to recapture the ultimate meaning of life and its values. Science must work along with divine wisdom to humanize and to build up a just and fraternal society (8).

True continuous conversion to Christ will benefit society, a "progressive integration of the gifts of God and the demands of his definitive and absolute love in the entire personal and social life of man" (9).

Two principles help the Church to integrate with culture. First, the culture's compatibility with the gospel, and second, communion with the universal Church. Then marriage and the family can be helped towards the full restoration of the covenant with God's Wisdom, Jesus Christ.

God created mankind in his own love image (11).

> Creating the human race in his own image and continually keeping it in being, God inscribed in the humanity of man and woman the vocation and thus the capacity and responsibility of love and communion.

Love is man's chief and most fundamental vocation, an incarnate love, including both body and soul. This love call can be heard either in marriage or celibacy.

Sexual love is not limited to biology, "but concerns the innermost being of the human person as such." Sex can only be truly human if it is an integral part of the love by which man and woman make a life commitment in total self-giving. This totality responds to the demands of responsible fertility, which includes the transmission of values by both parents.

The institution of marriage is

> an interior requirement of the covenant of conjugal love which is publicly affirmed as unique and exclusive in order to live in complete fidelity to the plan of God, the Creator.

Freedom in fidelity shares in God's creative Wisdom.

> As the love between God and His people is reflected in the affection of husband and wife, so marital infidelity mirrors the people's rebellion against God. Even when they err, God still loves them and so He remains for them a model of fidelity (12).

The love of Christ and His Church fulfills the love of God and His people, revealing the original truth of marriage. "The marriage of baptized persons thus becomes a real symbol of that new and eternal covenant sanctified in the blood of Christ" (13), so that husband and wife can love each other in the Spirit, as Christ loves His Church. Thus marriage is a sacrament of the New Covenant.

Conjugal love "is elevated and assumed into the spousal charity of Christ, sustained and enriched by his redeeming power." Since husband and wife are bound to each other as are Christ and the Church, their marriage is a memorial, actuation and prophecy of the Christ Event.

Conjugal love aims at a deep personal unity—one heart and one soul, indissoluble, faithful and fertile. Marriage is ordained for the procreation and education of children (14). Marital love is a gift of new life, which is "a living reflection of their love, permanent sign of conjugal unity and a living and inseparable synthesis of their being a father and mother."

Marriage and the family are a complex of interpersonal relationships (15), through which we are introduced both to the human family and to the family of God, which is the Church, building up both society and the ecclesial body.

Marriage and celibacy are mutually supportive (16). Celibacy can anticipate the eschatological marriage of Christ and His Church, and can give one a real spiritual parenthood within the Mystical Body of Christ. Like marriage, it demands fidelity to the covenant, and gives hope to the many millions of reluctant celibates in the world today.

John Paul II tells the Christian family to become what it is, namely, an intimate community of life and love, fulfilled in the Kingdom of God. The Christian family "has the mission to guard, reveal and communicate love," reflecting God's and Christ's love of man.

First the Christian family forms a loving community of persons (18). For "without love, the family cannot live, grow and perfect itself as a community of marriage and the family." The first love communion is between husband and wife (19), in fidelity and mutual self-giving, support and sharing. It is perfected through Christ in the sacrament of matrimony, reflecting the unity of his Mystical Body.

It is a unique and indissoluble union (20), reflecting the love of God and His people, Christ and His Church. As Jesus Christ is God's eternal "Yes" to man, so husband and wife say "Yes" to each other, and so are a sign of fidelity to an unfaithful world.

The faithful union of husband and wife is the firm foundation on which is built the communion of the whole family in love (21). The Holy Spirit through the sacraments is the source of the union of Christ and His domestic church, the family.

The Christian family should promote love and unity in a school of deep humanity in care, service and sharing. Parents and children, should minister to each other, reconciling differences for family unity. Family communion promotes the dignity of all its members, male and female, young and old (22). God gave equal dignity to men and women, as did Jesus and Paul. In the kingdom there will be no distinction between male or female.

Though women have equal rights to participate in public life, "the true advancement of women requires that clear recognition be given to the value of their maternal and family role" (23).

Home and family work are important and so should not suffer by comparison to work outside. Moreover, mothers should not be forced into other occupations to the neglect of home and family. In today's society we find many offenses against female dignity including: oppression, discrimination, poverty, pornography and prostitution. The divorced, widowed and other singles suffer most (24).

A man, as husband and father, should respect his wife as a friend, his charity reflecting the love of Christ for His Church (25). Moreover, his affection for his wife and children fulfills his fatherhood. When this is absent, harm can come to the family. Husbands should also avoid oppressive machismo.

Respect for children was taught by Jesus and Paul, as well as by the modern United Nations (26). Children need material, social, emotional and spiritual support, guidance and protection from conception onward. Moreover, there should be mutual respect between the young and the old, both in the family and in society (27).

Marriage and the family cooperate in the creative love of God (28), transmitting by procreation the divine image from person to person. Fruitfulness, the sign and effect of marital love, is also found in the education and training of the family. Spiritual traditions must be handed on to the next generations.

The Church stands for life in the face of modern reluctance to transmit life (30), due to fear, materialism, selfishness, or whatever. "The ultimate reason for these mentalities is the absence in people's hearts of God, whose love alone is stronger than all the world's fears and can conquer them." The Church sees in each life God's "Yes" in Jesus Christ and so defends it against contraception, sterilization and abortion.

Sexuality is "a value and task of the whole person, created male and female in the eyes of God" (32), preserving mutual self-giving and procreation in the context of true love. Through marital chastity, in the light of man's natural and supernatural vocation, there is an inseparable bond between the unitive and procreative. And so, if one separates the two ends, he manipulates and degrades his partner in a frustrated self-gift.

But the infertile periods may be used without manipulation or alteration, since this partakes in God's plan. At the same time, they recognize the spiritual and corporal character of conjugal communion with tenderness and affection, so that sex is fully human and not just an instrument of bodily pleasure.

The Church as a teaching and healing mother sympathizes with the difficulties of married life (33). But there cannot be a contradiction in God's plan. Moreover, the Church must use all means, including psychological, medical, moral and spiritual to help married couples.

On their part, husband and wife need humility, patience, strength, trust, prayer and the sacraments. "The gift of the Spirit, accepted and responded to by husband and wife, helps them to live their human sexuality in accordance with God's plan," as a sign of Christ's love for His Church.

John Paul II recommends marital chastity which esteems nuptial sex, defending love against selfishness and aggression. Periodic continence, far from harming a marriage, can enhance it.

"In God's plan husband and wife are called in marriage to holiness," in cooperation with God's grace (34). Sacrifice is necessary in order to deepen love and intimacy, and the whole Church should support the spouses.

Education is a projection of procreation towards a fully human life (36), and so the parents are the primary educators. Education starts in a family atmosphere of love, faith and charity, "that a well-rounded personal and social development will be fostered among the children."

The family is the first school, and the right and duty to educate follows the right to give life. Hence, it cannot be entirely delegated to others.

Parental love, the source of life, is also the animating principle and norm of education, with kindness, goodness, service and the selfless teaching of values (37).

"The family is the first and fundamental school of social living. As a community of love, it finds in self-giving the law that guides it and makes it grow," spreading to those outside the family circle.

Parents should also teach their children a selfless and fully personal sex education, in which there is a gift of the whole person on love. Moreover, schools should cooperate with parents in this important matter.

The sacrament of marriage gives parents the authority and grace for the Christian education of their children (38), sharing in the authority of God, Christ and the Church—a true ministry of the Church in building up her members.

"The family, called together by word and sacrament as the church of the home, is both teacher and mother, the same as the world-wide Church." Parents lead their children through faith and love of Jesus Christ, as brothers or sisters of Christ, temples of the Holy Spirit and members of the Church (39). The Christian family, transmits the gospel and Christian initiation, and is a school of following Christ, by example, word, prayer, and introduction to the sacraments and liturgy.

The family is the primary educator, collaborating with other schools. Both Church and state should support this home education (40). Moreover, family training should also prepare for the apostolate to those outside, especially the poor, abandoned, sick, old, prisoners, etc. (41).

The family is the primordial cell of society.

> The very experience of communion and sharing that should characterize the family's daily life represents its first and fundamental contribution to society (43), respecting each other's

dignity in dialogue, acceptance, service and solidarity. Thus the family is the primary school of social life, giving example and stimulus to the broader scope of society.

The family is the "most effective means for humanizing and personalizing society," giving virtues and values, respecting the personal rights and dignity, so necessary in modern anonymous society. The family must reach out beyond itself in hospitality to those in need, and in political and social action to transform humanity (44).

Society, in its turn, has the duty to defend and support the family, but always honoring subsidiarity so that the state never usurps the rights of the family but rather gives help where needed on economic, social, educational or other levels (45).

Some modern institutions and laws violate family rights (46). For example, its right to exist and prosper, to generate and educate children, its right to intimacy and stability, freedom of faith and the practice of religion, social and economic aid to the poor, fair housing, right of expression and representation and to form associations, the protection of children from drugs, pornography and other abuses, the right to wholesome recreation, the right of the elderly to a good old age and happy death, and the right to emigrate.

The Christian family has special graces and responsibilities (47). The sacrament of matrimony gives new life to marital love and a special vocation to the kingdom of God in the world, a social, political and economic witness for the poor and disadvantaged. Moreover, there is a spiritual communion between all Christian families (48), "an inner energy that generates, spreads and develops justice, reconciliation, fraternity and peace among human beings." The Christian family witnesses to the kingdom of God in the world.

The Christian family must participate in this kingdom of God (49), the life and mission of the Church. The Christian family "is a living image and historical representation of the mystery of the Church."

The Church, as mother, generates, educates and builds up the Christian family by word and sacraments imitating the self-giving love of Jesus Christ, and communicating Christ's love as a saving community.

The Christian family is an intimate community of life and love in the service of Church and society (50). It participates in the prophetic, priestly and kingly mission of Jesus Christ and the Church.

Furthermore, the Christian family shares its spiritual riches with other families by mutual love of spouses and family, generosity, fidelity, etc. It is a believing and evangelizing community imitating Christ the prophet (51). Only through faith can the Christian family see itself as "a sign and meeting place of the loving covenant between God and man, between Jesus Christ and his bride, the Church."

This begins in the preparation for the reception of the sacrament of matrimony. "This sacrament, in essence, is the proclamation in the Church of the good news concerning marital love." The sacrament of marriage is a profession of faith in and with the Church, and prolonged in married love and life. God, who called the couple in marriage, continues to call them in marriage. The domestic church needs evangelization and continual education in the faith.

The Christian family should be ministers of the gospel to each other and to those outside. Baptism and the sacrament of matrimony give grace and transform society. In the midst of a materialistic and secular society, the home is the main place where authentic catechesis can be taught and learned (50).

The family must educate children for life in their proper vocation. The parents' attempts at evangelization are often mixed with suffering and sometimes ill-received, as was that of the apostles. Family evangelization should also be in cooperation with the Church's evangelization (53).

The Christian family should evangelize the world within its own circle, and outside as well, teaching by word and example (54). Before they can evangelize, they must first be in dialogue with God (55), as a priestly people, sharing in the priesthood of Christ.

The sacrament of matrimony is vivified by Christ, and in dialogue through him with God, by prayer, sacraments and self-giving. "In this way the Christian family is called to be sanctified and to sanctify the ecclesial community and the world."

The sacrament of marriage gives mutual sanctification and worship (56), with special graces of healing, charity, etc. Jesus Christ abides with the Christian family through the whole of married life, as in the larger Church. Thus "arises an authentic and profound conjugal and family spirituality," inspired by God, Christ, the cross and resurrection, consecrating the world to God.

Matrimony and the Eucharist go together (57). Thus normally the sacrament of marriage is received at Mass. Since in the Eucharist Christ celebrates His nuptials with His Church bride, it is fitting that it also be the wedding feast of husband and wife. The whole family becomes one body in the Eucharist and shares in the wider community of the Church. The sacrament of reconciliation heals ailing couples and families.

The priesthood of the family, through Baptism and the sacrament of matrimony, transforms daily life by the Eucharist and family prayer. "Communion in prayer is both a consequence of and a requirement for the communion bestowed by the sacraments of Baptism and Matrimony." Where two or three are gathered in Christ's name, his presence is there (Mt 18:19-20).

Family prayer marks God's loving intervention in family history. Birth, marriage, separation, homecoming, thanksgiving and petition, feast days, death—all occasions of prayer. The Christian parent should teach prayer to the children by example (60), by preparing for the sacraments, calling on the saints, etc.

There is an important link between public liturgy and private prayer (61). Family prayer prepares for and leads the way to public liturgy, such as Baptism and the Eucharist.

If the family is the domestic church, then it should encourage home liturgies and celebrations, morning and evening prayers, blessings, scripture readings, and abridged office, preparation for the sacraments, devotions to the Sacred Heart and to Mary the mother of Christian families, etc.

Prayer is essential to the family (62).

> The Christian family's actual participation in the Church's life and mission is in direct proportion to the fidelity and intensity of the prayer with which it is united with the fruitful vine that is Christ, the Lord, a living union with Christ in prayer, liturgy and sacrifice.

Like the larger Church, the Christian family has a vocation to lead all to Christ (63). "Their love, purified and saved, is a fruit of the Spirit, acting in the hearts of believers," and constituting the moral commandment of life, called to serve God and neighbor in Christ's royal service.

Seeing the image of God in all as children of the Father, the Christian family extends its love outwards (64). "Thanks to the love within the family the Church can and ought to take on a more homelike or family dimension, developing a more human and fraternal style of relationship," and be open to those outside the Church, as well, seeing God in all.

The Christian family should not remain closed in on itself, but be open to the whole community in justice and concern. It is a fundamental duty of the Church to provide pastoral care for the family (65), in order to help it along its pilgrimage to full participation in the kingdom of God. "Future evangelization depends largely on the domestic church," extending its help to other families in need.

Today's climate demands special preparation for Marriage (66), by the Church, society and the family itself. Remote preparation for marriage begins in childhood with instructions, prayer, catechesis and good example. Proximate preparation presents marriage to the young couple "as an interpersonal relationship of a man and woman that has to be continually developed." Sexuality, parenthood, education, finances, job and apostolate are important facets to be discussed. Immediate preparation includes premarital inquiries, counseling, and courses which cover the medical, social and doctrinal sides of matrimony.

The sacrament of matrimony should be so arranged that impediments are avoided, consent is valid and the form is correct. The rites may include approved local customs (67). The liturgy should inspire a full pastoral commitment with community participation.

What about nonbelieving Christians and marriage? The matrimonial commitment is according to the will of God and His grace. The preparation and the marriage itself can help even a nonbeliever on the way to salvation (68).

Even if the couple only want a church wedding for social prestige, at least they implicitly agree to Christ and the Church's plan for marriage. The pastor should not refuse them, since they can receive the grace of the sacrament. However, if they explicitly and formally reject what the Church intends in the sacrament of matrimony, the pastor should refuse to witness the marriage (68).

Pastoral care after the wedding encourages a true community of love in mutual service and active sharing in family life. Especially, young couples starting out need the Church's support. The Church should be a family of families, helping each other.

The Church inspires beginning families to communion and service, harmonizing "the intimacy of home life with the generous shared work of building up the Church and society," helping the Christian family to grow in the Lord.

The parish in union with the universal Church is the closest to the Christian family. Pastors and assistants should be specially trained in marriage and the family on all levels: medical, social, psychological, educational and spiritual.

The Christian family itself, in virtue of the sacrament of matrimony, must be a part of the mission of building up the kingdom of God (71). As apostles of the family, parents through the Christian education of their children teach them faith, chastity and life preparation, vigilance against threats to marriage and the family, preparation for their gradual and responsible inclusion in the Church and society, vocational guidance, mutual help and a wider apostolate to all those in need.

Associations of families are encouraged, inspired by Christian values to give mutual aid, (72). Moreover, the Christian family should be active in political and social associations, preserving morals, guiding family planning, seeking justice for minorities, etc.

The clergy should take a special interest in the welfare of the Christian family (73). The bishop should make his diocese a family of families, while the priests and deacons have more direct contact with the family on moral, liturgical, personal and social levels. As fathers, brothers and teachers of the Christian family, they should be knowledgeable in the teachings of the magisterium on marriage and the family.

Both pastors and laity reflect the prophetic mission of Jesus Christ in word and example. Christian families and pastors should dialogue with theologians, doctors and experts on marriage and the family under the guidance of the magisterium.

Men and women religious are also important to the family apostolate (74). Reflecting the eschatological wedding between Christ and His Church, their chaste inclusive love is open to all families, and especially to abandoned children, the poor, handicapped, sick, old, divorced, through their counsel, marriage preparation, hospitality, retreats, etc. Lay experts such as doctors, lawyers, sociologists, marriage counselors, psychologists, and scientists can also support marriage and the family (75).

Modern social communications can either inspire or tear down the Christian family (76). On the one hand, they can build up family life, and educate parents and children. On the other hand, irresponsible media can destroy Christian values of sexuality, love, marriage and the family.

Pastoral care is needed to face the many threats to marriage and the family today (77), on cultural, economic, social, juridical, spiritual and other levels. For example: migrants, refugees, minorities, single parents, alcoholics, handicapped, ideologically divided families, abuse, teen families, old families, etc. Mixed marriages are growing today (78). The Catholic party still has the obligation to raise the children in the faith as far as possible. Nonetheless, pressure should not be put on the non-Catholic spouse to change religions. However, a proper preparation and an understanding of the Catholic religion is important. Moreover, the Catholic partner should be a witness of Christ in the family.

Mixed marriages can have an ecumenical impact, if the Catholic spouse is firm in faith, giving a" basis and motivation for expressing their unity in the sphere of moral and spiritual values." Moreover, Catholic and Protestant clergy may cooperate in the wedding rites.

There is also an increasing number of marriages between Catholics and the non-baptized. Although there should be respect for the non-Christian religion, often there is no religion at all, so that safeguards are necessary in order to preserve the faith of the Catholic spouse.

Irregular marriages are also of pastoral concern (79). For example, trial marriages are unacceptable experiments with human beings. The marriage of the baptized cannot be temporary, since it reflects the permanent union of Christ with His Church. Moreover, sexual relations are a sign of total self-giving of body and soul in charity. Also some for economic, social or psychological reasons live in free unions without civil or religious ceremonies. Some cultures require such an arrangement before the formal marriage, but this can be harmful morally and socially.

Pastoral care should try to prevent these unions and to regularize them, where possible, fostering fidelity and spiritual maturity. Public authorities ought to provide favorable conditions for marriage and the family, such as guaranteeing work and a family wage.

Though a purely civil marriage is a type of commitment, it is open to easy divorce (82). Pastors should encourage these couples to have their marriages regularized, so that they can receive the sacraments. Separation should be only a last resort (83). The separated and divorced need the support, understanding, forgiveness and love of the Church.

The divorced and remarried are a special worry (84). They are still members of the Church and so may pray, attend Mass, raise their children in the faith, etc. "Let the Church pray for them, encourage them, and show herself a merciful mother, and thus sustain them in faith and hope."

However, the divorced and remarried are not allowed to receive Holy Communion. Why not? Because their second marriage contradicts "that union of love between Christ and the Church, which is signified and effected by the Eucharist." Also, their full participation in the Church would tend to weaken the indissolubility of marriage.

In order to be reconciled, they must repent and live in a way that does not contradict the indissolubility of the first marriage. If they cannot separate from their second spouse, they should live as brother and sister.

Though the Church professes her fidelity to Christ and is concerned for the innocent abandoned spouse, she also encourages the divorced and remarried to do penance and charity in the hope of God's grace.

Many today live without a family through no fault of their own because of poverty, bereavement, divorce or whatever (85). The doors of the great family of the Church should swing wide open for those who have no natural family.

"The future of humanity passes by way of the family" (86). All must show the family special love, fostering its values and potentialities, protecting it from danger, and creating for it a proper environment.

The family needs to restore its confidence in nature and grace, its divine mission, and its loyal following of Christ. It needs to hear the good news, but the good news also includes the cross of Christ. All family support groups should collaborate towards the rapid and integral advancement of the family.

The holy family of Nazareth is the model Christian family. Joseph, worker and guardian; Mary, mother of the domestic church, obedient to God and a sorrowful mother; Christ, king of families, present in the Christian home as at Cana. The Christian family cooperates in His kingdom of truth, life, sanctity, grace, peace, justice and love.

Pope John Paul sums up his teaching on the family in these words:

> I entrust each family to him, to Mary and to Joseph. To their hands and their hearts I offer this exhortation. May it be they who present it to you, venerable brothers and beloved sons and daughters, and may it be they who open your hearts to the light that the Gospel sheds on every family.

MODERN CANON LAW

We have seen the origins of the marriage canons in medieval times, led by popes, decretalists and canonists, and based on many theses from Roman law.

Modern canonists, under the leadership of Cardinal Felici, have worked for many years revising the ancient codes. Here are some of their conclusions concerning marriage.

The marriage covenant, in which man and woman live their whole life in intimate union by the nature of the covenant for the good of the spouses and their children, was raised by Christ to the dignity of a sacrament for baptized Christians, giving the unity and indissolubility of matrimony a new strength.

While divine and canon law govern marriage, society controls its civil effects. The pastor guards marriage and the family through preaching, catechetics, premarital preparation, proper ceremonies and the sacraments.

Permission is still required for a mixed marriage. Both spouses should be properly instructed, and the Catholic party should promise to bring the children up in the faith.

After discussing the proper preparation for marriage, and obstacles to a valid contract, the code notes that the free consent of two capable parties makes the sacrament of marriage. Marital consent is the act of the will by which a man and woman give and receive themselves in a mutual irrevocable covenant for the constitution of marriage.

Of course, free consent is sometimes hindered by mental illness, lack of mature judgment, psychosexual imbalance, ignorance, error, force, etc. (5). To be valid, a marriage requires the assistance of a bishop, pastor, or delegated priest with two witnesses (6).

The effects of marriage (9). The valid sacrament of matrimony gives a perpetual and exclusive bond. Sacramental grace strengthens the spouses in their consecrated state. Husband and wife have equal rights and duties in marriage, including the right to educate their children as they wish.

The separation of spouses (10). A ratified and consummated marriage cannot be dissolved by any human power. A non-sacramental marriage may be dissolved for a good reason, for example, in favor of the faith. Moreover, the Pope may dissolve a ratified and non-consummated marriage for a proper reason. Husband and wife must cohabit unless separated for a just cause such as adultery or personal danger. From this random glance at the revised marriage canons, we can see that the ancient traditions of the threefold good: sacrament, fidelity and child, plus unity and indissolubility, have been preserved.

However, a valid consent now takes into consideration psychological, judgmental and even faith factors, allowing a broader base for annulments. Moreover, a more cautious preparation is stressed to heal these deficiencies. In arranged marriages of former times, there was a careful investigation of family backgrounds, which helped insure the stability of the union. The sudden individual decisions of modern marriages have often had regretful results.

So, despite increasing pornography, premarital sex, divorce and remarriage, the Church tries to preserve the sanctity of love, sex, marriage and the family. It has been an uphill struggle since the beginning and probably will remain so. In defending the unborn, the old, the innocent spouse, the children, she leaves herself open to the criticism of the strong, powerful and the pleasure-seekers.

In part two we will see some of the problems facing love, marriage and the family in contemporary society. They differ little from the vagaries of the past in kind, but not in degree.

PART TWO
TODAY

CHAPTER NINE

If A Man Meets A Virgin, Who Is Not Betrothed (Dt 22:28)

Among most early peoples premarital sex is not a great problem, since marriage follows shortly after puberty, and virginity is highly prized. Also, the sexes often are separated.

In modern society, with marriages delayed and puberty arriving at an earlier age, plus the constant mixing of the sexes, lack of chaperonage, and the encouragement of sexual promiscuity by the media and peer pressure, it is extremely difficult to avoid premarital sex.

ADOLESCENT LOVE

As a child moves into the teen years, his or her emotional development hits highs and lows. Also, this is an age when their middle-aged parents are prone to breakup. Some youths flee an unhappy home to what they hope will be a better situation in a sexual liaison, drugs or even death.

The pre-adolescent especially needs personal intimacy. He or she begins to acquire new extrafamilial relationships, first with peers, and then with members of the opposite sex. Some pre-adolescent same-sex companionships are prolonged into homosexuality.[1]

The need for contact, tenderness and adult participation continues into pre-adolescence. Peer pressures are strong and the dread of ostracism great, "the fear of being accepted by no one of those whom we must have as models for learning how to be human" (261). The pre-adolescent needs intimate exchanges with fellow, friend, or loved one in order to find satisfaction and security.

Loneliness, an experience which has been so terrible that it practically baffles clear recall, is a phenomenon ordinarily encountered only in pre-adolescence and afterwards (261).

Deprivation of companionship in pre-adolescence can affect personality development. They become lonely people simply because they never had normal relations with others. "Loneliness reaches its full significance in the pre-adolescent era and goes on relatively unchanged from henceforth throughout life" (262).

Loneliness is more terrible than anxiety, for the pre-adolescent will risk anything, even to leaving home or a chancy liaison with a boy or girl, to relieve the terrible pain of loneliness.

As a child enters early adolescence—and the age is getting younger—genital interests first arise and so a desire for heterosexual intimacy. H. Sullivan (263) notes three needs in early adolescence: personal security, intimacy and lustful satisfaction.

This is a time of trial and error, fear of taboos and pregnancy. And so the three needs collide! Loneliness is the basis of the frantic search for lust, security and intimacy. Yet approach-avoidance tensions and taboos are counter-productive.

Frustrated genital dynamism along with loneliness accelerates restlessness, lowers self-esteem and can disturb the personality. Moreover, family disapproval of intimacy, ridicule, criticism, and jealousy lead to furtiveness and risk-taking.

Inhibitions, loneliness and introversion can turn an adolescent to fantasy and autoeroticism. Not only can one not satisfy his or her need for intimacy all by oneself, but this usually escalates loneliness.

The entirely exlusive use of autoerotic procedures can contribute to the prolongation of warp, which, in turn, contributes to the continued handicap for life of the person concerned (271).

The lonely introvert is unable to develop normal relations with the opposite sex due to feelings of inferiority, etc. He flees to pornography, fantasy or prostitutes. Actually, the models he admires do not exist, except in his fantasy. Why? Because plastic surgery, silicone implants and air brushes cover bodily defects to enhance the illusion of perfection. The imagination has been called the crazy man of the house.

Though one can use imagination creatively, it also can be an escape from the real world.

> The incorrigible dreamer works at his own estrangement by pulling himself away from adjustment to what really is—which alone yields sanity.[2]

By avoiding others, the dreamer lives in a fantasy world—the road to annihilation, decreation and disintegration. There is a difference between normal sexual fantasies and an escape into an unreal world.

Moreover, along with fantasy often comes masturbation—an imperfect sexuality, at best. Guindon (277-8) points out some of the dangers of masturbation, namely, the priority of genitality over affection, and the priority of ego over other-directedness, or narcissism. "It does happen that young masturbators fall so deeply in love with themselves that going out of themselves to others proves to be an exremely painful task." Are they ever really present to others?

The third priority is imagination over real sex objects. "Masturbation easily becomes the handy evasion when things go wrong," seeking consolation in dreams and fantasies. Often this sexual immaturity is prolonged into adult life.

Masturbation is a refuge from loneliness, boredom, disappointment, failure, and life in general, a type of escapism as in drugs or alcohol. Moreover, masturbation is hedonistic, narcissistic ipsation. "One whose body becomes the erotic object of his tenderness and of his affection" is totally self-sufficient.

> The whole symbology of autoeroticism displays a pretense of closing the circle of humanity within oneself. This is what is typically acted out: curling in upon oneself all sense polarized in one's center, enclosed, hungry for oneself, autoerotic (282).

This leads to distantness and the avoiding of affectionate contacts. Asocial people such as imbeciles and idiots masturbate frequently. It mirrors their estrangement from society, "and constitutes a kind of prototype for those who use the same corporeal language because of spiritual emptiness" (283).

Though the masturbation of youth may be tentative tries at sexuality, it partakes in some way of ipsation. Moreover, the young autoerotic often becomes an old autoerotic. Adolescent masturbation is often an attempt to escape from the tensions of daily life, and although one feels guilty, he still prefers the guilt to the loneliness and frustration. Though masturbation seems to be a deviation, some see it as normal because it is so common. But it is possible to have a common deviation.

A restless search for intimacy is characteristic of adolescence, accompanied by a certain separation anxiety. Here there can be an identity crisis and a tension between the search for independence and the desire to be wanted. Too old to be daddy's little girl or mama's little boy, but too young for serious outside intimacy. Wanting to love and be loved, yet running from love's obligations. Hoping that one's self-gift will be accepted, yet depressed and frustrated when it is turned down.

LIAISONS

Teenage liaisons are becoming more and more common, with many ending in pregnancy, and either abortion or a child mother trying to raise a baby against almost insurmountable odds. Sometimes the two lovers are fleeing an unhappy home situation, which may include battling parents, divorce, poverty, alcoholism, family abuse, etc.

Some parents push their children too early into male-female relationships with dating, dancing, kissing, ring exchanges and even going steady at twelve years of age. The media, too, have glorified kiddie porn and kiddie sex, suggestive fashions, music, etc. However, the earlier they start their sexual experimentation, the sooner they will go on to something more daring. Guindon asks

> are we not responsible for all the alleged premarital debauchery going on by starting young adolescents on an escalator of progressive sexual intimacy, when we know that they will have ten or more years at it before marriage? (381).

Two reasons are often given for premarital intercourse. First, premarital continence is unhealthy, and second, it is necessary for sexual development (385).

Is the sex drive compulsive? Obviously in divine providence it was created strong, otherwise the human race would die out. Man can educate his instincts, integrating them into his daily life. Emotional strength comes from training the libido, not from constantly giving in.

Some feel that premarital intercourse can be harmful to later sex development, simply because sex is removed from love and marriage. Also, early promiscuity can lead to boredom, *deja vu* and even impotence in later life.

> The evidence is that the habit of premarital intercourse can serve to enslave rather than liberate, can gradually reduce enjoyment rather than augment it, and produce neurotic rather than zestful men and women (389).

Freud notes[3] that the physical value of erotic needs is reduced with their easy satisfaction. Courtly love teaches us that obstacles and restriction heighten libido. While in decadent societies love is empty and worthless, Christian asceticism erected barriers that escalated love.

Is there a correlation between premarital sexual continence, social energy and cultural develpment? Promiscuity certainly seems to herald society's downfall.

What about the argument that premarital intercourse is necessary to test compatibility and to insure proper sexual adjustment as one would test drive a car before buying it? Marriage is constant adjustment from beginning to end and most of the crises are difficult to anticipate except in a most general way.

Furthermore, current research has shown that the importance of sexual compatibility to the happiness of marriage has been blown way out of proportion.

Practice will not make perfect sexual adjustment, "because it is not a question of technique, but of affection and love" (391). "People with premarital coital experience, especially with a variety of partners, are substantially less likely to end up happily married" (Duvall and Packard, 392).

Obviously, the mystery, expectation and anticipation have been robbed from marriage. For, in a sense, the couple is already married. As we have seen, in the Jewish and medieval traditions betrothal plus coition equaled matrimony.

Furthermore, there is a certain avoidance, and even loathing for the person with whom one has had sex, plus feelings of guilt and discomfort. There are also dangers of venereal disease and possible pregnancy. Of course, the child born out of wedlock suffers most of all.

With increasing birth control and abortion, it would seem that premarital relations would be less risky. However, the number of illegitimate babies born in the USA has been steadily increasing. Though there is less of a stigma to unwed motherhood today, still, by and large, it is looked down upon, and being a bastard will never be something to be proud of. Furthermore, although the government will give aid, the mother has to bear 90% of the responsibility for raising the child, and her chances of marrying well later on are slim, indeed.

Two options are adoption or abortion. Adoption, though helping a childless couple to have a family, can be traumatic for mother and child, especially later on. Abortion, although allowed by law, does not respect the right to life of the child in the womb. It is clearly an economic decision. $200 for the abortion versus $100,000 to raise the baby to adulthood, plus twenty years of responsibility. Today 1/3 of all pregnancies end in abortion, (including those of many teenage mothers) about 1.5 million a year. Government, parents and boy friends encourage this to avoid involvement, expense, embarrassment and responsibility. Pregnancy is seen more and more to be a type of disease, like a tumor to be excised and thrown away.

Obviously, it all starts with irresponsible sex. Where does promiscuity stand today *vis-a-vis* virginity? In a recent college survey, students rated virginity as the least desirable quality for a future spouse. They rated honesty, integrity, and friendliness as the most important qualities. However, honesty and integrity, are rarely found without sexual control as well. These virtues are interdependent, as are their opposite vices.

Yet, a promiscuous girl is looked down upon. Some feel that boys prefer to have sex with casual acquaintances rather than with the special girl whom they want to marry, the future mother of their children. Often the girl sees the intercourse as some sort of commitment to the future. However, when many males sense this, they disappear. Obviously the breaking off of such an intimate relationship leads to pain, fear and feelings of rejection, and a reticence to begin new relations with others. Of course, males can experience the same traumas when their liaison is broken up by the female partner. Too much intimacy too young is risky in many ways.[4].

Peer pressure is an important deterrent to chastity, but can the two-in-one of premarital intercourse be totally without meaning—casual? Are you totally the same after the experience as you were before? If not, the act was a lie, using the other as an instrument of pleasure.

Promiscuity makes sexual maturity almost impossible. There is a perpetual search for "more joy," and the inability to postpone pleasure. Guindon (415) sees promiscuity as "the result of emotional troubles, of feelings of inadequacy and of other similar personality problems." Usually it is a deviance not in isolation, but linked with truancy, drugs, profanity and alcohol. Often it is really a sign of weak sexuality (415).

Promiscuity has made the use of prostitutes unnecessary among the young. Here, again, economy is a factor. The degradation, inhumanity and commercial love of prostitution is mirrored in promiscuity. What about loving intercourse between two unmarried people? Guindon (423) distinguishes between the foreplay of two singles in search of a life partner, and coitus which is two in one flesh.

There is a danger in blind love, loving love itself, instead of a person, the beloved, for this can lead to promiscuity.

> Heterosexual genital practice which develops outside the framework of a decisive mutual commitment frees eroticism to follow its inherent tendency: satisfying itself only for the moment in short-term pleasures (425).

The flesh itself is ephemeral, as are its pleasures, so there are no long term commitments to the flesh. Flesh and sex do not cause love but rather are love's effects. Premarital sex does not lead to love. Many marriages fail because they are founded on a fleeting sexual compatibility, rather than on a transcending love.

Since premarital sex is a trial, and not in the marital conditions of commitment and love, it can deceive. These temporary liaisons exclude the firm foundations of marriage: children, common life, shared responsibilities, etc. (426). Since premarital intercourse lacks the care of parenthood, it is not a fertile love. "All the theses in the world will never change the biological fact that coitus is also the procreative act" (427). Dissatisfaction is inevitable when this is frustrated especially among potential mothers.

Guindon also feels that trial liaisons frustrate mutual availability. Irresponsible sex is easier, since in it one "gets all the fun without any obligation" (428). The other can easily be dropped for a new relationship. Furthermore, fornication is a prelude to adultery, for both are irresponsible fun, recreation without procreation.

Does this mean that there should be no contact before marriage? Affectionate love is necessary for mating—talking, walking, holding hands, kissing. How far should we go? Positive action should proceed from true love and not *vice versa*. The boy's reaction is quicker, while the girls's response is more gradual. The goal is to achieve a sexual bond which is the seal and the expression of love, a goal which no orgasm-seeking sex will ever fulfill.

Once a partner has been chosen, the future husband is more restrained. He sees his girl as the mother of his family, so he accommodates himself to his future spouse's needs. Engaged couples do a lot of talking together, making plans, etc.

How about intercourse for engaged couples? We have seen that the medieval Church saw this act as the consummation of the marriage. Premarital sex, like marital sex, should not be selfish pleasure seeking, but rather a selfless giving and commitment and so not separated from its responsible procreative end.

Of course, it will happen since instincts are weak and accident-prone. Efforts should be made to foresee risky situations. Premarital sex which expresses love is quite different from that which does not.

SINGLE ADULTS

We have been speaking largely of adolescents, who are feeling their way, establishing positive relationships and making sexual errors.

What about older people? The age of first marriage is approaching the mid twenties, and the increasing number of divorces has pushed adult singles to around the 50 million mark, more than one for each married couple.

As we have seen, there were times in the past when the future looked dim, for example, at the end of the Roman Empire, when the single life was more appealing than bringing up children in a very uncertain world. In these and other apocalyptic times, governments encourage marriage and the family in order to keep the country and its military forces viable. Also longer lives have increased the singles' population, with more women than men as the years increase.

In the modern nuclear, small house family with one or two children, there is little room for adult singles, divorced or widowed. Also, married women sometimes feel threatened by the presence of a single woman, and do not want to be reminded of the future possibilities of divorce or widowhood. As a result, the single woman is more or less ostracized from coupled society. The irresponsible, swinging single is largely a myth. Most unmarried adults are lonely widows, divorcees or handicapped, with little hope for sexual activity or marriage.

Though the modern high standard of living has enabled singles to live self-sufficient lives, it has done little to solve their love frustration and loneliness. The single needs someone to love and to be loved by, someone to get up and go to work for and to come home to at night.

It is this lack of intimacy, and the escalating loneliness, that drives people to singles' bars, to stave off as long as possible their return to an empty apartment or condominium. Some send in their *résumés* to lonely hearts clubs, introduction columns, etc., in the hope of establishing a meaningful relationship.

Loneliness can lead to a host of ills, both mental and physical. Most patients in hospitals are lonely singles. Singles are more vulnerable to life's pressures simply because they have to face them alone. There is no one to care if he or she is sick, hurt, fired, retired, or dies— no one to understand.

In the past unattached singles, either never married, divorced or widowed, were looked down upon as losers by normal coupled society. But now that they number more than 50 million, they have an economic clout that makes business and advertising sit up and take notice: soup for one, smaller houses, apartments, vacations for one, etc.

Some are forced into single life because of an unfortunate experience in childhood, an early rejection, family heredity, over-education on the part of the woman, while others go the route of divorce or bereavement.

Saturday night seems to be the worst for a lonely single, home alone in an empty apartment with a silent phone. Singles bars beckon, where the unattached woman feels like a piece of meat on display, and roving males feel free to exploit her. Why else is she there?

Single men seem to need sex more than their female counterparts. This feeds the multi-billion dollar sex industry including: porn, movies, TV, prostitution, massage parlors, etc. But all this is immature, irresponsible sex, without a sense of intimacy or commitment, only pleasure.

The single can be doubly frustrated: with no spouse, he or she is an unwilling celibate in a sex-oriented society. The myth of easy sex propagated by the media makes the life of a single even more difficult.

As the median age for marriage advances, some are opting for unmarried liaisons, while others are postponing marriage till they are well established in their professions. Though the number of those who live in an unmarried state with a member of the opposite sex has increased, they are only about two percent of all households.

In a youth-oriented society, there seems to be a feeling that old age is a myth, which modern science has made obsolete. There will be plenty of time for a family after one's career is well founded, but the prime child-bearing years are under thirty. All sorts of complications from infertility to deformed babies can result from postponing childbirth. Surrogate mother and rent-a-womb companies have been proposed as solutions, but both are clear violations of the two-in-one of matrimony.

Some singles are called to sublimate their sexual drives for the service of others. Freud notes that the Church had the highest motives for recommending virginity and celibacy for its ministers. Relatively few are called to this lifelong continence. What of the other 95% of singles? Some have discovered, much to their surprise, that they can get along quite well without sex, despite the brainwashing of the media in the opposite direction.

Actually, morality and practicality are not far apart, as many tribal societies have taught us. Thus strict sexual mores are good for both individuals and the group. For example, promiscuity causes much more pain than pleasure in the long run. Hinduism tells us that pleasure is *maya*, an illusion, something we seek, but never find. And in the end our pleasure becomes pain.

Sexual liberation is really a contradiction in terms, for promiscuity, fornication, adultery, masturbation, far from releasing our tensions, are the most depressing forms of enslavement. As in Hinduism, true freedom (moksha) is only attained through self discipline (dharma).

Chastity is charity, love, joy, and its opposite can only lead to hate, pain and depression. Sex in marriage, Christian tradition teaches us, is good, but outside of the marital union, it can harm.

CHAPTER TEN

God Blessed Them
(Gn 1:28)

SACRAMENT

Though some would claim that since marriage is only a civil contract, it can be terminated at any time by the parties involved, the history of matrimony belies this. The sanctity of marriage is found in many cultures, either modeled on divine nuptials or blessed by the ancestral spirits.

In the Genesis story, God joined Adam and Eve for their mutual support and to help Him perfect and populate the earth and He blessed their union. Later, he gave the *Torah* to guard the sacredness of marriage against the deviations of the wandering yetzer. The prophets honor the union of husband and wife as the *hierogamy* of Yahweh and Israel. As God is loyal to his errant bride, so the husband should forgive and seek out his misled spouse.

The New Testament expresses the holiness of Christian wedlock by comparing it to the marriage of Christ with His Church. Karl Rahner comments:

> Marriage objectively represents this love of God in Christ for the Church. The relation and attitude of Christ to the Church is the model for the relation and attitude that belongs to marriage and is mirrored by imitation in marriage so that the latter is something contained in the former.[1]

The mutual consent of the spouses is the sacrament. Rahner explains, "It is because this conjugal consent is itself one of the acts in which the Church's own nature is brought into activity, because in this consent of her members she herself manifests herself as the mystery of the union between Christ and mankind" (110).

Bride and groom do an act of the Church by administering the sacrament to each other. Marriage contributes in a special way to the union of Christ and the Church, bearing witness that "in the Church Christ has espoused humanity irrevocably to himself" (111).

Christian matrimony also reflects God's threefold image. Its holiness mirrors His sanctifying Spirit. From the beginning marriage was God's healing gift to mankind, and especially blessed by the Spirit of His Divine Son.

The Christian Church has always honored matrimony as a holy and divine institution, and has condemned those who disparage this sacred bond, from the Gnostics and the Manichees to the Albigenses.

Though Paul includes Christian nuptials in the mystery of Christ and the Church, wedlock can be desecrated by adultery and so needs law, either *Torah* or canons, to protect it. And the bishop or his representative blesses it.

If marriage belongs to the full constitution of the Church, it must be sacramental, for the Church is the sacrament of Christ, and the Church is seen in its smallest form in the family. It is "a genuine community of the redeemed and sanctified, whose unity can build on the same foundation as that on which the Church is founded, the smallest of local churches, but a true church in miniature."

Christ Himself is the Ur-Sacrament manifested in His Church, His Mystical Body and bride. The groom and bride reflect Christ and His people in their union, forming a new cell of the Mystical Body, or an *ecclesiola* which grows and spreads from generation to generation. If husband and wife operate independently of the central *telos* (end) of the Mystical Body, they become a cancerous growth and so must be healed for the good of the whole Church.

Christ is in the world through His visible body, the Church, and He will remain with her till the end of days. The tiny cells of His body are microcosms of the macrocosmic hierogamy, enduring indivisible and indissoluble. Cells and body are interdependent, but the cells must cooperate in the central direction of the body which they reflect in their genes.

As the Mystical Body of Christ is the macrochurch, so the family is the mini version. Modeled on Jewish roots, early Christian liturgies were home-centered. As numbers increased, basilicas were built or adapted, and attention was fixed on them rather than on the *ecclesiola* of the home.

The Christian husband and wife recapitulate the union of Christ and His Church, which is a special sacred event, *kairos*. Upon this is based marriage's sacramentality and indissolubility, for in the *kairos* there is no material succession as in the *chronos* (ordinary time). The ups and downs of marriage are chronological happenings, but the bond of matrimony is perpetual (*kairos*) and unchanging.

Jesus Christ, the perfect spouse, is prefigured in Adam. As Adam initiated marriage, so the Messiah, the Last Adam, begins its sacramentality in a special incarnational way.

> With Jesus there appears in the world the spouse par excellence, who can as the 'Lord' and 'Last Adam' save and reestablish the true conjugality that God does not cease to wish for the benefit of the first Adam.[2]

Christ renews the primordial authenticity of the couple, overcoming Mosaic hardness.

> In his eyes man and woman can love each other from now on, as God from all time desires that they should love, because in Jesus is manifested the source of love which established the kingdom.

The original couple became in Christ and the Church what they always should have been in the eyes of God.

> Christ draws into his energy the conjugal love of the baptized, visibly part of the body of Christ, that is, the Church, in order to communicate to it the authenticity which outside of him this love would lack.

The Last Adam appropriates and makes the conjugality of the first

Adam to be in accord with the visible Church in which conjugal love is consecrated to the Lord. It so becomes a sacrament, through which Jesus Christ gives grace.

The spouses witness to the Church that they are promised to conjugal life, and expect from Christ the help to fulfill their vows. The mystery of Christ and His Church glows in the couple consecrated to him, whose union they recapitulate. Their conjugal love is deepened, reflecting back to Christ, who gives them his blessing and grace.

The sacrament of matrimony consecrates to Christ "the love of the baptized spouses so that Christ may realize the transforming of his own mystery in them." Their union in Baptism is renewed on the level of love vowed in Christ. In other words, this brother and sister in the Lord are now joined in a special union for the good of the Mystical Body of Christ.

"Their conjugal act in free giving to each other, consecrates them also to him who is the spouse par excellence and who will teach them to become themselves perfect spouses" (203). The personal mystery of Christ, participated in Baptism, penetrates the human marriage bond.

> This becomes sacrament only if the future spouses freely consent to enter into the conjugal life, pronouncing their vows in Christ into whom they are incorporated in Baptism.

It would seem that if there is a deficiency here, for example, if the couple does not vow *in Christ* in good faith, there could be a lack of sacramentality, or at least a certain inefficaciousness.

But when the two believing spouses minister the sacrament of matrimony to each other in good faith, as baptized members of the Mystical Body of Christ, the two cells fuse into one growing, expanding organ of the Body.

"They are ministers as living members of the body of Christ in which they exchange their vows without ever making of their decision, which is irreplaceable, just the pure emanation of their love" (303).

The sacrament of marriage, then, is a part of the Ur-Sacrament of Christ and the Church in which husband and wife share in a special way. In their consent the Church is "the sign and guarantee of the gifts of the Spirit that the spouses receive in communicating themselves to each other as Christians." As Christ is His Church, so the couple, as *ecclesiola*, are one with Christ.

Matrimony is a sacred institution so that husband and wife not only fulfill obligations to each other, but to the way of life which is essential to the welfare of Church and society, as well. As O'Callaghan notes,[3] "Marital consent is the dedication of man and wife in partnership to a Christian mission in the Church and the world," to integrate themselves as Christians, procreate and Christianize the world.

Husband and wife are one, not so much because they are one flesh and one bone, but because together they form a single member of Christ's Mystical Body. But is not the sacrament dependent on the mutual love and consent of the spouses? If they renege on their vows, or if their love wanes, what happens to the sacrament?

The sacrament of matrimony is not just a personal agreement which can be decided by the bride and groom alone, a lease on a new home, or a job contract. No, it is sealed in the Mystical Body of Christ and in the hierogamy of Christ and His Church. So, although affection may dwindle, though infidelity may come, the sacrament endures. Man cannot destroy a sacrament any more than he can demolish the union of Christ with His Church, for Christ is His Church. However, by his unbelief, he may either not receive the sacrament or at least frustrate its efficacy.

Insofar as marriage participates in the divine union, it is both creative and redemptive, for God is love, and in the sacrament of matrimony *eros* shares in this loving, creative and redemptive *agape*. How can marriage be redemptive? Insofar as it shares in the love by which Christ cherishes and redeems His Church. Paul told husbands to love their wives as Christ embraces His Church. This is *agape*, enduring, patient, kind, forgiving, expanding, centrifugal.

"Every sign of affection between husband and wife is an expression of the will to communicate the life of Christ to the other and is the actual communication of that life." If the believing spouse can consecrate the unbelieving spouse, as Paul tells us (1 Cor 7:14-16), how much more can two believing spouses sanctify each other?

In Christian marriage, *eros* is restored to God as *agape*, sacramental love. *Agape* is self-denying, self-giving, self-sacrificing, accepting and tolerating the trials and faults of others and so participating in the redemptive love of Jesus Christ.

> The whole family unit lives in an atmosphere of grace, not in virtue of any element added to it from outside, but in virtue of the fact that it is a Christian family, a cell in the body of Christ, an *ecclesiola*, charged with the task of handing on the faith and extending the community of charity.[4]

Christ raised up and sanctified marriage to help the Church, His Mystical Body, in its tasks of redeeming fallen creation. The Christian husband and wife continue Christ's mission of redemption.

The acts of the Church are the acts of Christ, the Great Sacrament, the Word of God, living in His Mystical Body. Husband and wife work together to establish and spread the fullness of Christ's Body. In Baptism they put on Christ. They receive His grace-giving body and blood in Holy Communion, and their marriage signifies His loving presence in His Church. In all the sacraments, Christians touch Christ, and He communicates with them. So, Christians in their marriage signify and incarnate Christ in themselves. Where two Christians are united, the presence of Christ is there. They are not two Christians side by side, but united by God, love, *agape*.

Marriage is a sacred gift of God to Adam and Eve, sanctified and incarnated by Christ in His living union with his people. Is this a temporary gift at the moment of consent, or a permanent grace throughout all of married life? If it parallels the union of Christ and His Church, it should be perpetual. For if marriage were only a temporary human contract, it would not be indissoluble, and consequently would be open to attacks on every side.

REALITY

Roman law stressed the mutual consent and affection of husband and wife, but once marital love faded, divorce could easily be obtained. Christianity, basing matrimony on the archetypal hierogamy, tried to underline the permanence of the state. The Fathers of the Church, medieval decretalists, theologians, and the popes and councils opted for the perpetuity of the marital commitment.

For example, Robert Bellarmine (WORKS 2.790) says that the sacrament of matrimony is more than just the moment of consent, but rather lasts through the whole of married life. In this it is similar to the Eucharist, which is more than the presence of Christ only in the words of confection, or in the reception of communion, but remains afterwards in the altar of repose.[5]

Theologians teach three basic elements in matrimony. First, the consent or contract (*matrimonium in fieri*), the sacramental sign (*sacramentum tantum*), second, the marriage bond formed by the consent and raised by Baptism (*matrimonium in facto esse*), and third, conjugal love, demanded by and expressing the word, sacramental grace (*res tantum*), human love supernaturalized by the grace of union, *agape*.

So the bond of marriage effected by the sacramental rite is a sacramental reality (*res et sacramentum*). "The bond is intrinsically elevated to be a permanent supernatural symbol, effectively signifying the love of the bridal union of Christ and the Church, to be shared and lived, in grace and conjugal charity, by the Christian spouses" (29).

The Christian pair unite as cells of Christ's Body, an integrated part of the whole, and so they participate in the central *telos*, enlarging and spreading the Mystical Body. These fused cells cannot be split apart any more than the Body itself can be cut away from Christ.

The reality of marriage, then for Christians is the grace of conjugal union, enabling husband and wife to live out their marriage with all its obligations and privileges, ups and downs, with charity, healing the wounds of suffering and elevating natural love. This reality is the covenant of charity (agape) between Christ and His Church. "In effect, it intensifies and deepens the very bond of union in the Mystical Body. And by that very token, intensifies and deepens the union of Christ and the Church, and effects what it signifies" (55).

The whole Mystical Body is perfected by the sacramental bond of marriage, so the Body is most concerned that the wedlock will succeed. As the early patriarchs arranged the marriages of their youths for the welfare of the whole tribe, and the Roman *patres familiae* approved nuptials which would enhance their families, so the Church, under its *pater familias*, the bishop, must safeguard the sacrament of matrimony for its own fruitful growth and health. For, if marriage succeeds, the Mystical Body will flourish. If, on the other hand, Christian matrimony fails, the Body will be weakened.

> The sacramental marriage bond is a consecration to a special function within the Mystical Body, viz., to represent, to make visible, the brideship of the Church with Christ, giving to the actual married life a definite religious and typically 'Christian' character (57).

This elevates the natural marital love so that it reflects the charity between Christ and His Church. The permanent sacramental sign of marriage, *in facto esse*, is the common love life of the Christian spouses. As in the Eucharistic presence, so husband and wife are perpetually consecrated to each other.

> Their community of life is thus a visible sign of manifestation of this inner invisible bond, steeped in the mystery of Christ and the Church, and thereby a sign effective of the grace of union binding them in an ever deepening charity to each other and to Christ (64).

Pius XI, in his encyclical *Casti Conubii*, drew the parallel between the permanence of marriage and the Eucharist, as did many modern authors.

Dietrich von Hildebrand comments on this sacred union.[6]

> The most intimate communion of love in Jesus and for Jesus, which belongs to Jesus and brings about the sanctification of both spouses, in which the two persons are one in flesh and have been allowed to participate in the creation of a new being by God, a community elevated to a sacrament as an image of the union of Christ and the Church.

The husband gives Christ to his wife through his love, while the wife presents Christ to her spouse through her tender affection. Thus they are ministers to each other in Christ. They see the presence in Christ in each other through the sacrament of matrimony.

Through the centuries, various groups have tended to look down on the physical union of husband and wife as something inferior, a weakness of the body or even as slightly shameful. Gerke responds,

> *Copula maritalis*, consummating marriage, must have a sacramental character, since it completes, perfects, *'consummates'* the sacramentality of marriage . . . the following acts of bodily union are the same nature: an expression *in actu secundo*, of the contracted supernatural bond, and a continuation in deed or act, of the mutual self-donation, in words, on the wedding day (119).

Moreover, the marriage bond, the inner essence of marriage, is experienced in the whole common life of husband and wife, not only in intercourse, but also in eating, talking, recreating, working, and praying together.

How does the assimilation of the Christian into the union of Christ and His Church differ from that of the other sacraments? The two, husband and wife, are not absorbed into the marriage of Christ and His Church as two separate individuals, but rather as one person.

Their whole marriage is sacramentalized so that the couple grows in charity, and the Mystical Body is built up. The two are one flesh, this does not mean only one physical substance, but rather one person, body and soul.

So a virginal marriage is not a contradiction in terms, for it points to the future *eschaton* when there will be a non-physical union in Christ. Most elderly couples enjoy a spiritual rather than a physical oneness before they enter the kingdom. In modern society the body has been overstressed, but when the whole of married life is seen, the spiritual side is of greater and more lasting importance.

Vatican II, as we have seen, taught the sanctity of marriage blessed by the presence of Christ. Authentic married love is enriched by the presence of Christ in the union, which he blesses. Thus the Christian spouses are consecrated by the sacrament, and penetrated by the Spirit of Christ. They teach each other by example and word, and their children honor and respect their parent-teachers. Thus the whole Christian family, as a cell of the Body of Christ, reflects the marriage of Christ and His people, his living presence in His Church.

The Lord gives many gifts to the couple, including supernatural love, healing and perfecting in grace and charity. Sealed in Christ's sacrament, this love will remain ever faithful.

With so many so-called Christian marriages breaking up today, some may wonder if they were sacramental to begin with. It would seem that if one or both of the spouses did not believe in Christ or the sacrament of marriage, that this would at least truncate the sacramentality, and so weaken the wedlock.

Thus we see "shotgun" or "jailbreak" marriages, church weddings "to please mother," and "career" unions in which each spouse goes his or her own way toward professional advancement with no children to hinder. There are also trial liaisons in which the couple have no intention of receiving the sacrament, living as Christians or of raising their children so, if they have any. Some unions involve successive or simultaneous bigamy. Are these living members of the Mystical Body of Christ? Can they validly confect and participate in the permanent and unique sacramental union of Christ with His Church?

CHAPTER ELEVEN

What God Has Joined
(Mt 19:6)

In the trinitarian model of marriage, the Holy Spirit is the sanctifier, while the Son is the image of fidelity in His everlasting union
with His Church.

Mutual support has always been an end of marriage, going back to
Adam and Eve. It is not good to be alone. Although marital companionship and pleasure are sought after today more than ever, there
seems to be less and less of both, with increasing adultery, chancy
liaisons, easy divorce and other family abuse.

Since pleasure is an illusion, as we have seen, it would be a mistake
to make this the central goal of marriage. This is only asking for
frustration, and the frantic seeking of sexual excitement outside when
home life gets dull.

If the perpetual loving friendship of marriage is to last, it must be
based on the indissoluble hierogamy and fidelity of Christ and His
Church, and its recapitulation in the sacrament of matrimony.

MONOGAMY

Anthropologists tell us that monogamy has a very early origin. It is
the archetypal ideal, and Jesus said that it was so in the beginning. But
over the millennia, both simultaneous and consecutive polygamy
blossomed. Sometimes it was for social and economic reasons, for
example, when large numbers of men were killed in wars or on
dangerous hunting expeditions, polygamy was necessary for tribal

survival. Also, polygamy could be related to wealth and prestige. Chiefs and the wealthy can afford more wives than the poor, and their harems add to their prestige and income, both in child-bearing and in labor.

We have seen the growth of divorce in both Israel and Rome until it was allowed for almost any reason at all. Christianity, from the beginning, taught the monogamous ideal, though there were times and places in the history of Christianity when divorce was allowed for various reasons.

Today simultaneous polygamy is still common in rural sub-Sahara Africa. Although Mohammed approved the plurality of wives it is no longer the custom in westernized Islamic countries, such as Turkey. Divorce and consecutive polygamy are just about everywhere today, even in the stricter branches of Christianity.

Some Marxists would claim that monogamy is an unnatural state forced on society, enslaving wives and children to work for the husband's capital. One goal of Marxism has been to liberate house-wives from their prison-like homes for labor in the factories.[1] Initially, the Soviets eased divorce to further weaken the capitalistic nuclear family. Then, according to the Marxist ideal, two property-related aspects of marriage will disappear, namely, male supremacy and the indissolubility of marriage. Of course, the varied duration of married love makes wedlock unstable without an underlying transcendent value.

Russian Marxism placed matrimony under the jurisdiction of the state, with the weddings taking place in government offices rather than before the priest in church. Divorce was made easy until the leaders realized that the fabric of society was being undermined.

Herbert Marcuse seems to carry the Marxist anti-monogamy theory a step further in order to desublimate sexuality and mono-gamy.[2] He feels that a desublimated sex can create ideal civilized relations, making life and work more pleasurable, giving immediate gratification rather than the mediate joy of strict monogamy.

The liberalized sexuality of society, industry, government, educa-tion and the media in the 1960's and the 1970's reflects this attitude as well. Are monogamy, sexual sublimation, and mediate pleasure, artificial impositions on society for the selfish capital of the patriarch? Or are they rather the natural God-given orientation of marriage?

Modern doctors, such as Walter Umbricht and James Lynch, have studied the effects of monogamy, adultery and divorce, fidelity and infidelity, on the health of their patients. They find that true, faithful married love is healing, while false, unfaithful affection wounds. Ovid and Andrew the Chaplain would agree, in their treatises on the remedies of love.

Dr. Umbricht notes[3] that since marriage is man's most important social relationship, two in one, if the two are split, at odds, unfaithful, it will affect the health of the individuals. For example, it is common for bereaved spouses to be depressed and even despondent at the loss of their better half. Sometimes, if they are elderly and infirm, the shock of one's partner's death can be fatal. Parallel traumas accompany adultery and divorce.

Anthropologists find monogamy in primitive peoples, as we have seen. Rather than being forced on society by the state or Church, it seems to be the natural way, though various forms of polygamy have crept in over the long history of man. Always, somehow, the ideal is in the background. For example, in many polygamous societies the first wife is the official lifelong spouse, who runs the household, gives advice to the patriarch, etc. Subsequent consorts take on a lesser role.

Monogamy is compatible with human nature, rather than an artificial arrangement which grinds against man's disposition. Therefore we might expect problems where it is ignored. With over one million divorces a year in the United States, and lonely millions suffering broken, adulterous, divorced or bereaved lives, what is the clinical evidence?

All doctors are familiar with the love triangle and its devastating effects. For example, a middle-aged husband, trying to recoup his youth by going out with a younger woman and finding his sexual power diminished or impotent. Or the attempt to live a normal life with a family in one home and a consort in an apartment, perhaps in another city. Or the young widow seeking sexual relief from a number of partners, only to sneak home to her children each night, depressed, angry, frustrated, ashamed and guilty.

The strained emotions between husband and wife over adultery lead to weakness, anger, nervousness, frustration, insomnia, exhaustion, frigidity and even murder. Is divorce the answer? Sometimes you hear people say that a certain couple would be better off apart because of his adultery or her drinking. This flies in the face of the "for worse" of the wedding vows. Also, it ignores the biblical tradition of forgiveness, healing and compassion. No one is hopeless in God's eyes, for He is ever loving and merciful, no matter what the fault.

Probably the children suffer more than the spouses in a split-up. Certainly a main reason for the indissolubility of marriage is the proper care of the offspring.

In a divorce situation, the youngsters are often shifted from one parent to another in an atmosphere of tension and rivalry for affection. Sometimes they are left with a grandmother or in a boarding school. Frequently they are the victims of omnigamy, in which both parents remarry, so that the young ones do not feel wanted in either household. Many of these take to the streets as juvenile delinquents, prostitutes, etc. Because of the rising divorce rate, some predict that most black children, and as many as 1/3 of white children under the age of 16 will see their parents break up.

Augustine comments on what a shameful thing it is when a mother is preparing for her second wedding at the same time as her daughter's first nuptials. There is hardly a sadder sight than a wedding picture of middle-aged newlyweds surrounded by their disillusioned progeny. Can they believe adults when they hear them say with straight faces "till death do us part" for the second or third time?

Dr. Umbricht remarks, "The healthy, natural and psychological balance which is of supreme importance for all mental and physical health is not supplied by this upbringing."[4]

No one would be so foolish as to say that separation should never be. Paul allows it for serious reasons, but he will only allow remarriage in the case of the unbelieving spouse leaving. Though separation may be necessary, the "innocent" victim should be compassionate and forgiving. None of us is sinless, and sometimes the so-called innocent party can be the cause or at least the occasion of the mate's escapades. The doctor sees the physical and mental value of monogamy. Freely assumed, indissolubility brings peace and confidence, giving physical and psychological security and calm.

Indissolubility aids fidelity, lessens anxiety and conserves nervous energy. Each individual has his or her limit of nervous tension, which is strained to the utmost by infidelity, divorce and the like. Moreover, in happy monogamy frigidity is rare because of the spiritual harmony between husband and wife. Family life is more tranquil and healthy.

> Monogamy seeks to overcome uncontrolled impulses and by this means protects the honor of the wife and mother. Healthy, indissoluble monogamy helps to form that fundamental mental attitude which is an essential condition of physical and psychological health.[5]

Patients frequently come to their physicians with all kinds of symptoms, from mental illness to cardiovascular problems, which are ultimately traced to marital strife, triangles, divorce and the like. Seldom do these victims see a religious or moral basis of their difficulties, so the priest or the minister is the last one on their list of people to see.

FRIENDSHIP

Friendship is one of mankind's most delightful experiences. However, many of our close associations are short range, such as childhood pals, roommates in school, business partners, professional colleagues, neighbors, etc. In our highly mobile society, friends necessarily change frequently, so there is an even greater need for stable, long-range relationships.

That marriage is the deepest of personal friendships we see in the story of our first parents, where God created Eve as a friend and companion for Adam. Moreover, this two-in-one union is reflected in the hierogamy. In ancient times anyone who would break this up by adultery was considered as a murderer, and worthy of capital punishment.

True love moves towards unity, while hate flees. *Agape* is the love of benevolence in which I wish happiness and welfare for my beloved, as Aquinas tells us. Dietrich von Hildebrand comments,[6] "In love we pour this very goodness into the soul of the beloved, we caress his (her) soul."

A person in love, breaking through his self-centeredness, seeks to bond with another. "He discloses his deep secret exclusively to the beloved and the beloved discloses her secret to him." This is what the Bible means by "knowing." Moreover, this mutual self-gift is a dynamic font of new life. But this sacred exchange is open to desecration.

> I degrade His dignity as a person first, because he becomes a means for my pleasure: and secondly, because I accept the fact that he throws himself away, that he betrays his secret, that he accomplishes a false donation and stains himself by a desecration (25).

Love, enthusiasm, and admiration are common human responses to value. But this loving affirmation of the other is not a seeking of personal happiness. Happiness is the result of love, not a means to it.

Love, charity, presupposes that the beloved is precious, beautiful, worthy of love. Love is a value response, not just the fulfillment of a need. I desire to make my beloved happy, giving up myself, yet retaining my individuality.

Spousal love is a lasting, vowed friendship between husband and wife, a total self-donation based on the sacred indissolubility of the archetypal hierogamy. Moreover, fidelity demands that the couple reserve their mutual donation for each other.

Marital union is a deep emotional experience including love, companionship, and value and meaning to each other. Husband and wife try to balance each other's needs but this is not always possible, for desires are not simultaneous.

There is a certain incarnational aspect of marriage. As God became man, taking on human form and living in union with His Church, so, in a sense, husband and wife incarnate themselves, taking on each other's body. Over the years their mutual exchange grows and deepens until many couples begin to look like twins.

Their unity imitates Christ's oneness with His people. Divorce would seem to be an attempt at splitting Christ from His Church. Can one who has divorced and remarried communicate with him whom he has repudiated? His second marriage no longer reflects the unique matrimony of Christ with His Church.

> If the Church could give the sacrament of unity to those who have broken with her on an essential point of the mysteries of Christ, she would no longer be the sign of the witness of Christ, but rather a counter-sign and a counter-witness.[7]

Nevertheless, Christ and His Church have mercy on weak and sick members of his Body, for if one limb is crippled, the whole body is affected. On the other hand, if all its members are strong, the entire body is vigorous.

The Church blesses their holy matrimony in which they irrevocably promise themselves to each other. However, if they make mistakes, the Church is a kindly mother. For example, she no longer excommunicates divorced and remarried couples. Though they are sick, it is not for the good of the whole to amputate them.

Perhaps they married too young when they were not psychologically or emotionally ready. Or maybe they are a couple from different religious traditions, one of whom does not believe in the sacramentality or the indissolubility of marriage. Many cases in Church courts reflect these situations.

But the Church must, as God, does, fight infidelity for the good of all. Some mis-marriages can be dissolved if non-sacramental. Even the divorced and remarried are not cast from the kingdom, but they should live as Christians and try to avoid scandal.

Paul Ramsey bases the fidelity of husband and wife on the archetypal union of Adam and Eve, without premarital or extramarital unions. Like Adam and Eve, husband and wife are naked and alone in their garden. "They rejoice as beings encountering and knowing one another across this bodily act."[8]

Here sexuality is not so much psychological or physiological, but rather ontological. It is the word (*logos*) of one human being to another (6). However, man in his weakness has the capability of acting irresponsibly.

As God clothed the naked and ashamed Adam and Eve, so He

gives us marriage to cover up our concupiscence. However, many people are reluctant to call marriage a remedy, which might imply some sort of weakness in man. Ramsey responds,

> With marriage we lonely fallen human beings are 'clothed' by the merciful hand of God as by 'garments of skin.' God has ordained marriage to restrain and remedy the defects in us to protect us against the threats which imperil our true good (19).
>
> It (marriage) is the dwelling place in which human life—in community—may be preserved against the storms of mankind's propensity to insult and injure one another through the misuse of God given sexuality.

Matrimony is God's gracious, healing gift to man. Man's fidelity makes marriage possible, like Adam and Eve before the fall. However, his infidelity makes matrimony necessary, like the union of Adam and Eve after the fall.

The very vows of the wedding anticipate life's problems: better/worse, richer/poorer, sickness/health. *Better, riches* and *health* put little strain on a marriage. But *worse, poverty* and *sickness* are the true tests of love. In a sense, no one is truly a husband or wife until his or her spouse becomes a burden. It is only when failure, bankruptcy, layoffs, sin, cancer, insanity, or senility come, and a spouse becomes a drag, that marriage is stripped of its glamor to its essential self-sacrifice.

The sacrament of matrimony is a garment which naked, weak, mistake-prone human love needs. "He becomes trustworthy only to the degree he is able to promise today what he will do tomorrow." He swears that he will give to the utmost of his ability. Sometimes there is little hope of reciprocity, a contract of unlimited liability. True love is vulnerable.

"To promise permanence means, in part, to acknowledge that at best man remains prone to sin." Sin may invade his very highest emotions. We cannot trust ourselves without a marriage covenant, which remedies and preserves our fidelity.

People change over the years. "You are not the same man I married." "And you are not that cute little loving girl I was so attracted to, either." The human body is constantly in transition, as is the mind.

We grow older, balder, and some people tend to get worse. Thus a social drinker may end up an alcoholic, or a girl about town may become a promiscuous housewife. Husband and wife see each other's bodies deteriorate as in a mirror. Face lifts, diets and exercise try to prolong youth, and sexual sorties attempt to rejuvenate waning libido. Certainly there must be something more fundamental to marriage than two aging bodies with their diminishing potencies.

Unless there is something unchanging, a human promise touching God's eternal covenant and drawing grace from it, the partners will grow apart. Although weak human nature needs the remedies of matrimony, it hankers to escape from the hospital to the Dionysian groves.

Recent studies show a certain ambivalence towards extramarital sex.[9] On the one hand, there seems to be a rather high rate of infidelity (50-85%). Yet, on the other hand, many (70%) feel that adultery is always wrong. Perhaps this is the dichotomy between the monogamous ideal and weak human nature.

A common excuse for adultery is sexual frustration, followed by curiosity, revenge, ennui and recognition-seeking. Subconscious motives may range from the need of stroking the inner child, to rage at one's partner, to proof of masculinity or femininity. Though adultery may sometimes be understandable, it endangers the stability of the marriage and fosters guilt, suspicion and reciprocity. It hurts all those involved including husband, wife, children and the third party. Can a marriage survive adultery? The prophets and Jesus advise forgiveness. God forgives the adulterer and so should we.

In modern society, the mixing of the sexes at work, play and in the professions causes much tension in the home. Thus a husband or wife may spend more time with a colleague of the opposite sex than with their spouse. There are more than ample opportunities for wooing, falling in love, liaisons, rendezvous, etc. Business trips and conventions are times of temptation for lonely spouses. As more and more wives enter the business world, chances for sexual mistakes double.

If physical unity is overstressed in matrimony, then when the couple are bodily apart, there can be a feeling of incompleteness. However, if husband and wife are one in soul then they are united even when they are far apart.

If the Holy Spirit is to accompany the single spouse to work or on a trip, he or she must be on familiar terms with the Spirit while at home. Where the two Christian mates are together, the Spirit of Christ is between them, even if bodily separated.

Finally, when the two are one flesh, body and soul, one person, they cannot fail to be a font of new life and love.

CHAPTER TWELVE

Be Fertile And Multiply
(Gn 1:28)

In the trinitarian archetype of marriage's threefold good, as the Spirit is the sanctifier, and the Son is the paradigm of fidelity, so the Father, is the image of parenthood.

PROCREATION

In His providence, God planned that man and woman would continue His work of creation in order to people the earth. Procreation is a divine mandate and part of man's God-given responsibility. Two basic needs meet in marriage, as we read in the book of Genesis—the desire for companionship and the obligation to continue the race.

While the personal good of marriage, with its mutual support and love, has been stressed in recent times, this has been especially enhanced by the attraction, and sometimes the necessity, of dual careers for husband and wife, and by the relative ease of modern family planning.

Motherhood as a career has reached an all-time low in prestige. Grace Hechinger comments, (NEWSWEEK, 5,1,81, p 19).

> Mother's job has no status in a society which rewards the single-minded pursuit of money and success. Her role clashes head-on with the real values of an achievement-oriented culture. The qualities needed to nurture, to put the needs of others ahead of our own, are directly opposite to those needed to "make it" in

the outside/corporate world. A mother's job is to train her children to enter a world whose values differ sharply from those she herself lives by her relationship with them. No wonder there is confusion on all sides.

Furthermore, mother's amateur status has been placed even lower by experts: pediatricians, child psychologists, orthodontists, sociologists, etc. Many mothers work outside the home because they have to, in order to keep their standard of living at a certain level, but there remains a certain tension between the outside career and motherhood. In many cases the second is slighted in favor of the first.

Some are shocked that procreation should still be considered as the primary end of matrimony. But when one looks at the history of wedlock, he sees that this has almost always been the case from primitive tribes to clan society, advanced cultures such as Israel and Rome, and in much of Christian tradition.

The main concern of tribal society is the fertility of the bride and the production of warriors and workers for the prosperity of the group, and the continuation of the ancestral line. As we have seen, both the Jews and the Romans required parents to procreate. The Romans called marriage matrimony, or motherhood, and the Christian Church passed on this child-centered theme.

In agricultural societies children have economic value as workers, and so large families are encouraged. But in urban industrial cultures, children can be liabilities, costing much more than they produce. So the tendency towards small families. Some countries are offering bonuses to support parents who have more little ones in order to try to counteract this downward trend in the population. Although some countries such as India, China and Japan are overpopulated, the world, as such, is not.

Though mutual affection seems to be the primary end of marriage today, nevertheless, the childless union is, indeed, empty. For a while the couple may feel self-sufficient and fulfilled in their careers, with many hobbies, shows, trips and other pleasures. However, they are headed for a lonely old age with no progeny to rejoice in or worry over.

With infertility a common problem due to artificial forms of birth control, postponed pregnancies, etc., and a high abortion rate, it is difficult for spouses without children to adopt.

Bonum est diffusivum sui. The good spreads. It can never be totally self-contained, centripetal, but rather must flow into others, centrifugal. Thus God who is all good and all love diffuses His goodness in the creation of infinite galaxies and myriad species of life. It is His plan that man and woman imitate His diffusive goodness in procreation.

This is the principle of superabundance, not mere instrumentality, for the means have a value independent of the end to which they lead. "The same act, which in its meaning is the constitution of the union has been superabundantly made the source of procreation."[1]

> The God-given essential link between the love of man and woman and its fulfillment in marital union on the one hand, and the creation of a new person on the other hand, has precisely the character of superabundance which is a much deeper connection than the one of mere instrumental finality (97).

The meaning (*logos*) is marital union, whose end (*telos*) is procreation. The two-in-one flesh culminates in the penetration of the egg by the sperm. Artificial birth control separates meaning from end, frustrating superabundance.

> Every active intervention on the part of the spouses, which eliminates the possibility of conception through the conjugal act, is incompatible with the holy mystery of the superabundant relation in the incredible gift offered by God (98).

If man freely elects to participate in the hierogamy, he must also cooperate in the divine plan. This in no way indicts those who are naturally incapable of procreation because of age or disability, for these couples are not intentionally frustrating God's plan.

Paul Ramsey, too, reminds us that the act of love is generative.[2] "Whether or not a child is engendered, the act itself is procreative." Intercourse is both unitive, as the expression and the strengthening of love, and procreative for the engendering of children. We procreate for God, who stays in the background, preferring to create through men and women.

To us has been given this great commission that in the act of sexual intercourse we are to be present as codeterminers with God there at the beginning of human life, which henceforth transcends all human determination (4).

Man and wife codetermine with God the existence of another human being. What an honor and responsibility. Their one flesh unity passes into the one flesh of the child, who is both the symbol and the effect of their oneness. As the Fathers tell us, the child *is* the one flesh of the parents. So when the one flesh of the child is deliberately frustrated, it is difficult to see how the parents can be two-in-one.

Today there is much concern over the ends of marriage; which is primary, which secondary, and so on. Though Augustine wrote in the Roman Empire, which demanded marriage for the sake of children, he described the good of marriage as threefold, child, fidelity and sacrament, not three goods, but one.

Ramsey remarks, "Procreation sets marriage apart from other acts and relations in the whole field of human community; and it is therefore called primary" (7). Can intercourse as an act of mutual love be separated from intercourse as an act of procreation, crossing out the divine intention?

But may not husband and wife plan their family according to means, health, etc.? Yes, but by their very design they are saying that the child they will have will be from their one flesh and not outside this union.

Clearly, extramarital intercourse separates recreation from procreation and the good of the child, and so it goes against God's plan. Either no child is allowed, or, by accident, an illegitimate foetus is conceived, and, more often than not, aborted. Or if it is born, usually left without support by the father.

Extramarital partners do not "take into account the gracious claim God placed upon their lives when he linked their unity with the one flesh of the child" (11). How can one be a father and not a husband, a mother and not a wife? Making love outside of matrimony still implies parenthood. Some states demand child support from unwed fathers, though this is difficult to enforce. Others declare the real fatherhood of one who only inseminates a woman artificially.

Society must take the responsibility for these unwanted children. In clan and tribal society an infant born out of wedlock was welcomed as a member of the extended family. Today, however, some governments encourage birth control and abortion rather than incur the heavy expense of raising the child to maturity.

A responsibility to both God and society is violated when sexual love is separated from procreation. Sexual love of its very nature is procreative. The unity of the flesh of the parents cannot be split from the one flesh of the foetus.

Some feel that the perfect contraceptive will solve all problems, so that people will be free for premarital and extramarital affairs, and the state would not be burdened with the support of unwanted bastards. Even if science comes up with a magic potion, it will still be violating the cosmic plan. As Ramsey writes, marriage "consists in a covenant whose matter is the giving and the receiving of acts which tend both to unique one-flesh unity between the partners and to the unique one-flesh of the child between them" (13).

CONTRACEPTION

Some today seem to look upon pregnancy and childbirth as pathological conditions to be prevented or relieved by drugs or abortion. The opposite is true, namely, that pregnancy is natural, while the potions and abortive procedures wound nature, harm fertility, and so are pathological.

Although the Church has guarded the procreative end of marriage through the ages against sterilization, contraception and abortion, she has never taught that parents should have unlimited families. They must act responsibly in cooperation with God, Church and society.

There have been times in history when the desire for pleasure has overridden the divine plan for procreation, as we have seen. Probably this has been the reason for the fall of so many advanced cultures. The wealthy and educated classes and leaders had little time for offspring, while, at the same time, they encouraged slaves and peasants to produce more children to supply more workers, and so more wealth and leisure for the rich.

Eventually the small ruling classes fell to the overpowering numbers of the lower castes, so we end up with shacks and hovels replacing the palaces, temples and culture of the wealthy and powerful. Though Rome tried to force its citizens to reproduce, it was not enough to forestall slave uprisings and barbarian invasions.

One of the big fears in the American South before the Civil War was that the large numbers of black slaves would take over from their white masters. This led to repressive measures against the slaves, which eventually brought about the war between the states.

Can man become extinct? Probably many species of plants and animals, and even tribes and nations, have become extinct because of frustrated teleology.

Birth rate in the United States dropped from 25/1000 (1955) to 15 (1975) with a slight rise to 16 in 1980. The fertility rate stands at 68/1000 women from 15 to 44 years of age, with approximately 2.2 children during the fertility span of each. Later marriages, birth control, and abortion all contribute to the decline.

Some feel that fewer children necessarily mean a higher standard of living. However, recessions, inflation and unemployment seem to accompany lower birth rates.

Governments are concerned that the lower classes be taught birth control and be shown the value of abortion and sterilization, perhaps in fear that they may outproduce the wealthy elite, and also to save government expense in child support. On the other hand, some countries are offering bonuses to those with larger families, in order to help build up a dwindling population.

There have been times in history when man has limited marriage and reproduction because of short food supplies, disastrous wars or bad economic conditions. Some postponed marriage till after the prime reproductive age. Others joined monasteries or convents.[3]

Disease and war have always been population controls. One reason for the population explosion in India has been the conquest of childhood diseases in that country.

Moreover, it is clear that child-loving primitive people did not have hut-to-hut babies. Though it is true that some tribes practiced the exposure of baby girls, the natural way of child spacing was through normal breast-feeding. This sometimes continued for several years, during which time husband and wife slept in separate dwellings.

The only absolutely safe methods of birth control are sterilization and continence. To my knowledge a serious study has not been done on the psychological and physiological effects of sterilization. However, many have tried to have the operation reversed, showing some dissatisfaction.

Dr. Walter Umbricht notes some of the medical contraindications of various types of contraception.[4] Any foreign object placed within the body, be it pessary, IUD, jelly, etc., can cause inflammation, infection or even cancer.

Condoms would seem to be harmless. Dr. Umbricht responds, "In the course of time the sensitivity of both partners is dulled. If intercourse is practiced in this way over a certain length of time, a mutual dislike not infrequently sets in." It is a barrier, divisive and psychologically bad for the relationship, the opposite of two-in-one.

Interrupted intercourse also "is very harmful and often of serious consequences to the health of both husband and wife. It causes nervous troubles which express themselves in insomnia, irregularities of the heart, anxiety states, frigidity and so on." Progestin, which suppresses ovulation and alters cervical mucous, can be abortive, so that the fertilized egg cannot attach itself to the wall of the cervix.[5]

The pill creates an artificial pathological condition in the female body, and may cause cancer and thromboses. It is perhaps too early to see what effects the pill will have on the second generation.

Ironically, some go to the doctor out of fear of pregnancy as if it were an illness, and even have the foetus excised as if it were a malignancy. In fact, the real pathology lies in the use of artificial chemicals and devices. Babies are not foreign objects, and motherhood is not a disease. Contraceptives can have other deleterious effects. Dr. Umbricht comments,

> It is a common experience to find sterility in a large number of patients who have used contraceptives of whatever kind over a long period. This serious consequence may appear even if it is not always desired as a permanent condition.

The newly modified rhythm method of natural family planning, by which fertile periods are accurately measured, will be discussed in a later chapter. It is precise, and safer than most other means now in use.

Some of the anovulants are abortive, and abortion is the ultimate contraceptive. Gary Wills[6] points out that 1/3 of the pregnancies in the United States during 1980 ended in abortion (1.5 million).

> Science and society are out of sync. The most humane of sciences, medicine, can now treat as patients those whom the law says lack an essential human attribute: rights. Mothers can kill any foetus that medicine can treat.

In the same hospital you will find a premie (premature baby) living peacefully in an incubator while doctors and nurses hover over it, feed it artificially, monitor every function, etc., while down the hall another premie lies dead in a garbage can, killed by aborting knives, saline solution or whatever.

May the foetus ever be sacrificed to save the life of the mother? The advances of modern science and medicine have made this a rare case. Doctors say that in most cases the termination of pregnancy is pointless and can even be counterproductive, although a cancerous uterus may be removed.[7]

The placing of an artificial barrier between husband and wife, not only strikes at the very root of marriage, but parallels the excommunication of the Christian from Christ. Kindregan notes,[8]

> The life God has given them and the power of passing it on to others is not a thing to be used lightly. Birth limitation, regardless of the method employed, does present a danger that our love and respect for life will be diminished.

The domino effect can lead to child abuse, youth suicide and euthanasia. If life is cheap in the womb, it is cheap everywhere.

Vatican II (*Church in the Modern World*, 50) speaks of the child-orientation of marriage. Not wishing to make the other ends of marriage less, the couple should be ready, "with stout hearts to cooperate with the love of the Creator and the Savior, who through them will enlarge and enrich His own family day by day."

Bonum est diffusivum sui. Agape is centrifugal. Parents cooperate in the self-diffusing love of the Creator, and interpret this love, taking into account the welfare of the family, society and the Church.

Husband and wife must harmonize their conjugal love and respect for human life. There is a danger in breaking off marital relations, which can lead to infidelity. "True contradiction cannot exist between the divine laws pertaining to the transmission of life and those fostering authentic conjugal life" (51).

Paul VI also emphasized the child-centering of marriage and the dangers of contraception in his historic encyclical on *Human Life* in 1968, as we have seen. Besides undermining marriage, it can easily make women the means of men's pleasure and open the door to extra-marital affairs. This is not an idle fear, for many women have expressed this concern to their doctors and psychiatrists.

Jonathan Schell notes[9] that marriage solemnizes love, giving inward feelings outward form. "In swearing their love in public, the lovers also let it be known that their union will be a fit one for bringing children into the world." And the witnessing world shows its stake in its own continuance.

Though marriage is a personal action, it also belongs to everybody, and "lays the foundation for the stability of the human world that is built to house all generations."

But when the future orientation of love and marriage is lost, they become contraceptive, selfish, solitary, ephemeral, impersonal, detached and pornographic. Moreover, momentary sex pleasure can never substitute for the long-range joys of future hopes.

Parental love anticipates the child and is unconditional. "It does not attach to any quality of the beloved, it only wants him to be." So the child is conceived of the unconditional superabundance of his parents' love and fruitfulness.

It is obvious that generation does not end in conception. The long-range responsibility and expense of child raising has scared some into abortion clinics. Just as God creates and then guides the world, so parents procreate and then train their young ones, leading them along the path to salvation.

As Christ perpetually offers His body as food to His Church, so parents pledge their bodies to each other, and together give their one flesh to their children, their domestic church. They do this not only in generation, but also in a lifelong communion of nourishment, care and education.

CHAPTER THIRTEEN

He Who Disciplines His Son
Will Benefit From Him
(Si 30:2)

Education means "to lead out." The potential in the fertilized egg is actualized, fulfilled, developed to maturity. Generation does not end with intercourse. This is the tragedy of premarital or extramarital sex, divorce and dual parental careers where the children are neglected. In conceiving a child, parents incur the responsibility of raising it to maturity.

PARENTS

Marriage is holy because it participates in God's creation, including not only the planting of the seed, but also its nurturing, guidance, watering and pruning.

Education begins even before conception, for heredity and family traditions play important roles. Clan societies examined minutely the backgrounds of the prospective bride and groom. Are they children of healthy, happy, educated, prosperous, law-abiding parents?

From the moment of conception, the learning process evolves. What a marvelous teleology prompts the fertilized egg to split and divide, absorb nutriment from its mother, develop small arms and legs, tiny fingers and toes! More and more doctors tell us of the importance of prenatal development. Anything that goes on in the home affects the growing foetus. Do mother and father drink, smoke, fight, take drugs? Or are they prayerful, calm, loving and peaceful?

Hinduism teaches us a lesson in its prenatal sacraments, which begin with the parents' intercourse. If the child is prayed for several times while in the womb, its chances of being born well and with a good religious foundation are excellent.

Some maintain that, since the foetus is a part of the mother, she may elect to do with it what she wishes. However, the baby is the one flesh of both mother and father, with its own unique individuality, a human person with all rights and privileges, including life.

What if there is a defect in the infant? Would it not be better to terminate the pregnancy than to burden society with a child who is armless, or deformed in another manner? All attempts at developing a genetically perfect society in the past have failed. Moreover, there are certain factors that cannot be accurately measured in the womb, namely, determination, courage, ability to overcome obstacles, and God's providence and grace. Furthermore, most handicapped adults feel that their lives are meaningful, and are happy that their existence was not destroyed before they even had a chance to be born.

Modern methods of examining the womb can see the little one move about, flex its limbs, express pleasure and pain. Moreover, modern medicine can treat and heal many prenatal illnesses. And when the baby is attacked by abortion knives or salt solutions, it fights for its life.

Today, obstetricians promote natural childbirth as being better for mother and child alike. Moreover, they respect the ancient tradition of keeping mother and child together, so that she can love it and feed it the natural way. Studies have shown that the child is much healthier and saner, than when separated from the mother at birth. The learning process, begun in the womb, continues after parturition.

If education is a continuation of procreation, child abuse is a projection of abortion. Child abuse can take many forms, from actually striking the infant to passive neglect.

All the infidelities of marriage, from adultery to divorce, are also forms of child abuse. The youngsters suffer most of all, buffeted from one parent to the other, living with relatives, in foster homes or institutions, lost in the throes of omnigamy. Is it sometimes better for the children if battling parents split up? This is hard to say, but healing, forgiveness, and charity are far better than recriminations, revenge and hate.

Parents are the primary educators by word and example. We all know the small boy who imitates his daddy, cutting the lawn and reading the paper, and little girl who copies her mother's cooking, cares for the baby, or who likes to dress up like mommy in high heels, long dress and lipstick. As we are made in the image and likeness of God, so parents procreate and educate in their own model.

Weaknesses and strengths tend to run in families. This is true of alcoholism, short tempers, abuse, infidelity, divorce and crime, but also of skills, patience, benevolence and kindness. Like father, like son. Behind many criminals lie dishonest parents and split homes, with no family pride because there is no family. On the other hand, in the background of kind, helpful souls often are found compassionate mothers and fathers.

In the bosom of the family with a Christian atmosphere of prayer and discipline, the child learns early his lessons of piety and morality. The importance of the early years cannot be overestimated. Both good and bad habits, formed early, are hard to break.

The child learns lessons in moderation, obedience, humility, gratitude, acceptance of correction, modesty, and chastity. Modesty in small children will prepare them for the inevitable attacks on their chastity as teens and adults.

In a sense, the whole family educates, for youngsters learn much from their older siblings, as well as from their parents. Especially in their early years, the parent or older brother or sister is the hero, the one to be looked up to and imitated, an inexhaustible source of guidance and knowledge. "Why, Daddy?"

Education includes not only intellectual development, but also the evolution of the child's whole personality on the emotional, social and physical levels. Discipline, friends, play, responsibility, nutrition, physical and mental health are all included.

As a boy's or girl's physical body grows, so also does the mind and personality. Hobbies and vocational interests should be encouraged. Also a sense of healthy independence should be fostered, giving them roots and wings.

Sometimes it is hard for parents to admit that their children are just temporary gifts of God. Mother and father are the trustees of God for their offspring, who will soon be off to raise families of their own, but the trusteeship carries heavy responsibilities.

Since parents imitate and take part in the union of Christ and His Church, they must train their young ones to be good members of the Mystical Body of Christ. Charity unites the family, as the Spirit is the Love of the Father and of the Son. Discipline without anger, respecting the person of the child. Together, parents and children help each other to heaven.

If parental responsibility in the education of their progeny is so great, what is to be said of a mother and father who—not out of necessity—have dual careers, and so rarely see their children? When they do come home, either the kids are out, or the careerists are too tired to communicate. Or else, they program a few hours of "quality time" for the youngsters.

Besides Marxism, American capitalism, too, is dedicated to the emancipation of housewives. This often has meant either the forestalling of children, or else placing them in commercial nurseries for 50 hours a week during a crucial period of their development.

It is unfortunate that our society forces some mothers, especially widows and divorced, to balance two careers in order to bring up their families. Grace Hechinger remarks.[1]

> Ironically, the women's movement reflects the same dilemma that troubles individual women. The initial concentration on creating new employment opportunities was a realistic response to priority needs. But progress has had the unintended consequence of making motherhood appear even less appealing to many younger women.

Puberty is a crucial time of formation. Though youths sometimes seem to reject their parents, and even feel ashamed of them in front of their peers, parental guidance is needed. Actually much teen rebellion is really the beginning of independence, the first tentative leap out of the nest.

Sexual mistakes during mating times are inevitable: masturbation, peer pressure, teen sex and even pregnancy. Contemporary highly educated and complex civilizations have postponed marriage till many years after the sexual powers have developed, with predictable consequences.

Youthful emotions are still developing and prone to ups and down, drug experiments and sexual mistakes. Pornography, ads, TV, movies and songs encourage sexual errors. Modesty, caution and parental approval of dates are a few prudent measures to avoid problems. Young people who are still developing themselves, are in no position economically or emotionally for the long-range commitments of marriage and family.

Whereas the mother's companionship and training are essential to the beginning years, the father is important as a guide and model for the maturing time.

Armand Nicholi[2] notes that the inability of many of today's youths to control their impulses is due largely to the declining influence of the father in the home. For example, a lack of sexual identity may be traced to cold, distant, rejecting, inaccessible, separated or divorced fathers.

About one half of American college students will drop out of school, about a third for psychological reasons. Nicholi finds two characteristics of these dropouts: isolation from their parents, especially their fathers, and apathy.

There is a whole culture of runaway children in the United States. Many end up as white slaves, trucked from one convention to the next till they either die of venereal disease, commit suicide or end up in some bizarre cult. Many are running from an impossible home situation. Often little attempt is made to locate them, for their parents may have divorced and remarried and moved on to new places. And when their mom and dad are so involved in their careers kids soon get the message that they are in the way. Most police budgets allow little or no money for tracing runaways.

Young schizophrenics usually have one or both parents missing. Drug addicts, too, often have a history of isolation from their families, especially in the early crucial years.

Nicholi also found that most motorcycle casualties had a frustrated anger at their fathers turned inwards to depression and self-injury. There was "a distant conflict-ridden relationship with the father who was critical of and inaccessible to the boy throughout the boy's life" (164).

"What has been shown over and over again to have the most profound effect on the character development of a child is a close warm relationship with both parents" (165).

Much child care today has shifted from the family to surrogate parents: baby sitters, social workers, nurseries, day schools, boarding schools, camps, and peers. There is much age segregation, in which the young and old eat, work, play and live separately, with no more extended family to absorb pressures.

There seems to be a progressive decrease in the amount of contact between parents and children in the USA. Moreover, the high juvenile crime rate probably is one of its evil effects.

Nicholi notes, "Only recently have we come to realize the full emotional impact on the child of the missing father" (165). The "famous father" syndrome is familiar. Here we have a man who is so busy with his career that he neglects the spiritual and emotional needs of his family.

> A parent's absence through death or divorce, as well as a parent's inaccessibility, either physically or emotionally, or both, exact a profound influence on an individual's emotional health or illness (166).

The adverse effect of truncated family life, through death or divorce or infidelity, in the children cannot be overestimated. Anyone who has taught or counseled these youngsters knows that they are wounded. They rarely smile, for a child or youth is too honest to simulate happiness.

SCHOOLS

Obviously, parents do not have the time or the expertise to handle all of their children's education. So they have the right and duty to choose a school which will continue what they have begun.

Since the purpose of Christian marriage is to form good members of the Mystical Body of Christ, a Christian education is necessary. The history of Christian education goes back to Jesus Himself and His teachings. The Fathers and monks continued this tradition with catechetical schools and, in medieval times, cathedral schools, colleges and universities.[3]

Today, more than ever, a good religious education is necessary, especially on the grammar and secondary school levels. Much good work has been done with special children's liturgies, plays, art work, community service, etc. However, many so-called Christian colleges are such in name only. They are caught in the morass of tenure, academic freedom and government regulations, in which atheists, agnostics and other unbelievers are allowed to teach with utter impunity.

Perhaps here we might make the important distinction between vocational and occupational education. All men and women have different talents and skills which encourage them to take up certain occupations. These range from farmer, engineer, teacher, or manager, to mechanic, doctor or accountant, but all have the same ultimate vocation, namely, union with God.

Since the Christian's vocation is union with Christ in His Mystical Body, his religious education should point in this direction. Though occupational training is important, it is, in a sense, an illusion, for the average person changes his or her occupation several times during a lifetime of work. On the college level, administrators cannot keep up with the swiftly changing occupational interests from pre-med to pre-law to pre-business. Environmental chairs went in and out with the wind.

At most, one's job lasts till retirement, and with a recession it often ends long before this age. Sooner or later, one's essential vocation should reassert itself. Though occupations change and become obsolete quickly, a man's or woman's ultimate vocation always remains the same, divine union. Of course, our occupations are necessary in order to help God subdue and fulfill the earth, but they are means to the end and not ends in themselves.

Vatican II underlined the right of the Christian, as a new creature, to a Christian education. Moreover, parents and Church have the right and duty to provide it, so that he or she may be knowledgeable in the mysteries of the faith, and allow it to grow in Christ (*Declaration on Christian Education*, 1).

Parents are the primary educators, and pastoral concern tries to ascertain even before the baptism of the child whether the parents intend to raise the child as a Christian. Procreation and education go hand in hand. If the child is to be born again in baptism, it is unfair to him or her if the mother and father have no intention of raising the little one as a member of the Mystical Body of Christ.

As we have seen, the family is the first school in which Christian virtues and morality are inculcated into the child. If family life is fractured, the school can do little, for at most it is a surrogate family. If the child is not trained in the love of God and Church in the home, the school has no foundation upon which to build. A Christian school can make a student from a good Christian home better. But what can it do for one from an un-Christian atmosphere? How can it recommend that children go to Mass on Sunday, if the parents never do?

Society has a duty to help and not to hinder Christian parents in the education of their children. Moreover, the Church has been given the teaching office by Christ. She educates through her liturgy, catechetics, homilies, media and schools.

The Christian school should be a community of love and gospel freedom. "It aims to help the adolescent in such a way that the development of his own personality will be matched by the growth of that new creation which he became in baptism," illuminating all by the light of faith (8).

Christian education should be incarnational, sacred and secular, vocational and at the same time, occupational. "Bound by charity to one another and to their students, and penetrated by an apostolic spirit, let them (teachers) give witness to Christ, the unique teacher, by their lives as well as their teachings" (8). They are partners with the parents in the development of the child.

Public schools, of course, are by their very nature non-religious, and so tend to deemphasize values and the vocational in favor of the secular and the occupational. Lack of ethical training, disciplinary problems, teacher strikes, inadequate funding, and questionable results in student achievement have forced many parents to transfer their children to religious schools.

Historically, all education began as religious or ethical teaching, from the Confucian schools of China to the Hindu Brahmins, Buddhist bikkhus, Jewish rabbis and the Christian educational tradition. The Hindus led the way, since for them knowledge *vidya* is sacred. Thus they have one sacrament *vidyarambha* in which the youngster begins to read and write, and another liturgy *upanayana* in which the adolescent boy is reborn in order to study under his Brahmin-teacher and spiritual father.

Purely secular education is of a relatively late origin, and is of questionable viability.

We have seen in the last two chapters the procreative and educational ends of marriage. Both seem on the wane today, as the fertility rate drops and schools close for lack of students.

With new opportunities opening up for women in business and the professions, there is less desire to tie themselves down for twenty or thirty years of child-bearing and the rearing of sometimes ungrateful offspring. What about me? Why not develop myself and gain more personal and material advantages with all this energy?

But it is the vocation of Christian parents to fill the earth, to complete the Mystical Body of Christ with new cells and members, and so to lead them to salvation in Christ. Although the progeny of the future may be deprived of certain physical luxuries, this is no guarantee that they will be unhappy spiritually.

In our discussion of procreation and its evolution into education, we have not mentioned the ongoing graces of the sacrament of matrimony. Too frequently young newlyweds look ahead with fear and trembling, as if they had to do it all on their own. Impossible! Marriage is a trinity: lover, Love and beloved, where God is Love. In a holy and sacramental marriage He is in their midst, and in a Christian union He is there in the Spirit of His Son.

Family planning is not only the concern of husband and wife, but also of the Creator, for in His divine providence, He cannot create unless the parents procreate. God should be included in family planning through prayer, reception of the sacraments, and the asking for guidance. "Ask and you shall receive" (Mt 7:7). "Where two or three are gathered in my name, I am in the midst of them" (Mt 18:20).

We sometimes forget that there is a kind, loving and caring divine providence. "Are you not worth more than sparrows?" (cf. Mt 6:26; Lk 12:24) At the same time, we should use our own intelligence to co-plan with God for the future, remembering always that man proposes, while God disposes. The Almighty may not want a husband and wife to have any children, or He may wish them to adopt homeless waifs. Ask, seek, pray, trust!

CHAPTER FOURTEEN

Exclusive And Inclusive Love

The one flesh of marriage is not one physical body, but rather one living person. The body changes from year to year, cells die, tumors and wrinkles grow, teeth and hair fall out, but the single living person is the same. Flesh, in the biblical sense, can also refer to a moral person such as a clan, or even the whole human race.

We in the West have been conditioned by Greek philosophy to see the spiritual soul as imprisoned in the material body. Hinduism, on the other hand, teaches that all partake in the same Self, *Atman* or Person, *Purusha* with the physical body only a passing illusion.

Husband and wife can be perfectly one flesh without bodily union, even when separated by a great distance.

We saw how the good of marriage must diffuse itself in children, but it does not stop there, for it keeps spreading throughout society.

CREATIVE CONTINENCE IN MARRIAGE

Ordinarily, we do not associate the words "continence" or "chastity" with marriage. Rather, we think of a nun or a priest or a monk dedicated for life by vows to the service of God and man.

However, from earliest times we find marital continence practiced in almost all cultures in preparation for feasts, rites, prayer, war, hunts, planting and harvesting, and during pregnancy and menstruation.[1]

In Hinduism, newlyweds refrained from coitus for the first three nights in order to insure a good beginning. Moreover, the Hindu *vanaprastha*, retired from procreation and family life, is a celibate in the service of others. The sublimation of sexual energies into a higher union is found in many Indian traditions.

In the first century Jewish rabbis separated from their wives for a while for the sake of *Torah* study, and the *Shekhinah* of Yahweh accompanied them. Paul advises Christians to do the same for a time for the sake of prayer.

The chaste man of one wife was chosen for early Church offices. Some even held that this fidelity to one spouse should be kept after the death of the beloved. Furthermore, the early Christian communities, following ancient traditions, required continence before the Eucharist and during Lent.

Though some may feel that man's sexual instincts are irrepressible, modern psychology contradicts this. The main reason for the recent sexual revolution is overstimulation. As Hinduism tells us, there is a direct link between the mind and the sex organs.

Marital chastity not only does not hinder love, it safeguards and even escalates it. There are many circumstances in the life of a married couple when they must observe continence out of love. Separations for business or professional reasons are more and more common. Even in the home, the continence of a healthy spouse can be a creative act of love towards his or her indisposed mate.

In this continence there is not less love, but more. And how about an elderly couple, no longer fired by the passions of youth? Their love is often deeper and more intense than the ardent bodily union of young sweethearts.

Contemporary research has shown that the sexual revolution of the 60's and and 70's overstressed the importance of sex in marriage. In fact, many couples were found who were happily married without a highly active sex life.[2]

> Sex, or the lack of it, apparently only becomes a problem when couples try to match idealized standards popularized by books and movies. Researchers stress that the key for each couple is determining what's right for them.

Gabrielle Brown[3] corroborates this evidence. She found that if a spouse did not measure up to the mystical ideal of sexual powers, he or she may be accused of infidelity, frigidity or just not caring.

Some feel that if sexual activity does not increase in marriage, that something is wrong and so they should seek it outside. However,

> the change toward lessening sexual activity may be indicative not of the failure of a marriage, but of a higher level relationship between the marital partners. It has been found that in the most successful, committed marriages, sexual response may, indeed, diminish in its localized expression—while changing into another kind of response (131).

But some may mistake the diffusion of sexual energy (sublimation) for its absence. Is the marriage on the rocks? No, just elevated to a higher level. "As the sexual response in marriage becomes diffused, the opportunity for intimate love increases" (132). This is fine if the progress of the couple is equal, but often it is not, so patience is required.

Is sex absolutely necessary for a happy marriage? The marital act should be symbolic of the spiritual union of the couple. However, this can also be expressed non-sexually. Happy marriages do not necessarily have perfect sex relationships, but, by and large, the couples do not worry about it.

Ironically, the sexual revolution may have made sex less important in marriage, because it was anticipated so much in premarital life. Here abstinence can enhance marital love, rather than cool it. "Celibacy may be regarded as a way to 'spiritualize' sexuality in order to refine the experience of love further" (138). The same thing over and over can be boring, but when it is redirected, one can find new ways of courting one's spouse, reexperiencing love in a purer sense, with intensity, courtesy and kindness. Thus there arises a more subtle exchange in thought, looks, hugs, kisses, energy, richer emotional and spiritual bonding.

Of course, celibacy in marriage should be a cooperative endeavor. "Celibacy or sexual activity chosen in the service of love is the context in which a couple makes its decision." Fulfillment, service, charity, growth in love take precedence. If sex, or celibacy helps, let the couple decide.

Some couples report that celibacy keeps their hearts open to each other, just like falling in love all over again (147). People who are best friends have the least need of sex. And when sex is had with a view to children, it is an act of love, self-giving, something divine.

But is not marital continence a contradiction? Or an unnatural state of tension? Charity and chastity are two sides of the same coin. Charity means one is dear to me, and chastity means I discipline my appetites for the sake of my beloved. One is necessary for the other, so marital chastity is really marital charity. Far from harming a marriage, sexual abstinence actually builds up libido, as Rabbi Gelles notes.[4]

> It (separation) brings the couple a time of physical rest; revives in them a feeling of attraction; is a reagent against the danger of satiety, a constant threat, with its consequent marital lassitude; and finally, proves how necessary it is to be able to control the demands of the flesh.

Love means control, not blind instinct. Human love is much broader than the sexual drive. Probably, the lassitude of which the rabbi speaks is responsible for more marital disintegration today than any other factor. The continual use of artificial birth control, and overuse of the genital faculties, can lead to boredom, frigidity and even impotence. Here periodic continence would be a positive force for the strengthening of marriage, rather than weakening it.

MARITAL CONTINENCE AND THE KINGDOM

There are many ancient traditions of marital restraint for the greater good of mankind. Hinduism has famous *vanaprasthas* such as Buddha and Ghandi, who traded *kama*, exclusive sexual affection, for *ahimsa*, universal love to ease the sufferings of the world.

Judaism and Christianity offer similar examples in their rabbis, monks, nuns and priests. Almost all cultures have some type of sexual sublimation in preparation for their liturgies.

Some have accused the Church of overstressing celibacy. This probably reflects a time when the Romans honored their virgins and celibate priests. *A fortiori*, Christians should, too. However, all the Fathers insisted that celibacy is the daughter of marriage. Moreover, they taught that chastity plays as important a role in nuptial life as among singles albeit of a different degree.

Many modern professions require periodic separation of husband and wife, or at least a sublimation of marital pleasures for career demands for the good of society, for example, the armed services, transportation, merchant marine, space exploration, international diplomacy, worldwide business, medicine, politics, etc. Here a spiritual union of the couple has to transcend bodily closeness.

Mary and Robert Joyce[5] see marriage not so much as a narrow exclusive exchange of selves (you and me against the world) as a hand-in-hand giving of themselves to the world. Here sublimation, far from being self-interested and centripetal, is centrifugal, moving out to others. The one flesh is not merely the union of husband and wife, but includes society as a whole.

Mary Joyce feels that if the source of human sexual energy is given a chance to expand and assimilate the emotional and physiological energies of sex, there would be an increase in spontaneous chastity, and the marriage would be born again in a deeply sublimated union of husband and wife. Then continence would not be a source of frustration and fear, but rather the foundation of a deepening love, an evolution from exclusive to inclusive affection.

But can one be morally sexually fulfilled without coition? Husband and wife can be interior to each other without intercourse, which is only one way to interiority. "Their indirect sexual relationship is just as physical, though in a different way, as any direct sexual union between them. This fact is central to the meaning of sublimation in marriage" (48).

The mental and spiritual side of sex needs to expand. "Freedom to be one's sexuality in communion with the being of the world is the gift of true sublimation." Celibacy and marriage still seem to be contradictory. However, they are complimentary, for one must be able to live alone with oneself before he or she can join another in community. This is an open aloneness, a "being love" rather than "making love" (51).

If God is Love, then one can hardly "make Love." But we can "be Love," having God within us and giving Him to others. "If the spouses are able to express the being of sexual love without necessarily making love in a genital manner, then they are able to make love in freedom rather than out of necessity" (52).

I have had the privilege of witnessing the deep tender love of a husband for his paralyzed, bedridden wife, and the kind affection of two golden jubilarians, all without genitality. This is being love, the spiritual side of sex, the deeper, conditioned and non-compulsive side.

Mary Joyce calls celibacy an interior marriage, androgyny, if you will, the union of *anima* and *animus*, Eve and Adam, *yin* and *yang*. This is the ancient archetype and the goal of the *eschaton*.

The inclusive love and charity of matrimony extends outside of the immediate family. Mary Joyce remarks, "Love for the being of the universe is the primordial meaning of marriage. In the union of husband and wife, the whole world waits to be reborn" (65).

In this, marriage is cosmological, as prefaced by the archetypal hierogamies. In wedlock there can be an interior presence to each other by a shared love for the world. Thus "marital communion does not need direct intercourse to be a complete and consummating union of the spouses" (66).

Marriage and celibacy lean on each other, and, in a way, include each other, especially if celibacy is considered as an inner marriage. Thus Hindus honor *Shiva*, the celibate proto-yogi ascetic and ardent spouse of *Shakti*. Both marriage and celibacy are within the capacity of most people. This is especially true today, when singles make up such a large part of the adult population.

Matrimony needs independent celibates as paradigms of true sexual freedom, and singles also need an archetypal androgyne. "A person who cannot remain a virgin, cannot marry well. He may have to marry in order not to burn (1 Cor 7:9). But if this is so, he is not marrying well" (140).

Mature spouses should be able to choose continence or not, depending on the circumstances. Both continence and coition can express love. As *Ecclesiastes* says (3:5), there is a time to embrace and a time not to embrace. The mature marriage will not be an exclusive, private affair, but will be open, inclusive, cosmic.

Though many teach that marital intercourse is the central act of matrimony, all acts that husband and wife share are unifying—prayer, work, play, meals, sleep.

More than ever, today there is a need for inclusive love, for being love, rather than making love. So many are unloved and unwanted, for example, babies about to be aborted, abused and runaway children and wives, divorced, widowed, elderly, sick, insane, and prisoners.

"The human community needs and can sustain many and various kinds of husband and wife and other man-woman teams, increasing and filling the earth with a co-creative love" (178).

FAMILY PLANNING

In recent years, many have found the various methods of artificial birth control to be ineffective, unsatisfactory and even dangerous. However, new studies of fertility cycles, plus accurate measurements of temperature and vaginal variances, have given us a natural, accurate and safe method of family planning.[6] Some still fear that continence during the fertile periods may harm the marriage. Yet, as we have seen, continence can also be a sign of love.

What about spontaneity? Some maintain that continent periods destroy the impulsiveness of married love. However, if the central marital act is being love, and not making love, any creative restraint is a part of the love life.

Others feel that continence is as separative as artificial birth control. But rather than being contracoital, it is trans-coital. Of course, tension can arise between the desire for coitus and the need for family planning. Dr. John Marshall remarks,[7]

> The need to express love by coitus cannot always be fulfilled here and now, even though it may, in one way, be more desirable that it should be. . . . If coitus is to serve its true purpose in marriage, it must always be a considerate and responsible act between two fully accepting human beings.

Is it not harmful to postpone an overwhelming desire for sex? For example: some claim that a woman's libido peaks during her fertile period. Dr. Marshall replies, "It need not be psychologically dis-advantageous, for postponement for a short time, when accepted for reasons of love, can enhance subsequent fulfillment."

Coition, then, is not a mechanical instinct, which must be answered here and now, but rather it is a loving choice. "In loving a woman and seeking to serve her through coitus, man must consider and respect her pattern of fertility and infertility in accordance with what he sees to be required by the demands of creative love" (203).

Continence can be an act of love, and natural child spacing can be a safe and reliable way of family planning, so that each child gets the care it needs and the mother can safeguard her strength. "In this way the practice of periodic continence is not a negative thing, but it is a positive instrument used in the work of building a Christian family."[8]

Whereas continence may well be an act of love and consideration, artificial birth control can easily make a woman an instrument of man's pleasure. Restraint can be positive and creative, sublimating sexual love into charity, and so fulfilling the spiritual potential of sexuality. Creative continence can enhance the good of the whole family, and those outside as well, in an ever expanding charity.

AMORIZATION

Teilhard de Chardin calls this evolution from exclusive to inclusive love, amorization, "in which men acquire the faculty of associating together and reacting upon one another no longer purely for the preservation and continuance of the species, but for the creation of a common consciousness."[9]

In this conspiracy of love there is a deepening of self in which there is a coming together of man, hominization. "By a sort of inward turn towards the other, its growth culminates in an act of giving and excentration" (55).

Teilhard sees love evolving towards a collective approach to the divine. Love is motion towards the Omega (God) from the smallest microbe to man, with a gradual growth of interiority, inwardness, consciousness, self-mastery and amorization. From a simple instinct in lower animals, it develops to a high spiritual level in man.

Teilhard agrees with Hinduism and modern psychology that man's principal sex organ is his mind, "that is responsible both for the superior aspects of love and the possibility of mastering his genital reflexes."[10]

Love is social. It takes the radical inwardness of beings and unites them. Beginning in the love of husband and wife, it expands outward. "In amorizing the world, in amorizing society, man is on the march toward the God of love, that Omega Point of supreme convergence" (37).

The dedicated celibate gives up exclusive for inclusive love, or, as the Hindus would say, *kama* for *ahimsa*. Sydney Callahan writes[11] that the Christian celibate "witnesses to the Christian hope and belief in the primacy of community beyond the kinship through exclusive love."

The first vow (yama) of Hindu religious life is ahimsa or inclusive love, to which the following vows of brahmacharya (chastity) and aparigraha (renunciation) are closely allied.

So in Christianity the priest or bishop should be the true spiritual father and the nun (Sanskrit, nana, mama) the true spiritual mother of the Christian community, the family of families.

Their universal parenthood and love is more important today than ever since so many lack parental love due to the breakdown in modern family life.

Moreover, he or she validates the asexual lives of the young, old, sick, bereaved, divorced, paralyzed, imprisoned and lonely, the *anawim*, a large portion of the people of God.

By his or her renunciation of the exclusive one flesh union with a single person, the consecrated celibate is called to open him or herself to the one flesh of all, the total family of God. This is done by imitating God's universal fatherhood, the goal of amorization, but, at the same, time, not forgetting the mutual interdependence of celibacy and wedlock, the interior and exterior marriages.

CHAPTER FIFTEEN

Fill The Earth And Subdue It
(Gn 1:28)

VOCATION AND OCCUPATION

Hinduism sees three main pillars of married life: *artha* (occupation, material prosperity); *kama* (pleasure, including sex); and *dharma* (moral conscience) which keeps the first two on target, namely, man's vocation of *moksha* (liberation or salvation).

Artha includes all the things that man needs for the material comfort of his family: job, money, house, power and security, etc.

All through his life man heads towards *moksha*, guided by *dharma*. But only in the married state, *grhastha*, are *kama* and *artha* important. Here he builds his family and fortune, supporting both the old and the young. But when gray hair comes and he plays with his grandchildren, he retires from work, and *kama* and *artha* wane so that he has more time to spend in the service of others.

Western patterns are parallel, with work a substantial foundation stone in the life of the householder. The Judaeo-Christian tradition is ambivalent about work, for example, the *Book of Genesis* shows God as a worker, creating and forming heaven and earth and mankind.

Far from being an anthropomorphism in God, work rather seems to be a theomorphism in man, for God gave man the mandate to complete His work (Gn 1:26). He purposely left His labor unfinished so that man can carry on where He left off. Yet when Adam and Eve's sin entered the picture, spoiling God's plan, the earth became uncooperative, so that toil and sweat were needed to raise food and provide shelter (Gn 3:17-19).

In His mercy, God gave man a rest day which recapitulates the peace of paradise and anticipates the *parousia*, in which the bliss of sacred time will replace the dead weight of chronology.

Jesus, the Messiah, through His Incarnation, recreates and blesses both matter, and work which perfects matter. He also consecrates labor through His carpentry, which He learned from His father, Joseph.

Some of Jesus' apostles earned their way by fishing, while Paul was an expert tent-maker. He criticized the Thessalonians for stopping their work to await the *parousia*. No work, no food (1 Th 4:11; 2 Th 3:10-12). Works alone are not what Paul wants, but rather work consecrated by faith in Jesus Christ (Gal 5:13; 1 Th 1:3) (Also Jm 1:25).

The Desert Fathers, plus Augustine, John Cassian and Benedict, see work as a remedy for man's laziness and temptations. Work and prayer give a happy, healthy balance to human life. The work ethic was strong in Reformation theology, and some see this as a factor in the Industrial Revolution.

Marx and Engels preached against the exploitation of workers by owners, stressing their rights to the profits from their own labor. Popes from Leo XIII to Pius XI and John Paul II have promoted the dignity of work and the rights and duties of laborers.

Today's job takes about one-half of our waking hours or more, if you include preparation, travel, and actual time in production. Some who equate their occupation with their vocation spend almost all their time promoting their careers, to the neglect of their families.

But, as we have seen, one's occupation is an illusion, especially in a changing and mobile society with automation, computers, depletion of material and energy sources, moving population and a lower birth rate. All of these factors make the job market more and more tenuous. The average worker changes his occupation several times, and his employer even more, over a lifetime of labor.

WORK AND THE FAMILY

Work is a natural right of the head of the family to earn the means necessary to support his loved ones. But work is a means to this end, so that family life should never be subordinated to career, as John Paul II reminds us.[1]

Work is an important influence in the education of the family, helping them to become more human by working for and with each other. "The family is simultaneously a community made possible by work and the first school of work within the home, for every person."

John Paul II sees family and society as historical and social incarnations of the work of past generations. Moreover, our present labor prepares the way for those generations that lie ahead.

This was God's plan in asking man to subdue the earth. Work is for man's benefit, not vice versa, otherwise he would be a slave. In the old farm economy the whole family worked together, from grandparents to children, and marriages were more stable. The coming of industrialization separated the fathers for factory tasks, while most of the mothers remained at home to care for the children. But in modern society, women have moved into the factory and office alongside of the men. With new options and independence opening up for married women, the divorce rate has also climbed.

Today, about 60% of mothers with children under 18 work outside the home. Many of these are single parents or wives whose husbands do not earn enough to support the family.

The "greener pastures" myth has lured some women to outside jobs with a hope of dynamic, creative and self-fulfilling work. But the fact is that most women workers are in boring clerical and service jobs with little chance for advancement. Some find the price of success in the business world too high, and long for children and close family relationships. However, those who have tried to have babies in middle age have run into all kinds of medical and emotional difficulties.

John Paul II feels that the mother's role in society should not be denigrated (19). Children should have proper care, love and affection, "that they may develop into responsible, morally and religiously mature and psychologically stable persons." It is society's duty to see that mothers are free to raise and educate their little ones properly. If this is not done, society and the family are endangered.

This brings up a problem we have mentioned before, namely, society's low view of motherhood in comparison with success in the business or professional worlds. "Just a housewife," is often given in an embarrassed manner in answer to a query about a woman's occupation. What an indictment of our modern society, which tends to look down on motherhood in comparison to more visible and more financially rewarding occupations.

Since most children's mothers work outside the home, this brings up the problem of latch-key kids, who leave school to go home to empty houses. This situation has led to an increase in juvenile crime, drugs and sexual errors. As John Paul writes, where motherhood is neglected, the whole of society suffers.

DIVINIZATION OF LABOR

When the work-oriented Pilgrims came to America, the Indians could not understand why they worked so hard. The Pilgrims, on their side, could not understand why the Indians would not work. The Indians did work for sustenance, but not to acquire private property, and they had faith that the Great Spirit would provide them with enough if they respected His natural gifts.

Why work? To make money? To acquire property? To raise a family? To get security for old age? Routine jobs can be boring, and can lead to alcoholism, high absenteeism and low productivity.

Modern industry has tried to humanize labor with incentives, varied jobs and hours, and by allowing a certain amount of self-determination. Man is ambivalent towards his job. He hates the routine, yet he lives in fear of being laid off. Moreover, his firing or retirement can be a traumatic experience in an occupation-centered society.

There can be a solution to the boredom of the daily job routine by spiritualizing our labor. For example, by integrating our occupation into the overall vocation of man to fill and subdue the earth and continue God's work of creation. God put iron, copper, coal, oil, silicon and aluminum into the ground to be used and developed. He made the soil fertile, and watered it to produce food, but all with man's help.

Luther pointed out that all occupations are equal in God's eyes: farmer, iron worker, clerk, housewife, minister, doctor. All are called by their God-given talents to do their own task in the development of creation.

Teilhard de Chardin has helped modern Christians to see the spirituality of matter as incarnated and sanctified by Christ.[2] For

Teilhard, salvation does not consist in abandoning the world, but rather in building it up to free the spirit hidden within matter. For example, he writes to a businessman, "Because you are doing the best you can, you are forming your own self within the world, and you are helping the world to form itself around you" (36).

Christ divinizes our activities, expanding our energy, helping us to put on Christ, joining our wills with God's *telos*, using matter as He intended. Our intention can divinize our job, giving a soul to our actions in a Christification of work. "No one lifts a finger to do the smallest task unless moved by the conviction that he is contributing infinitesimally (at least indirectly) to the building of something definitive to God's work" (56).

While divine teleology builds up the world according to God's plan, sin, telic decentralization, tears it down.

The final solution to the problem of work is that all endeavor cooperates to complete the world in Christ Jesus. Material reality exists through our souls for God.

In my occupation I use matter to help God subdue the earth and, at the same time, to aid me in my ultimate vocation of salvation and divine union. Christ attains His plenitude in creation, and we help Him to complete His creation—an ongoing process. By my work I coincide with the creative power of God, not merely as His instrument, but rather as His living extension, sharing His love for the end.

Through our job "we complete in ourselves the subject of the divine union and through it again we somehow make to grow in stature the divine term of the one with whom we are united, our Lord, Jesus Christ" (63). As Christ incarnated matter by emptying Himself in order to become man, so we use up our energy and flesh, turning them into material goods and services.

Are work and prayer incompatible? Rather, they are complimentary. If we cooperate in God's *telos*, our work is a prayer. *Laborare est orare.* "By virtue of the creation and still more of the Incarnation, nothing here below is profane, for those who know how to use it" (66).

Our work builds the kingdom of heaven, and heaven draws us through our God-given talents and labors, immersing ourselves in God and His *telos*. We should never attempt any task without first realizing its significance and constructive value in Jesus Christ. It then becomes a thing fulfilling its natural end, linked with the all-embracing work of the Incarnation.

Although many are not conscious of advancing God's kingdom through their work, the Christian artisan divinizes the world in Jesus Christ.

Labor, as *Genesis* tells us, is hard, and matter uncooperative. In this we are engaged in God's struggle to overcome evil in the world. The farmer fights hunger; the tailor, nakedness; the contractor and carpenter, homelessness; the doctor and nurse, sickness. Our setbacks along the way are just steps towards the ultimate victory, for the divine *telos* transfigures our failures.

"Jesus on the cross is the symbol and reality of the immense labor of the centuries which has little by little raised up the created spirit and brought it back to the depths of the divine milieu" (104). Christ brings spiritual power to matter through His Incarnation, a progressive sublimation in Christ Jesus. Matter slowly drifts towards spirit in contemplation, chastity and amorization.

We see the Incarnation especially manifest in the Eucharist. "The sacramental species are formed by the totality of the world, and the duration of the creation is the time needed for its consecration" (125).

There is a continual cycle in the Eucharist, as Simone Weil points out.[3] Thus farmers, viticulturists, bakers, winemakers, and distributors turn their flesh into bread and wine. Christ then changes the bread and wine into His body and blood. Then the workers, consuming the flesh and blood of Christ, return to the fields, vineyard, bakery, winery, etc. and make their Christified flesh into the bread and wine. Of course, parallels could be made with any occupation in which we seek to fulfill Christ's desire to consummate all things in the growth of the Divine Milieu.

In faith we are convinced that "the universe, between the hands of the Creator, still continues to be the clay in which he shapes innumerable possibilities according to his will" (135). Faith consecrates the world, while fidelity communicates with it.

In the *parousia*, the Son of Man will gather all the elements of the universe to Himself. We prepare for this by recognizing "the intimate connection between the victory of Christ and the outcome of the work which our human effort here below is seeking to construct" (152).

The more one perfects nature through his or her work, the more beautiful creation will be, and Christ finds a body worthy of Resurrection. To divinize and not to destroy—to surcreate. As God separated the land and waters, created plants and animals and formed man out of the earth, so we take up matter to form objects that continue God's plan for the universe.

RECREATION

The fatigue and boredom of work are due to the uncooperativeness of matter, and the sweat that God promised Adam, although He also gave man relief in the Sabbath.

The Supreme Workman, God Himself, gave the example of resting on the seventh day after His labor of Creation. So, in Jewish law, man and beast on the Sabbath eve must stop all work for a full day. The housewife cooks the Sabbath meals on Friday in preparation. In a special way she is queen of the Sabbath, spreading peace, rest and happiness in the home.

Why a Sabbath? Man is tired and needs rest, recuperation and recreation of body and soul. The Sabbath is sacred, Yahweh's bride, whom He meets in the temple at midnight. The seventh day is a time apart, *kairos*, sacred time, as opposed to *chronos*, measurable time. Work is tied to chronology: a five-day week, eight-hour day, overtime, etc. The time clock, the inexorable tyrant, must be punched in and out. Time studies attempt to speed up production.

Six days men and women work, preparing for and anticipating the Sabbath rest. The work week gets one ready for the Sabbath, not *vice versa*. The Sabbath is blessed, eternal, recapitulating God's everlasting rest. It is recreation time. Just as God created and then rested, so we alternate creation and recreation. Unfortunately, our modern culture is unable to rest, since it suffers from a restless dis-ease. Stores remain open seven days a week, and weekends are a frenzy of shopping, sports, trips, parties, and yard and household tasks, especially for dual career families.

But the Sabbath really means doing no work, no talk of work, no cooking, no long trips or sports. It is also a time of prayer, of honoring God. And it is a family day, a home day in which the family gathers together to pray, read scriptures, eat, sing, and be happy and at peace with each other. Some say that the stability of the Jewish family over the millennia is due in large part to the strict observance of this family feast of the Sabbath.

Summing up, work is a vital part of married life, for this is the period in which parents help God to fill and subdue the earth. However, one's occupation, like child-raising, is only a temporary phase. Moreover, the former should serve the latter, and not *vice versa*.

If one makes an occupation into a vocation, when layoff time or retirement comes—misery. Indeed, one's occupation should be inspired by the overall vocation to subdue the earth, uniting with God's will and *telos*.

Work can be exclusive, self-seeking, centripetal, for my career advancement, to make as much money as possible, acquire as many material possessions as I desire, to maintain a predetermined standard of living, based on peer pressure or "keeping up with the Joneses." Or, the job can be inclusive other-serving. Thus I use my God-given skills to support my family and to help improve the earth and serve others, whether I am a garbage collector, janitor, housewife, policeman, farmer, auto worker, doctor, nurse, lawyer, teacher, salesperson, etc.

The smallest, dullest jobs such as turning bolts on an assembly line sweeping the floor, contribute to our fellow man and to God's overall plan. There can be an incarnational aspect in all of our work. God calls us to salvation and divine union in our vocation, but He leads us to our occupation through the skills that He gives us. Sometimes, because of the economy and job market, we are forced into a job not compatible with God's gifts. This is where some of the misery promised to Adam crops up, but perhaps our talents can be channeled into a hobby.

In married life, work and family are two interlocking foundation stones, both God-given, spiritualized by the Incarnation and aided by grace to build up the earth and the Mystical Body of Christ.

In the last stage of life, children leave home, occupation ceases, and the vocation to divine union once again reasserts itself, pointing us towards eternal life, as earthly goals fade into the background.

CHAPTER SIXTEEN

My Son, Take Care Of Your Father When He Is Old (Si 3:12)

Traditionally, romantic literature concentrates on young lovers, from the *Greatest Song* of Solomon to the medieval troubadours and modern love stories. But young lovers become old lovers.

Our society is gradually getting older because of the lower birth rate and longer lifespans. By the year 2000, 16% of the population will be over 65, and Social Security and pension fund administrators are worried. As we have seen, excessive birth limitation has been an important factor in the disintegration of civilizations in the past. It could happen again.

When does old age come? Bodily deterioration has been observed even in the young. Is 50 old, or 60, or 70? A lot depends on one's heredity. Teens see their fiftyish parents as ancient. "What did they do in olden times?" Insurance companies are hard-nosed about signing up older people.

Modern culture has worshipped youth. In fact, rarely is an older person asked to appear as an advertising model, except for laxatives or denture cream. There is nothing sadder than an older person trying to recapture lost youth through cosmetic surgery, sexual escapades, etc. Whatever old age is, the clock can never be turned back.

EMPTY NEST

Probably the first milestone of advancing age is the death of one's parents. You are next. Then the departure of the youngest child for college can be traumatic, with the large home, empty rooms, rusting swings, deflated basketballs, etc. Surely there are mixed feelings. There is relief from the responsibilities of parenthood, but now husband and wife must face long years together. Marital tension and even divorce surface at this time, especially if they have kept together for the sake of the children.

But the youngsters are temporary gifts of God, placed under the trusteeship of the mother and father for 20 years or so out of a total of 75 years. Child-raising is the privilege and duty of the middle phase of life, giving the offspring roots and wings.

In later middle years, when child-rearing is past, sex desires wane, and menopause and male climacteric come, with personality and endocrinal changes. Sometimes the couple will have unequal desires in later years, bringing tension, unhappiness, and perhaps infidelity. Here it takes understanding and patience on the part of both spouses.

In a sex-conscious society, when sexual enjoyment wanes, one is apt to feel frustrated, deprived and depressed. But if sex is seen as a good but temporary gift of God, its diminishment in old age should be accepted as being as normal as its gradual evolution in youth.

Diminishment of the physical side of sex means that nature feels that one is too old to be conceiving and raising children. It is a natural devolution for the good of the species. Here the child orientation of sex is learned from nature's school. The deeper meaning of spiritual love and charity asserts itself more strongly as the bodily urges lessen.

FILIAL PIETY

After the children have flown the nest, parents begin to see old age creeping up on the horizon. Often it is a very thoughtful time, for they see their own parents failing and dependent. They know that if they treat their parents well, their children will have a good model to follow when they themselves reach the age of sickness and debility.

We have talked much of parents' obligations towards their children. But what do their offspring owe mom and dad? Many cultures teach filial piety towards their elders, from the Confucian ethic to the Hindu *sannyasis*. The fourth commandment says: "Honor your father and mother," and enjoy a long life.

Ben Sira (Si 3:1-18) teaches that one who reveres his father, atones for his own sins. Moreover, he will be given good progeny, and the Lord will hear his prayers and grant him a happy and extended time on earth. God blesses those who respect their father and mother. "Glory not in your father's shame." For this is also a disgrace for his children.

"My son, take care of your father when he is old, grieve him not as long as he lives." Even if he is cantankerous and mentally ill, be kind to him. God will remember those who are good to their parents, and will bless them and forgive their sins. But his wrath will fall upon those who despise their fathers and mothers.

Children owe their ancestors and parents filial piety, obedience and respect. In China, filial reverence was a pillar of clan society, with violations severely punished. For example, the ancestors were often consulted in family decisions and celebrations. They were offered food and entertainment. Moreover, the ancestral tablets adorned every home in an honored place. Modern Marxism tried to destroy this deference to the olders. However, the Cultural Revolution was soon rejected for a return to respect for the ancients. There is a close relationship between honoring the dead ancestors and the living elderly. If we ignore one, we will forget the other, since they are links in the same family chain.

Once the extended family of clan society disappeared, in favor of the small nuclear household of urban industrial society, elderly grandparents and parents, far from being respected as patriarchs and matriarchs, become burdens on society.

It is true that many elders value their independence. And it is a wrenching decision to send mom or dad to a nursing home, for their children see the same fate awaiting themselves. Many elderly today live in bare apartments in unsafe sections of the city, with inflation eating up their tiny pensions, with few visitors and silent phones. When we visit nursing homes and extended care facilities, we see long rows of patients in wheel chairs, staring into space. Where are their children?

Some are busy with dual careers, climbing the ladder of success and prosperity. Others are totally wrapped up in their own offspring: orthodontist appointments, Little League games, ballet lessons, etc. The important grandparent-grandchild relationship is missing in many homes, a relationship beneficial to all three generations.

RETIREMENT

With the compulsory retirement age raised, more are staying on the job to fight off the roads of inflation. However, young workers resent the oldsters hanging on to block their promotions, or even force their layoffs due to the rules of seniority.

We mentioned the ambivalence about work. I can't stand it, yet once laid off, I miss it badly. In our occupation-centered society, retirement or layoff can be traumatic, leaving one feeling deprived, stripped of meaning, worthless. However, if the overall vocation of life to divine union is seen, then the retirement years can be viewed as the Sabbath of Sabbaths.

As the weekly Sabbath is a day of prayer, peace, and rest, the very purpose of the other six days, so the Sabbath of life should be a time of tranquility, contemplation and divine union, the goal of our working days and a prelude to eternal life.

WIDOWHOOD

Perhaps the greatest illusion of marriage is that of "growing old together." Since men often marry younger women, and women tend to live longer, widows have always been a rather large segment of society.

One of the earliest fights in the Church was the protest that the Hebrew widows were favored over those of Greek-speaking Jews. Paul advises the widows of his communities to serve as continent grandmothers to the Christian churches. Many wealthy widows became deaconesses serving the poor, and some started convents in their homes. Paula and Melania come to mind.

About one-sixth of all women over 21 are widows, and 70% of women over 65 are single. However, most old husbands are not alone, again because men marry younger women and usually predecease their wives. "Widow" is from the Sanskrit, vidh, meaning "gracious, poor."

Since people tend to identify wives with their husbands, when the male spouse dies, the widow is cut off from former married friends. Single women are generally not welcome in coupled society. Sometimes they are seen as a threat, and other times they just do not fit into the social world of the married.

Now that the extended family is a thing of the past, many widows are holed up in large homes or tiny apartments, with withering pensions and few social contacts. Psychiatrists recognize widowhood as one of the most traumatic shocks of life. For example, it is not unusual for bereavement to kill the surviving spouse among elderly couples.

Stress can be measured in life change units, and 200 of these are about all one can handle.[1] The death of a spouse (100) generally tips off a crescendo of shocks: financial problems (38), mortgage (31), change in living conditions (25), alteration of personal habits (24), social changes (16), poor eating habits (15), children leaving home (29), another death in the family (63). These stresses easily pile up, till, one is forced into some type of nervous bankruptcy for his or her system to survive.

What about sex? Paul advises widows to live chastely, giving good example to the younger women. But if a youthful widow feels that she must marry, she may do so. Sexual tension in a highly stimulating atmosphere can be dangerous for a widow. There is always a lingering doubt, a subconscious loyalty to her dead husband.

Intercourse with old family friends is most unsatisfactory for both parties, and usually ends up destroying the friendship. Liaisons with younger partners are no more satisfying. Moreover, it is clear that the widow's sex life is not child-oriented, as that of a mother should be.

Actually few widows (10%) remarry, so widowhood is the final stage of life for most women. If they overidentify with the temporary marital stage of their lives, or are too dependent on their husbands, there can be a rough adjustment when their spouse dies.

Here an overall view of life's vocation to divine union may help. In early Christianity, the widows gathered together to pray, support each other and help the community.

Even today there is a sisterhood of lonely single women, consoling newly bereaved members of society. Go to any Catholic church for early Mass, and you will see many widows assembled for prayer, for their widowhood brings their vocation to divine union to the fore. Now there is only One who cares for them. Not children or relatives or former employers, but only their heavenly Father whom they will soon worship for all eternity in company with their dear husbands.

DIVINIZATION OF DIMINISHMENTS

Old age is a diminishment, retirement is a diminishment, children leaving home are diminishments, the death of a spouse is a diminishment, ill health is a diminishment.

Teilhard de Chardin sees suffering and diminishment as a part of cosmic evolution.[2] Pain and passivities wake us up, turning us away from lower delights towards things that endure. They expiate life's errors, spiritualize and purify.

While youth lives in the future in hope, ambition and illusion, old age often looks back, discouraged and depressed, on frustrated hopes and emphemeral works. We made mistakes, committed sins, had breakdowns. Our efforts seem useless and our sufferings barren.

But Christ leads us in the primacy of humility and suffering. His kingdom makes its progress by "the way of relinquishment, of blood and tears, the way of the cross." It is through a painful metamorphosis, life through death, that the divine cosmos germinates from the ruins of the old earth (53).

We are caught between heaven's design and earth's ambition. But the cross is the sign of victory of duty over attraction, spirit over senses, good over evil. We have to resign ourselves, especially in old age, to being useless and ineffective. Hosts of failures are the price of the success of God's overall plan for the cosmos.

The more complex a creature is, the more open to suffering and diminishment, and a man is the most complex creature of all. But Christ gathers all the suffering of the world to Himself on the cross as cosmic suffering. Without Christ, suffering and sin would become the earth's "slagheap." The cross makes this a treasure. "There is a wonderful compensation by which physical evil, is humbly accepted, conquers moral evil" (68).

Suffering is a sacrament, the mysterious union between the faithful soul and the suffering Christ. When the soul reaches the end of its suffering, it knows that its most effective and peaceful work is to gather the sufferings of the world, soothe them and offer them to God.

We feel pain when our being is diminished. But, "Christ gathers up for the life of tomorrow our mystified ambitions, our inadequate

understandings, our uncompleted and clumsy, but sincere endeavors
. . ."3

Our soul has parasitic branches that reach out for evil. It has to be
purified before it can join God. It must "suffer a type of decomposition
and carry within itself the pain of the multitude." The grain of wheat
must die before it can sprout, blossom and bear fruit.

Though material things diminish, there is no unalleviated sadness,
but rather joy in the disappointment and collapse of earthly supports.
You alone are stable.4 Some day everything temporal will collapse, and
then God will raise up from the ruins.

The disappointments and the chains of life are blessed. "Blessed
. . . the inexorable bondage of time that goes too slowly and frets our
impatience, of time that goes too quickly and ages us, of time that
never stops and never returns." Blessed be death and the falling back
into cosmic forces (131).

The value of old age, diminishment, bereavement, suffering and
death, is that they are involuntary. Suffering gradually dissolves our
being, drop by drop, and replaces it with God. Though loving life, we
desire death, the destruction of our ego and absorption into Christ.

Christ is the boundless abyss in which we can relax from our woes.
"By growing less in *Christo Jesu* those who mortify themselves, who
suffer and grow old with patience, cross the critical threshold at which
death is turned into life."

In his *Divine Milieu*,5 Teilhard notes that our passivities comprise
about half of our existence, and increase as we age and our options are
closed off. Passivities are things done to us. We can only control things
in our lives in a very limited way. We suffer diminishments: frustration, disease, shock, disappointment, severances. All our diminutions
merge in death, which we should overcome by finding God in it (61).

In God's plan for the world, there must be diminishments before
the final victory, as soldiers die for lasting peace. God uses our
sufferings to mold us and make our losses into points of contact with
Himself. Our mini deaths are just foretastes of the final moment when
we will leap out of ourselves and into his arms.

We cannot win our fight against death, but Christ can win it,
transforming death into life. "God . . . must make room for himself,

hollowing us out and emptying us if he is finally to penetrate us" (68). He has to break us in order to remold us, and death completes our self-emptying. Our vocation is divine union and the pathway is through diminishment.

> Grant . . . that I may recognize you under the species of each alien and hostile force that seems bent on destroying and uprooting me: illness, old age, bereavement, losing hold. You are painfully parting the fibers of my being in order to penetrate to the very marrow of my substance and bear me away within myself.

By losing myself and being assimilated into Christ my death is a communion.

We accept suffering in faith, though still struggling against it. A human failure, but a divine success. Suffering seems to be so useless for the ill, the lonely and aged, while the world is filled with activity, work, play, sex, etc.[6]

Teilhard compares the world to a large tree in which some branches are twisted and dead, flowers wilted, fruit rotten, reflecting its long fight against wind, ice, snow, cold, disease, birds, bugs, etc. On the human level, labor, pain, failure are necessary parts of the cosmic scene. The progress of the world can only take place at the expense of failure and hurt, so suffering and pain are not useless. Rather, their victims "are simply paying for the forward march and triumph of all. They are casualties fallen on the field of honor" (50).

Like the tree, the Mystical Body of Christ is comprised of different organs and functions. Some parts are destined to help spiritualize and to sublimate themselves for progress and conquest. The contemplatives, the suffering, and the aged are driven out to themselves to help raise the world to a higher level, but this does not mean giving up. No, the sick and aged man or woman should cooperate in the transformation of human suffering.

> The world would leap high towards God if all the sick together were to turn their pain into a common desire that the kingdom of God should come to rapid frustration through the conquest and organization of the earth (51).

As old age creeps up on Teilhard, he becomes more aware of his own diminishments. "Stay with us Lord, for it is towards evening " (Lk 24:29). We should use the shadows, depressions, frustrations, enfeeblements and loneliness of later life. We have no more earthly horizons, but Christ, the Omega, gives hope, for old age comes from him and leads to him, Alpha and Omega.[7]

"Desperately, Lord Jesus, I commit to your care my last active years and my death. Do not let them impair or spoil the work I have so dreamed of achieving for you" (100).

Diminishment is a part of life, but it has a purpose in God's plan. When children are raised, job relinquished, bereavement comes and health fails, God is emptying us so that He can fill us up with Himself.

Elderly people have made a positive contribution toward subduing the earth and filling out the Mystical Body with their well-raised children. Now through their passivities they play an equally important role in the evolution towards divine union.

Yet their children should support their parents in their diminishments, helping them along the road to eternal life. And as Ben Sira says, God will bless them and forgive their sins.

CHAPTER SEVENTEEN

Marriage As Theomorphy

HIEROGAMY

The history of man is the history of the gods. Does man model his deities on himself, or is his human ideal based on the divine archetype? Do the marriages of the gods imitate human matrimony, or does man emulate the hierogamy?

Wherever we look, we see the marriages of the gods. Primitive peoples celebrated the wedding of father sky and mother earth. While the sky god inseminates his spouse with his fertile rain, she yearns for heaven with her misty breath.

Hinduism honors the marriages of *Purusha* and *Prakriti*, *Shiva* and *Shakti*, the love of *Krishna* and *Radha* and many others. Greece and Rome has married gods who did not always measure up to the ideal family. Judaism blessed the union of Yahweh and Israel, or Yahweh and his *Shekhinah*, while Christianity idealized the wedding of Christ with His people. Whereas Christianity worshipped the archetypal family of Father, Son and Holy Spirit, the medieval Jewish Kabbalists honored a divine quaternity of Father, Mother, Son and Daughter.

In all cultures, the union of husband and wife recapitulates the bonding of the gods. It commemorates the cosmic joining of heaven and earth, *yang* and *yin*. While the Jews relive the wedlock of Yahweh and Israel, or the King and his *Shekhinah* in marital coitus, Christians join in a special way in the nuptials of the Messiah King and His Church.

Mystics, from Gregory of Nyssa to Bernard and Teresa, see the union of the individual soul with God as a paradigm of the marriage of husband and wife, interior and exterior marriage.

The Trinity is the first family of Christianity, Father, Son and Spirit. In Jewish tradition, the *Shekhinah*, or Holy Spirit, is the mother figure and spouse of Yahweh. In Christianity the same Spirit unites with Mary, Yahweh's chosen one, in the conception of Jesus.

The Christian family is modeled on the divine archetype. Yahweh, from whose hand comes all creation, is the image of procreation, father and mother, "Male and female he created them."

God's Son, obedient to His Father, blessed marriage through His Incarnation, and, by His faithful union with His Church, is the type of fidelity between husband and wife. Moreover, in His obedience to Mary and Joseph, He teaches humility and respect to children of the Christian family.

The Holy Spirit is the Love of the Father and the Son. In Jewish tradition, the *Shekhinah* is represented in the home by the mother of the family, and accompanies her husband on trips. Moreover, she lies between husband and wife in the marriage bed.

In the Christian parallel, as the Holy Spirit binds Father and Son in love, so also this Sanctifier unites the Messiah King and His people. And as the soul of the Church, the Holy Spirit joins the Head to the Body and blesses the union of husband and wife.

The Christian couple have a divine mandate to build up the Mystical Body of Christ. Just as God gave Adam and Eve the command to fill the earth and subdue it, so the Christian pair must fill out the Body of Christ, and work the earth to bring it to fulfillment in Christ.

As in the human body new cells grow to insure life and health, so in the Mystical Body, husband and wife fuse to form new life-giving cells to expand the union of Christ and His Church, and strengthen it as well.

Man and wife participate in God's plan, for male and female he created them. They procreate for God, imitating the faithfulness of His Son. And the Spirit of God binds them together in sacramental love. Wherever two are gathered in His name, His Spirit is present. So the trinity of marriage; husband and wife and Christ's Spirit, three in one as the archetypal family is three in one. Lover, beloved and Love, as John and Augustine teach.

How can the Christian family emulate the Trinity in its daily life? Its vocation, as we have seen, is divine union. This is religion (Sanskrit, *yoga*), binding the household to God. In this the Christian home should be an *ecclesiola*, a domestic church. As we have seen, the Christian religion started out as a home-centered worship, like its Jewish predecessor. Through the millennia, partially modeling itself on the Roman government and cult, Christianity focused more on the basilica, cathedral and parish church.

In many cultures, although there are temples and shrines, the home remains the essential church where daily prayers and sacrifices are offered, and where the divine presence is welcomed in special ceremonies.

For example, the Hindus have a *puja* or prayer room with a small shrine, where the father of the family leads the home liturgies. China and Japan have ancestral tablets or sanctuaries where petitions and offerings are made, uniting the living and the dead.

Judaism is essentially a home religion with a beautiful liturgy welcoming the Sabbath bride, honoring the mother of the family and inaugurating the family day of peace and prayers. Also, *Rosh Hashanah, Yom Kippur, Chanukah*, Passover, Weeks, Booths, etc. are celebrated in the home. Each meal is blessed by *berakoth*, and the *Shema, Tephillah* and *Torah* are good friends. Early Christian families kept many of these family liturgies.

What can the Christian family of today do to make its *ecclesiola* a reality? The parents must teach by example, family prayer, Bible reading, reception of the sacraments, grace before meals, home celebrations for Thanksgiving, Advent, Christmas, Lent, Easter, etc.

Too many of our feasts have become merely secular holidays, with decorations, cocktails, big meals, presents and visits, with little thought of the family vocation to divine union.

Probably a central reason for the breakup of marriage today is the fracturing of the binding (religion) of the family to God. If man and woman are so alienated from God that their marriage no longer reflects the hierogamy, they are separating their domestic church from Christ, and its very existence is in peril.

A recent study of the American family corroborates this.[1] It showed that successful, happy families are united to God through an all-penetrating religion. The broken households made no mention of the faith, but only squabbling over money, property and visiting rights.

How can Christ be an honored guest in a Christian home, if His picture is never displayed, if He is never addressed? How can He be appreciated if His gifts are thanklessly received? How can He be a close friend, if He is never introduced to the children?

Today there is an explosion of mixed marriages. Unfortunately, in many of these one or both spouses have no belief at all. This makes any religious foundation in the home all but impossible. Sometimes they say that they will let the children decide what religion they will join when they become of age. If the important learning years have gone by without any religious teaching, how can they possibly decide? Certainly, the parents would not let their youngsters decide on important issues such as health, nutrition, education, etc. But when it comes to religion, they let them do whatever they want, which usually means to continue the indifference to God which the parents have taught by their example through the formative years.

EPILOGUE

We have seen the evolution of marriage from primordial monogamy, to environmentally conditioned polygamy, to its degradation in adultery, fornication, prostitution and easy divorce in more complex societies.

Judaism tells the story of man's monogamous beginnings in Adam and Eve. Yet starting with our first parents who are really Every Man and Every Woman, we are weak and prone to sin, the *Yetzer ha Ra*. But God gave remedies in matrimony and the *Torah*, His personal marriage contract with His Bride, Israel.

Jewish marriage was to imitate His loving and forgiving union with Israel. The prophets taught the meaning of marital fidelity, and the wisdom sayings and the *Talmud* guard the sanctity of wedlock despite widespread divorce. By medieval times, mystics see the union of the Messiah King with his *Shekhinah* Queen as the paradigm of Jewish marriage.

Jesus teaches a stricter view of matrimony, a return to the archetypal monogamy of Adam and Eve. Paul wrote that Christian nuptials should celebrate the Messiah's love for his people. The husband should sacrifice himself for his wife as the Messiah did for His followers. And the wife should honor and obey her spouse as the Church reveres her Head.

This monogamous tradition carries on in the Church's magisterium. Two in one flesh and Augustine's threefold good. Augustine answered the Manichees, who tried to degrade marriage, by asserting that matrimony is good, holy and blessed by God. Neither matter nor sex nor wedlock is unholy, for all are created in the image of God.

There is a certain ambivalence in the nuptial union between the monogamous archetype and man's weak nature. As the *Torah* and the *Talmud* helped straighten out the errant *yetzer* in Judaism, so the *Gospels*, Church law, penitentials and pastoral directives tried to hold the line in Christianity.

Though some might deny that marriage is a sacrament, few would question that it is sacred. It has always been linked with the nuptials of the gods. Christianity's model of the marriage of the Messiah to His people brings the grace of Christ to the Church through the union of husband and wife who generate new members of Christ's Body.

Unless marriage is a permanent source of grace in better or worse times, it is difficult to see how the spouses can weather the storms, especially today with increased promiscuity and divorce.

Ever since Adam and Eve, matrimony has been a deep personal friendship with mutual support, and to be secure it has to have a guarantee of permanence.

God told our first parents to fill the earth. Thus the two in one flesh become the one flesh of the child, which requires the stability of twenty years of guidance, example, education and support.

God also told Adam and Eve to subdue the earth. So, work is a necessary part of married life, bringing material blessings of food, shelter, clothing, education and recreation. But the job must always be a means to the end, rather than a goal in itself.

Where does the individual marriage fit into the overall plan of the kingdom? Two cells of Christ's Body unite to produce more living cells. This diffusive, centrifugal love should not stop with the nuclear family, but spread outside to the whole Body.

Good diffuses itself, as does love. It is not enough for husband and wife just to love each other. No, they must also procreate, for their love is of its very nature expressive.

When the children leave home, retirement comes, and the body grows weak, the children owe their parents the care which they gave them in their helpless days. Now the son or daughter becomes the parent.

The diminishments of old age, bereavement, ill health, and a feeling of uselessness and loneliness, can lead to a closer union with the crucified God. Moreover, these passivities can contribute to the overall good of Christ's Body.

There are many threats to marriage today including: the sexual revolution, dual careers, lack of religious ties, longer lives, boredom and attempts to preserve youth with younger partners.

In the last analysis it is the old tension between the ideal monogamy and weak human nature. Unless we take advantage of all the spiritual helps available, we will forget the archetype. Unless we are led by God's Spirit, and trust in His providence and the grace promised to us in holy matrimony, sanctity, fidelity and children can never unite in one holy communion.

Footnotes

Prologue

1. See A. Moffett, *"The American Family is Alive and Well,"* Saturday Evening Post, March, 1981, pp. 14-16.

PART I: YESTERDAY

Chapter 1   THE EVOLUTION OF MARRIAGE

1. R. Mohr, *"The Primitive Races,"* in Sex-Love-Marriage, F. von Hornstein and H. Faller, eds, New York, Harper and Row, 1964, p. 249.
2. J. Thiel, *"The Institution of Marriage*: an Anthropological Perspective," in The Future of Marriage As Institution, ed., F. Bockle, New York, Harper and Row, 1970, pp.13-24.
3. See J. Dennis, The Gbandes, A People of the Liberian Hinterlands, Chicago, Nelson-Hall, 1972, p. 84.
4. See V. W. von Hagen, Aztec, Man And Tribe, New York, Mentor, 1958, pp. 63-66.
5. See H. Driver, Indians of North America, Chicago, Chicago University Press, 1965, p. 267.
6. *"The Primitive Races,"* p. 255.
7. See Chiu-Chen Wang Liu, The Traditional Chinese Clan Rules, Locust Valley, N.Y., Augustine, 1959, p.78.
8. *Vatsyayana*, Kama Sutra, tr. R. Burton and F. Arbuthnot, New York, Capricorn, 1963.
9. Laws Of Manu 8/226, 227, Hindu Polity, *Ludhiana, Kalyani*, 1972.

Chapter 2   "IT IS NOT GOOD THAT MAN SHOULD BE ALONE" (Gen 2:18)

1. See R. de Vaux, Ancient Israel, New York, McGraw-Hill, 1961, pp. 19-23.
2. See S. Rosenberg, Judaism, Glen Rock, Paulist Press, 1966, p. 116.
3. See J. Mohler, Dimensions of Love, Garden City, Doubleday, 1975, pp. 192-211.
4. B. Patai, The Hebrew Goddess, New York, KTAV, 1967, p. 263.

Chapter 3   "FROM THE BEGINNING IT WAS NOT SO" (Mt 19:8)

1. See R. Batey, New Testament Nuptial Imagery, Leiden, Brill, 1971, p. 15.
2. See also J. Mohler, Origin and Evolution Of The Priesthood, New York, Alba House, 1969, chapter 2.

Chapter 4   "A COMMUNITY OF HUMAN AND DIVINE LAW" (Modestinus, D 23:2-1)

1. See O. Kiefer, Sexual Life In Ancient Rome, London, Routledge and Kegan Paul 1950, p. 8
2. See A. Berger, Encyclopedic Dictionary Of Roman Law, Philadelphia, American Philosophical Society 1953, New Series, 43, pt. 2.
3. See K. Ritzer, *"Secular Law and the Western Church's Concept of Marriage,"* in The Future of Marriage As Institution, p. 68.
4. See N. van der Wal, *"Secular Law and the Eastern Church's Concept of Marriage,"* in The Future of Marriage As Institution, pp. 76-82.
5. See L. du Chesne, Christian Worship, Its Origin and Evolution, London SPCK, 1949, pp. 433-34.

Chapter 5   "DEAREST COMPANION IN THE SERVICE OF THE LORD" (Tertullian to His Wife)
1. See W. Dooley, Marriage According To St. Ambrose, Washington, CUA Press, 1948 (D).
2. Confessions, tr. J. Ryan, Garden City, Doubleday, 1960.
Chapter 6   "THE GREATEST FRIENDSHIP" (Thomas Aquinas, Summa Contra Gentiles, 3:123-6).
1. The Art Of Courtly Love, New York, Columbia U. Press, 1941.
2. See J. d'Auvillier, Le Marriage Dans Le Droit Classique De L'Eglise. Gratian (1140)—Clement V (1314), Paris, Sirey, 1933, p. 6. This section owes much to d'Auvillier's fine research.
3. Liber IV Sententiarum, De Sacramentis, Florence, 1949.
4. Works of Bonaventure, Vol. 2, Paterson, N.J., St. Anthony Guild Press, 1963.
5. On the Truth Of The Catholic Faith, Garden City, Doubleday, 1956.
6. Summa Theologica, Madrid, BAC, 1962.
7. Commentary On The Pseudo-Economics Of Aristotle, See F. Parmisiano, "Love and Marriage in the Middle Ages," New Blackfriars, Vol. 50 (1969), pp. 599-623
Chapter 7   "A TRULY NOBLE, IMPORTANT AND BLESSED CONDITION," (Martin Luther, On the Estate of Marriage, 13)
1. See G. Wingren, Luther On Vocation, tr. C. Rasmussen, Philadelphia, Muhlenberg, 1957, p. 2.
2. Book Of Concord, tr. T. Tappert et al, Philadelphia, Fortress, 1959.
3. The Reformation Of The Sixteenth Century, Boston, Beacon, 1952, p. 46.
4. Canones Et Decreta Concilii Tridentini, Ratisbon, Manz, 1866, Sessio, 24, pp. 135-143.
Chapter 8   "A SCHOOL OF CHRISTIAN CHARITY" (John Paul II, 10:12-18, 6)
1. Papal Teaching, Matrimony, Benedictine Monks of Solesmes, tr., M. Byrnes, Boston, Daughters of St. Paul, 1963, p. 26 (PTM).
2. Casti Connubii (1939), Five Great Encyclicals, New York, Paulist Press, 1939, pp. 77-117.
3. The Pope Speaks, Teachings of Pius XII, M. Chinigo, ed., New York, Pantheon, 1957, pp. 70-75.
4. Documents Of Vatican II, New York, Guild Press, 1966, W. Abbott, ed.
5. Boston, St. Paul Editions, 1968.

PART TWO: TODAY

Chapter 9   "IF A MAN MEETS A VIRGIN, WHO IS NOT BETROTHED" (Dt 22:28).
1. H. Sullivan, The Interpersonal Theory Of Psychiatry, New York, Norton, 1953, p. 260.
2. A. Guindon, The Sexual Language, Ottawa, University of Ottawa Press, 1977, p. 230.
3. S. Freud, "On the Universal Tendancy to Debasement in the Sphere of Love," 1912.
4. R. May (Freedom And Destiny, N.Y. 1981) and C. Lash (The Culture of Narcissism, N.Y. 1980) have written well of the psychological dangers of sex without commitment.
Chapter 10   "GOD BLESSED THEM" (Gen 1:28)
1. The Church And Sacraments, New York, Herder and Herder, 1963, p. 107.
2. See "Christological Theses on the Sacrament of Marriage," G. Martelet, ORIGINS, 9/14/78, Vol. 8, No. 13, p. 202.
3. "Marriage as a Sacrament," in The Future Of Marriage As An Institution, p. 103.
4. IBID p. 108.
5. See L. Gerke, Christian Marriage, A Permanent Sacrament, Washington, CUA Press, 1965, p. 1, (G).
6. Marriage, London, 1942, p. 52.

Chapter 11 "WHAT GOD HAS JOINED" (Mt 19:6).
1. See F. Engels, The Origin Of The Family, New York, International Publishing Co., 1884.
2. Eros And Civilization, Boston, Beacon, 1955.
3. *"Monogamy as a Modern Problem,"* Sex-Love-Marriage, pp. 109-119.
4. IBID, p. 114.
5. IBID, p. 119.
6. Man And Woman, Chicago, Franciscan Herald Press, 1965, p. 12.
7. Origins, 9/14/78, p. 12.
8. One Flesh, Bramcotte Notts, Grove Books, n.d., p.6.
9. See B. Greene, *"A Clinical Approach to Marriage Problems,"* Ann Landers Encyclopedia, New York, Doubleday, 1978, and N. Lubenz, *"Why Some Husbands Stay Faithful,"* Reader's Digest, Oct., 1977, pp. 98-101, also the Hite Reports.

Chapter 12 "BE FERTILE AND MULTIPLY" (Gen 1:28)
1. D. von Hildebrand, Man And Woman, p. 94.
2. One Flesh, p. 4.
3. See J. Mohler, The Heresy Of Monasticism, New York, Alba House, 1970.
4. "Monogamy," p. 115.
5. C. Kindregan, Theology of Marriage, Milwaukee, Bruce, 1967, p. 114.
6. Newsweek, 6/22/81, p. 92.
7. See Dr. J. Zurcher, "Profanation of Marriage," in Sex-Love-Marriage, p. 104.
8. A Theology of Marriage, p. 116.
9. "Reflections, The Fate of the Earth, II, The Second Death," NEW YORKER, 2/8/82, pp. 90-92.

Chapter 13 "HE WHO DISCIPLINES HIS SON WILL BENEFIT FROM HIM" (Sir 30:2)
1. Newsweek, 5/11/81, p. 19.
2. *"The Professional Man and His Family; Areas of Conflict,"* in At The Edge Of Hope, H. Butt, ed., New York, Seabury, 1978, pp. 162-168.
3. See J. Mohler, The School Of Jesus, New York, Alba House, 1972.

Chapter 14 EXCLUSIVE AND INCLUSIVE LOVE
1. See J. Mohler, Sexual Sublimation And The Sacred, Cleveland, John Carroll University, 1978, pp. 182-195.
2. N. Heckmann, *"Sex Doesn't Determine a Happy Marriage,"* The Cleveland Press, 11/9/81, p. B10.
3. The New Celibacy, Why More Men and Women are Abstaining from Sex, and Enjoying it More, New York, McGraw-Hill, 1980, p. 128.
4. See L. Suenens, Love And Control, Westminster, Newman Press, 1961, p. 81.
5. New Dynamics In Sexual Love, A Revolutionary Approach to Marriage and Celibacy, Collegeville, St. John's University Press, 1970.
6. See J. Billings, Natural Family Planning, Collegeville, Liturgical Press, 1975.
7. Catholics, Marriage and Contraception, Baltimore Helicon, 1965, p. 151.
8. J. Marshall, The Infertile Period, Baltimore, Helicon, 1967, p. 104.
9. The Future Of Man, New York, Harper and Row, 1964, p. 54.
10. P. Chauchard, Teilhard De Chardin On Love And Suffering, New York, Paulist Press 1966, p. 25.
11. Beyond Birth Control, New York, Sheed and Ward, 1968, p. 85.

Chapter 15 "FILL THE EARTH AND SUBDUE IT" (Gen 1:28)
1. On Human Work, 9/15/81, Origins, 9/24/81, p. 232.

2. The Divine Milieu, New York, Harper and Row, 1960, p. 22.
3. First And Last Notebooks, London, Oxford University Press, 1970, p. 96.

Chapter 16 "MY SON, TAKE CARE OF YOUR FATHER WHEN HE IS OLD" (Sir 3:12)
1. See L. Caine, Widow, New York, Morrow, 1975, pp. 80-81.
2. "Cosmic Life," (2/24/16) in Writings In Time Of War, New York, Harper and Row, 1967, p. 43. See also J. Mohler, The Sacrament of Suffering, Notre Dame, Fides/Claretian Press, 1979, ch. 5.
3. "Struggles Against the Multitude," (1917) Writings In Time Of War, p. 111.
4. "Mystical Milieu," (1917), Writings In Time Of War, pp. 126-127.
5. New York, Harper and Row, 1960, pp. 51ff.
6. In Trait D'Union, 1933, quoted in Human Energy, New York, Harcourt, 1969, pp. 48-89.
7. "Retreat Notes, 1944-1945" in Hymn Of The Universe, New York, Harper and Row, 1965, pp. 98-100.

Chapter 17 MARRIAGE AS THEOMORPHY
1. "The American Family, an Endangered Species?" E. Newman and B. Rollin, NBC-TV, 1/2/79.

A Selected Bibliography

Andreas Capellanus, *The Art Of Courtly Love*, New York: Columbia University Press, 1941.

Augustine, *The Good Of Marriage, Marriage And Concupiscence, Continence*, (FOC), *Adulterous Marriages* (PL).

Auvillier, J., d', *Le Marriage Dans Le Droit Classique De L'Eglise* (1140-1314), Paris: Sirey, 1933.

Bailey, D.S., *Sexual Relation In Christian Thought*, New York: Harper and Brothers, 1959.

Batey, R., *New Testament Nuptial Imagery*, Leiden: Brill, 1971.

Bernard of Clairvaux, *On The Love of God*, tr. T. Conolly, New York: Spiritual Book Associates, 1937.

Bainton, R., *The Reformation Of The Sixteenth Century*, Boston: Beacon, 1956.

Berger, A., *Encyclopedic Dictionary of Roman Law*, Philadelphia: American Philosophical Society, Vol. 43, Part 2, 1953.

Billings, J., *Natural Family Planning*, Collegeville: Liturgical Press, 1949.

Bockle, F., ed., *The Future Of Marriage As Institution*, New York: Herder and Herder, 1970.

Bonaventure, *Liber IV Sententiarum*, Florence: ex Typographia, Collegii S. Bonaventurae, Quaracchi, 1937.

_____, *Breviloquium, Works Of Bonaventure*, Vol 2, Paterson, N.J.: St. Anthony Guild Press.

Briffault, R., *The Troubadours*, Bloomington, Ind.: Indiana University Press, 1965.

Brown, G., *The New Celibacy*, New York: McGraw-Hill, 1980.

Burrows, M. *The Basis Of Israelite Marriage*, New Haven: Yale University Press, 1938.

Callahan, S., *Beyond Birth Control*, New York: Sheed and Ward, 1968.

Corpus Iuris Canonici, Vol II, Graz: Akademische Druck, 1955.

Dooley, W., *Marriage According to St. Ambrose*, Washington: Catholic University of America Press, 1948.

Epstein, L., *Sex Laws And Customs In Judaism*, New York, KTAV, 1967.

Five Great Encyclicals, G. Treacy, ed., New York: Paulist, 1947.

Ford, J., and Kelly, G., *Contemporary Moral Theology*, Vol. 2, Marriage Questions, Westminster: Newman, 1963.

Fromm, V., *The Art Of Loving*, New York: Harper and Row, 1972.

Geiger, L.-B., *Le Probleme De L'Amour Chez S. Thomas D'Aquin*, Montreal: Institute D'Etudes Medievales, 1952.

Gerke, L., *Christian Marriage, A Permanent Sacrament*, Washington: Catholic University of America Press, 1965.

Gilson, E., *Wisdom And Love In St. Thomas Aquinas*, Milwaukee: Bruce, 1951.

Guindon, A., *The Sexual Language*, Ottawa: University of Ottawa Press, 1977.

Guitton, J., *Essay On Human Love*, New York: Philosophical Library, 1951.

Healy, E., *Moral Guidance*, Chicago: Loyola University Press, 1958.

Hildebrand, D. von, *Marriage*, London: Longmans, Green and Co., 1942.

_____, *Man And Woman*, Chicago: Franciscan Herald Press, 1965.

Hindu Polity (The Ordinances of Manu), A, Burnell, tr., Ludhiana: Kalyani, 1972.

John Chrysostom, *WORKS*, PG, SC, NPNF.

John Paul II, *L'Osservatore Romano*, 1979-.

_____, Origins, 1979-.

_____, *USA, Message of Justice, Peace And Love*, Boston: St. Paul Editions, 1979.

_____, *The Role Of The Christian Family In The Modern World*, Origins, 1981.

Joyce, M. and R., *New Dynamics In Sexual Love*, Collegeville, Minn.: St. Johns University Press, 1970.

Kanana, K., *The Theory of Marriage In Jewish Law*, Leiden: Brill, 1966.

Keenan, A., and Ryan, J., *Marriage, A Medical And Sacramental Study*, New York: Sheed and Ward, 1955.

Kerns, J., *The Theology Of Marriage*, New York: Sheed and Ward, 1964.

Kiefer, O., *Sexual Life In Ancient Rome*, London: Routledge and Kegan Paul 1950.

Kindregan, C., *A Theology of Marriage*, Milwaukee: Bruce, 1967.

Kinsey, A., et al, *Sexual Behavior Of The Human Male*, Philadelphia and London: Saunders, 1948.

Kippley J. and S., *The Art Of Natural Family Planning*, Cincinnati: Couple to Couple League, 1977.

Kippley, S., *Breast-Feeding And Natural Child-Spacing*, New York: Harper and Row, 1974.

Lasch, C., *The Culture Of Narcissism* New York: Norton, 1979.

Lewis, C.S., *The Allegory Of Love*, Oxford: Oxford University Press, 1951.

_____, *The Four Loves*, New York: Harcourt, Brace, Jovanovich, 1960.

Luther, M., *Works*, Pelikan and H. Lehman, eds., Philadelphia and St. Louis: Fortress (LW).

_____, *Selected Writings*, T. Tappert, ed., Philadelphia: Fortress, 1967.

Lynch, J., *The Broken Heart*, New York: Basic Books, 1977.

Marcuse, H., *Eros And Civilization*, Boston: Beacon, 1955.

Marshall, J., *Catholics, Marriage And Contraception*, Baltimore: Helicon, 1967.

_____, *The Infertile Period*, Baltimore: Helicon, 1967.

May, R., *Love And Will*, New York: Norton, 1969.

_____, *Freedom And Destiny*, New York: Norton, 1981.

McAuliffe, M., *Catholic Moral Teaching On The Nature And Object Of Conjugal Love*, Washington: Catholic University of America Press, 1954.

Mohler, J., *Dimensions Of Love*, Garden City: Doubleday, 1975.

_____, *Sexual Sublimation And The Sacred*, Cleveland: John Carroll University, 1978.

National Conference of Catholic Bishops, *To Live In Jesus Christ*, Washington: U.S. Catholic Conference, 1976.

Oraison, M., *Union In Marital Love*, New York: Macmillan, 1958.

_____, *Harmony Of The Couple* Notre Dame: Fides, 1967.

_____, *Being Together*, Garden City: Doubleday, 1971.

Ovid, *Works*, LCL.

Palmer, P., *Sacraments of Healing and Vocation*, Englewood Cliffs: Prentice-Hall, 1963.

Parmisano, F., "Love and Marriage in the Middle Ages," *New Blackfriars*, 50 (1969), pp. 599-608, 649-660.

Papal Teachings: Matrimony, Boston: St. Paul Editions, 1963.

Patai, B., *The Hebrew Goddess*, New York: KTAV, 1967.

Paul VI, *Human Life*, Boston: St. Paul Editions, 1968.

Periera, B., *Doctrine Du Marriage Selon St. Augustin*, Paris: 1930.

Pius XI, *Casti Connubii*, AAS 22 (1930).

Pius XII, *The Pope Speaks*, New York: Pantheon, 1956.

Rahner, K., *Church and Sacraments*, New York: Herder and Herder, 1963.

Ramsey, P., *One Flesh*, Bramcotte Motts: Grove Books, n.d.

Raterman, H., *Charity, Sex And The Young Man*, Cincinnati: 1970.

Robert Bellarmine, *De Matrimonio, Opera*, Vol III, Naples: C. Pedone Lauriel, 1972.

Rougemont, D. de, *Love In The Western World*, New York: Random House, 1956.

Sacred Congregation for the Doctrine of the Faith, *Declaration on Sexual Ethics*, Washington: U.S. Catholic Conference, 1975.

Schillebeeckx, E., Marriage, *Human Reality And Saving Mystery*, New York: Sheed and Ward, 1965.

Suenens, L., *Love And Control*, Westminster: Newman, 1961.

Taylor, G., *Sex In History*, New York: Harper and Row, 1973.

Tertullian, *Treatises On Marriage and Remarriage*, W. LeSaint, tr, ACW.

Teilhard de Chardin, P., *Divine Milieu*, New York: Harper and Row, 1960.

_____, *The Future Of Man*, New York: Harper and Row, 1964.

_____, *Activation of Energy*, New York: Harcourt, Brace and Jovanovich, 1971.

The Theodosian Code, and Novels and the Sirmondian Constitutions, C. Pharr, tr., Princeton: Princeton University Press, 1952.

Thomas Aquinas, *Opera*, Turin, Marietti, 1924-.

_____, *Summa Theologica*, Madrid: BAC, 1962.

_____, *On The Truth Of The Catholic Faith*, Garden City: Doubleday, 1956.

Vatican II Documents, W. Abbott, ed., New York, Guild, 1966.

Vatsyayana, *The Kama Sutra*, R. Burton, tr., New York: Capricorn, 1963.

Wingren, G., *Luther On Vocation*, C. Rasumssen, tr., Philadelphia: Muhlenberg, 1957.

Index